Legend

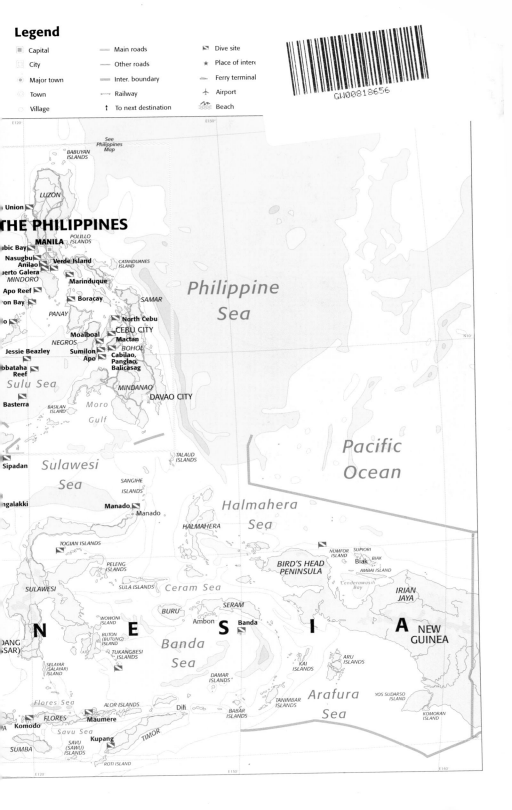

E120° E130°

See
Philippines
Map

BABUYAN
ISLANDS

LUZON

Union ◤

THE PHILIPPINES

MANILA POLILLO
ISLANDS

bic Bay ◤

Nasugbu◤ Verde Island CATANDUANES
Anilao ◤ ISLAND
uerto Galera ◤
MINDORO

Apo Reef ◤ Marinduque

on Bay ◤ Boracay ◤ SAMAR

PANAY

o ◤ North Cebu ◤

Moalboal ◤ CEBU CITY
NEGROS Mactan ◤

Jessie Beazley Sumilon ◤ BOHOL
◤ Apo ◤ Cabilao,
bbataha Panglao,
Reef ◤ Balicasag

Sulu Sea MINDANAO

Basterra ◤ DAVAO CITY

BASILAN Moro
ISLAND
Gulf

TALAUD
ISLANDS

Sipadan ◤ Sulawesi Pacific

Sea SANGIHE Ocean
ISLANDS

ngalakki ◤ Manado ◤

Manado

Halmahera

HALMAHERA Sea

TOGIAN ISLANDS NUMFOR SUPIORI
◤ ISLAND Biak BIAK

PELENG BIRD'S HEAD AMBAI ISLAND
ISLANDS PENINSULA
Cenderawasih
Bay

SULAWESI SULA ISLANDS Ceram Sea IRIAN
JAYA

SERAM

BURU Ambon Banda

WOWONI ◤
ISLAND

N BUTON E S I A
(BUTUNG) NEW
ANG ISLAND Banda GUINEA
SAR) TUKANGBESI
ISLANDS Sea ARU
ISLANDS
SELAYAR KAI
(SALAYAR) ISLANDS
ISLAND DAMAR
ISLANDS YOS SUDARSO
ISLAND
Flores Sea TANIMBAR Arafura
ALOR ISLANDS Difi ISLANDS
FLORES Maumere BABAR Sea KOMORAN
ISLANDS ISLAND
Komodo ◤
SAVU TIMOR
(SAWU) Kupang
SUMBA ISLANDS

ROTI ISLAND

E120° E130° E140°

Diving Malaysia and Southeast Asia

A GUIDE TO THE BEST DIVE SITES IN INDONESIA, MALAYSIA, THE PHILIPPINES AND THAILAND

Text by David Espinosa, Heneage Mitchell, Kal Muller, Fiona Nichols and John Williams

Edited by Fiona Nichols and Michael Stachels

PERIPLUS

Published by Periplus Editions (HK) Ltd.

Copyright © 2002 Periplus Editions (HK) Ltd.
ALL RIGHTS RESERVED

ISBN 0-7946-0132-4
Printed in Singapore

Distributors

Asia Pacific   Berkeley Books Pte. Ltd.
                      130 Joo Seng Road, #06-01/03
                      Singapore 368357
                      Tel: (65) 6280 3320
                      Fax: (65) 6280 6290

Indonesia   PT Java Books Indonesia
                      Jl. Kelapa Gading Kirana
                      Blok A-14/17, Jakarta 14240
                      Tel: (62) 21 451 5351
                      Fax: (62) 21 453 4987

Japan and Korea   Tuttle Publishing
                      RK Bldg. 2nd Floor 2-13-10 Shimo-Meguro
                      Meguro-Ku, Tokyo 153 0061
                      Tel: (81) 03 5437 0171
                      Fax: (81) 03 5437 0755

United States   Tuttle Publishing
                      Distribution Center
                      Airport Industrial Park
                      364 Innovation Drive
                      North Clarendon, VT 05759-9436
                      Tel: 1 (802) 773-8930, 1 (802) 773 6993

Cover Divers visiting Southeast Asia have the rare opportunity for regular encounters with large pelagics like the whale shark. Southern Leyte, Philippines. *Photo by Scott Tuason.*

Pages 4–5 Protected inner reef flats, like this one off Madang, Papua New Guinea, provide the ideal environment for communities of finely branching acroporid corals. *Photo by Roger Steene.*

Frontispiece Sites off Thailand's west coast are rich in hard and soft corals. It is due to this wealth that Richelieu Rock, a favorite among live-aboard operators, attracts thousands of the tiny, shiny glassfish that swarm in caves and crevices. *Photo by Scott Tuason.*

Contents

Photo by Scott Tuason

DIVING SOUTHEAST ASIA

Thailand

See page 173

Practicalities

Appendix

Contributors

Gerald R. Allen is one of the leading ichthyologists working today on Indo-Pacific reef fishes. He is the author of dozens of books, including Periplus Editions' *Marine Life*. He received his PhD from the University of Hawaii in 1971, and has been with the Western Australian Museum since 1974.

Charles Anderson is a British-born marine biologist who has been working in the Maldives since 1983. He authored a series of guidebooks to the marine life of the Maldives, and contributed to Periplus Editions' *Diving Indonesia*.

Michael Aw is a Singaporean photojournalist based in Sydney. He manages the environmental group Ocean Discoverers.

 **Gary Bell** is an underwater photographer based in New South Wales. With his wife Meri he runs the photo agency Ocean Wide Images, specializing in marine natural history photography. His work has been published worldwide, and he has received many awards including, for three years running, the Australasian Underwater Photography prize.

 **Ashley Boyd** is an underwater photographer based in Thailand. He has co-authored a number of publications on diving in Thailand. With thousands of dives under his weight belt, Boyd has built up an impressive body of photographic work. He continues to dive frequently, and now teaches underwater photography.

Clay Bryce has spent thousands of hours below water, photographing the marine life of the Indo-Pacific. He has co-authored five books, including *Sea Slugs of Western Australia,* and his photography and writing have appeared in magazines such as *Aqua Geographica* and *Ocean Realm*.

 **David Espinosa** is originally from San Francisco, and has travelled extensively throughout Asia, Europe and Latin America. David spent three years as a cruise director in Komodo, Indonesia. Now based in Singapore, he is currently the Features Editor of *Asian Diver* magazine. When he isn't diving, David is busy at his laptop, either recording his observations or diligently editing his underwater videos.

Lynn Funkhouser is a Chicago-based photographer, author, and environmentalist. In 1994 she received the Seaspace/PADI Environmental Awareness Award for actively promoting reef preservation.

 **Jack Jackson** is a British underwater photographer who has photographed underwater from the Red Sea to the Philippines. He managed a dive operation in the Red Sea for more than 12 years, and his photography has been published in a number of international publications. His work has also been featured in several well-reviewed exhibitions in Britain.

Ingo Jezierski is a Singapore-based travel photographer. He contributed to the photoediting of this book.

 **Burt Jones** and **Maurine Shimlock** are a Texas-based underwater photographic team who have worked extensively in Indonesia, Malaysia, and the Philippines. They run the photo agency Secret Sea Visions, and their work regularly appears in *Ocean Realm* and other magazines, as well as the monograph *Secret Sea*.

Heneage Mitchell is a British writer and editor now based in the Philippines. In 1980, while on leave from his job, he discovered how good diving the Philippines was. He quit the job, began exploring the islands and in 1983 set up a dive center in San Fernando, La Union. He is now a publisher, and his Samon Publishing Inc. produces *Philippine Diver* magazine.

Kal Muller is a photographer and writer who for the last two decades has specialized in Indonesia. He is the author of at least a dozen books, including the Periplus guides to the eastern Indonesian provinces and the ground-breaking *Diving Indonesia*. His photography and writing appear regularly in travel and dive publications.

Fiona Nichols is a freelance editor, writer, and photographer who was based in Southeast Asia for a decade, regularly diving these waters. Her published works include travel guides (one on Phuket, Thailand), photo features for travel magazines, and contributions to several guidebooks. She is now a freelance writer in Europe.

Mike Severns is a Hawaii-based photographer whose work has appeared in *Natural History, Islands, Aqua,* and many other magazines. Two monographs of his work have been published: the acclaimed *Sulawesi Seas* and *Molokini,* both co-authored by Pauline Fiene-Severns, a biologist. Mike and Pauline are also the writers of Periplus Editions' *Diving Hawaii and Midway.*

Michael Stachels is an editor who has been stationed in Singapore for over ten years.

Roger Steene is Australia-based, pioneering underwater photographer. He regularly teams with Gerald Allen, and his work has appeared in dozens of books, including several large-format monographs.

Shaun Tierney is a Londoner who has spent the last decade capturing images of the underwater world. His awards include the BG Wildlife Photographer of the Year and his work is often used in books and advertising. Shaun and his wife Beth, regularly contribute to magazines like *Asian Diver, UK Sport Diver* and *UK Scuba World.*

Takamasa Tonozuka is a Tokyo-born underwater photographer based in Bali. He has traveled throughout Indonesia and worked as a dive instructor, and now owns the Bali dive operation Dive & Dive's. His work has appeared in magazines and books in Japan, Hong Kong, and Singapore.

Scott Tuason is based in the Philippines and has co-authored two books, *Philippines Coral Reefs in Water Color* and *Anilao*, which won the Photography Award at the 19th Philippine National Book Awards and the Grand Prize at the 27th World Festival of Underwater Images in Antibes, France. His photos and articles have appeared in *Action Asia, Asian Diver, Philippine Diver, Sport Diving Australia, Sport Diver UK, Plongeurs International* and *Ocean Realm.* He is a founding member of the environmental group Concerned Divers for the Philippines and contributes photos to the World Wildlife Fund.

John Williams is a California-born writer and dive instructor now based in Thailand. He has been diving for two decades. He spent four years diving in the Caribbean and the Pacifie before settling on Phuket in 1987. He now runs the dive operation Siam Dive n' Sail on Kata Beach.

Robert Yin has been photographing Pacific reef fauna for over 40 years. His work has appeared in numerous publications and dive magazines.

Additional acknowledgements: The authors and editors would like to thank the following for their invaluable assistance:
Ron Holland and **Graham** and **Donna Taylor** of Sangalaki Dive Lodge; **Dr. Hanny** and **Inneka Batuna** of Manado Murex Resort; **Anton Saksono** of Pulau Putri Resort; **Michael Lee**, recreation manager of Berjaya Beach Resort; and **Henrik Nimb**, PADI course director and director of Master Divers, Singapore.

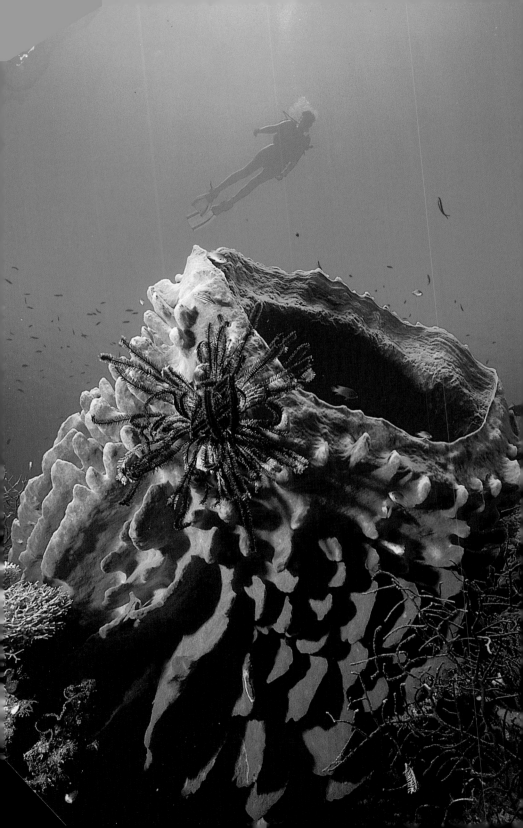

Diving Southeast Asia

A Bounty of Reefs, Wrecks, and Coral Gardens

Access

Visibility

Current

Coral

Reef type

Fish

Highlights

In subsequent chapters, the above symbols will provide at-a-glance information about dive locations

Whatever extraordinary notion possesses us, that first time, to strap on our backs a metal tank full of compressed air, fit fins to our feet, stuff an uncomfortable contraption in the mouth and a tight-fitting piece of glass across our eyes? Uncomfortable and inept, struggling and sweating, we lurch in our new uniform, wondering whether the effort is worthwhile. But our gracelessness soon vanishes as we tumble below the surface and move weightless through the water, drift with currents and have the chance to observe, often at close quarters, creatures large and small that we would never otherwise have imagined. It is quite simply a magic world and one which invariably seduces the novice diver. He is hooked on scuba diving.

Fifteen years ago, while snorkeling from a dive boat in the gin-clear waters of the Similan Islands, a divemaster friend suggested I don a tank and reg, and drop below the water to see what diving was all about. With little more comment, he told me to stick by his side, ascend slowly and remember to breathe out. Within minutes of descending, I was amidst a school of sweetlips, then visited by Moorish idols, and was enthralled by the pink soft corals sprouting from the reef like some exotic cotton wool. For some, that might have been enough, but when I caught sight of a blacktip shark (shark!), admittedly at the edge of the 20-meter visibility, I, too, was hooked. Within two months I had crawled the length of a public swimming pool where second-hand Band Aids were the only novelty to spot, had learned to control buoyancy somewhere under the diving board and was finally rewarded with a PADI open water certificate. Armed with this little plastic card, the real diving experience was about to begin.

For many a novice diver, education takes place after work in public swimming pools in the cold northern latitudes. Dive tables seem like just another bit of school maths and the idea of search and rescue, in a swimming pool, appears totally absurd. The promise of warm water and subtropical species is a lure but rarely a reality.

In Asia, one of the most species-rich areas in the world, diving is a whole different ball game. Water that hovers around the 25°C mark, a tropical climate that is tempered by sea breezes, more species than most books cover, and a wealth of different marine environments—not to mention idyllic sandy shores for surface interval picnics—make diving a special pleasure. Imagine learning in this particular environment!

Pioneer Divers

The sport has evolved quite radically in the last 20 years and this has something to do with both the Vietnam War and the oil industry. The former brought Americans who were used to recreational diving in the New World and who sought to enjoy their hobby when on R&R, notably in Pattaya, while the latter brought expatriates from

Opposite: Giant barrel sponge (*Xestospongia testudinaria*); Togian Islands, North Sulawesi. *Photo by Gary Bell.*

the United States, Europe and Australia to work in the fast developing oil business. Amid the personnel who came to work in the industry—in Thailand, Indonesia and Malaysia—there were plenty of professional divers and, often benefitting from periods of long leave and a fat salary, many of these people explored the region diving recreationally.

Today, you'll come across dozens of divemasters whose first experience of diving in Asia was at the bottom of the Gulf of Thailand, off platforms in the South China Sea, or from some deserted island in Indonesia. Working at depths that were measured more often in fathoms than feet, diving was not always a pleasure. But armed with the skills to withstand the most taxing conditions, recreational diving in more shallow waters, on reefs that were in pristine condition, was

a real pleasure even if the infrastructure for diving was largely missing. These pioneers of sports diving lugged their tanks from far-flung compressors, bartered with local fishermen and *bêche-de-mer* and pearl divers for a boat ride, and picked the brains of local mariners for reefs and shoals in a bid to find good diving. The rest was easy; life on shore in Southeast Asia was (and still is to some extent) inexpensive and they had no need of fancy hotels. Nipa thatched huts and simple meals in the local cafes were good enough.

But what about their buddies who were envious of their travels and fun? In the early seventies there were precious few places to learn to dive in Asia (Pattaya was one of them), and it was not until the last few years of the decade, with easier air travel and greater awareness of the sport, that the bulk of dive shops and operators finally began to open their doors to novices.

It was then that a number of saturated professional divers took a look at the area they had grown to love and decided to turn their skills to teaching recreational diving. All it took was a little capital and some formal qualification from one of the professional dive associations.

Growing Professionalism

The debate as to which of the professional dive associations is the best, is one which continues without respite. Despite the differences of opinion, it is PADI which has the greatest foothold in Asia and is constantly upgrading its services and instruction. You'll find that the majority of dive operators are PADI qualified and adhere to the standards set out by this American association. NAUI instructors also operate in Southeast Asia, as do BSAC, CMAS (and its regional Indonesian equivalent, POSSI) dive instructors.

Today there are four-score or so PADI 5-star operations in Southeast

Below: Striped triplefin (*Helcogramma striata*) resting on ball tunicates and soft corals. Tulamben, Bali. *Photo by Gary Bell.*

Asia, and more waiting for certification. But there are also too many fly-by-night operations run by locals who employ a dive instructor for a season and advertise themselves as professionals. It is advisable that you check out the qualifications and facilities of the dive operator before parting with any money! Borrowed boats may be okay, but borrowed BCs and regs are definitely to be avoided.

In the popular resorts of Southeast Asia, dive operators lure prospective divers with very inexpensive introductory and resort courses. These are fine, up to a point, but they really only qualify you to dive that resort. There is a lot more to diving than taking a resort course.

Furthering your dive education in Asia is, however, also an interesting option. Learning in a tropical environment is fun but perhaps a second, and deciding factor is the relatively inexpensive cost of upgrading skills. The major training centers in Pattaya, Phuket, Samui, Hong Kong, Singapore, Kuala Lumpur, Manila, Anilao and Jakarta offer courses right up to instructor level at prices that compare very favorably to courses in the Caribbean or Australia. Most popular courses are the Advanced Open Water and specialty courses—Wreck Diving, Photography, Night Diving, Navigation and Search and Rescue—which can be put to good use on a diving holiday. Indeed, a course need not interfere at all with a dive trip but can enhance it.

Eco-sensitivity

Another improvement in the dive scene over the last three decades is the growing awareness of environmental concerns which touch not only the requirements of recreational divers but the lives of locals and the flora and fauna. Finally, deforestation, discharge of sewage, oil and refuse in the sea, destructive fishing methods, as well as coral and shell collection, have all come under the environmental spotlight in Asia.

While lifestyles have not radically changed, some of the destructive practices have been curtailed and local governments have begun to set up marine reserves to encourage the regeneration of the marine

Above: Gorgonian fan (*Melithaea*) in the waters around Sumbawa, Indonesia. *Photo by Takamasa Tonozuka.*

environment. Of course, mangrove swamps that have been suffocated by silt do not recover overnight, nor do coral reefs that have been blasted by dynamite or repeatedly broken up by anchors and fins. But recover they do, albeit more slowly than from the blanket damage inflicted by natural disasters, and the results are encouraging. The marine environment rarely returns to what it was before damage, but it does recover and proliferate.

Where to Dive

So where do divers head for, and what can they expect to find in Southeast Asia?

Most diving has been centered on the Gulf of Thailand and from Phuket, in the Philippines from Batangas and the Visayas, in Malaysia from the East Coast and Sabah, and in Indonesia from Bali, Manado, and Flores.

Thailand In the search for pristine locations and big pelagics, Phuket-based operators have pushed out into the Andaman Sea as far as the Andaman Islands themselves, which are in Indian waters, and to the Mergui Archipelago in Burmese waters (Myanmar). They have also forged southward, toward the Malaysian border, where they have discovered, like their pioneering colleagues from Pattaya, untouched coral reefs and forgotten wrecks.

Philippines The diving fraternity in the Philippines has benefited from a burgeoning infrastructure in the smaller island destinations, and a proliferation of live-aboard boats which explore the Sulu Sea. The retreat of the United States military has opened once off-limits areas to the public.

Malaysia In Malaysia, the development of an infrastructure on a number of East Coast islands has made it easy for dive enthusiasts to enjoy some of the best coral reefs, while the country's premier dive spot in the deep waters off Sabah has developed into a real dive destination. Off Sabah too, the oceanic reef, Layang-Layang, has developed into a world-class destination for dive enthusiasts.

Indonesia A country with far-flung islands, Indonesia has developed resorts in tandem with the establishment of regular air connections, and in many of these diving and snorkeling are given priority. Outside flights to Manado have further opened up this fine dive site, and live-aboard boats have also made their debut, offering divers the chance to explore really remote areas like the Banda Sea.

Dive Topography

Most Southeast Asian reefs are fringing reefs, and most diving will be along the outer reef edge, often quite close to shore. The profile is sometimes gently sloping, and sometimes full of bommies and coral heads. But the region is perhaps most famous for its steep drop-offs, particularly in Indonesia and the Philippines. The wall at Bunaken near Manado is world-famous, and Menjangan, Komodo, Kupang, the Bandas, and Sangalaki also feature steep dropoffs.

The Philippines offers plenty of good walls—at Verde, Anilao, Nasugbu, Apo as well as a dozen more places. Malaysia offers fabulous walls at Sipadan and Layang-Layang, and even tiny Tenggol off peninsular Malaysia offers a good one.

And while not particularly widespread, Southeast Asia also has its fair share of wrecks. There are numerous war graves and vessels lost during World War II off Pattaya in Thailand, in the bay at Coron in the Philippines, and there are easily dived wrecks off Manado and Bali in Indonesia. Then there are fishing vessels that met an untimely end and even the odd dive boat or two.

In some places, artificial wrecks (tires, old buses and broken boats) have been sunk to encourage regeneration of reefs and their associated fauna. Singapore has done this outside its harbor waters; the Philippines and Thailand too have adopted this method.

You'll find that diving in Southeast Asia is generally on the continental shelf, but oceanic diving is possible too. This inevitably entails a trip on a live-aboard.

getting more sophisticated but less costly, dive courses are becoming more competitively priced and the cost of diving itself is getting more expensive—mainly because today's diver is a more sophisticated animal and not the hardy aficionado of yesteryear. In the Practicalities section at the end of this book you will be able to see how the cost of diving compares through the region.

Below: Juvenile round-faced batfish (*Platax orbicularis*). *Photo by Lynn Funkhouser.*

Live-aboard Diving

Live-aboard dive boats have made a big impact on the scope and range of diving. In Indonesia, live-aboard operations take divers to the Banda Sea, the islands north of Manado, and Komodo and other islands in the Nusa Tenggara provinces. Yacht chartering is becoming popular in Bali with holidaymakers who also enjoy diving. In the Philippines the fabulous reefs at Apo and those of Tubbataha, Jessie Beazley and Basterra are only accessible by live-aboards while other live-aboards and chartered yachts ply the small islands of the Visayas and Palawan. So do yachts and dive vessels in Sabah, Malaysia, that offer diving in remote offshore areas, while yachts and small motor boats (often converted fishing vessels) offer diving trips in Malaysian and the northern Indonesian waters from Singapore. Phuket, especially, has developed this industry, building new marinas to accommodate charter yachts and dive vessels. And, if you want to, you can dive in the Mergui Archipelago from Thailand, discover the reefs off the southeast coast by the Cambodian border in the Gulf of Thailand, or head for the absolutely virgin territory of the Andaman Islands. Well-equipped live-aboards are the only answer to reaching these remote areas.

When diving first started in the region, it was a cheap hobby once you had bought a regulator and other basic gear. Today, the relationship between learning to dive, buying the gear and getting going has changed. The gear is

Best of all, there are still many areas in Asia to be charted, let alone developed as dive destinations–areas that have, up to now, discouraged tourism and development, places that were off limits for political or commercial reasons, and spots where transport was almost non-existent. But it is only a matter of time before these virgin areas open up to enthusiastic divers.

— *Fiona Nichols*

Above: The easiest, and best means to explore Indonesia's vast expanse of islands is via live-aboard. Murex Resort's *Symphony* plies the waters north of Sulawesi, and the islands in between.

Diving in Indonesia

A Vast and Largely Unexplored Archipelago for Divers

An archipelago of over 17,000 islands, stretching more than 5,000 km from west to east, with a coastline of more than 80,000 km washed by tropical waters, Indonesia has the potential for fabulous diving. Indeed, the world's fourth largest country contains 10–20 percent of the world's coral reefs.

Indonesia is the least known of the world's best dive locations, but things are changing fast. The introduction of scuba gear and the beginnings of dive operations in the country go back nearly 20 years, and each year more new, exciting locations are opening their doors.

It will be many years before diving in Indonesia reaches its full potential because it has both great advantages and serious drawbacks. The advantages of diving the clear, rich waters of an uncrowded site or, better still, the virgin waters of an unexplored corner of the archipelago, need hardly be mentioned. Ask anyone who has dived in Indonesia. But the country's advantage is also its drawback—distances and remoteness conspire against all but the most adventurous or well-heeled diver. For those whose pockets are deep, a number of charter vessels and dive boats operate in the more remote areas of the country, offering keen divers a chance to really sample some of the most exciting diving in the world.

Interestingly, the country's most popular tourist destination—Bali—also has some excellent diving, including a superb wreck, and is the area of the country where the standard and number of dive operations is the highest. But good diving is not exactly located in your hotel lobby! Day-trippers, who sally forth from their luxury hotels in the south, should be prepared to travel an hour or more away from the urban areas to experience some of the best diving the island has to offer. In recent years, however, boutique and 5-star resorts have opened up in nearly every corner of the island, offering serious divers the opportunity to undertake a dive safari, stringing together a number of fantastic dive days without sacrificing time, energy or comfort.

In the Back of Beyond

As more and more dive operations open their doors, professionalism is certainly increasing. However, some stumbling blocks continue to thwart divers. The country's international airline will bring divers to the country with little hassle, but things slow down rather considerably from there onwards.

It is worth noting that excellent diving is accessible by direct overseas flights. Bali and Jakarta are linked to a score of international destinations. Manado also receives direct flights from Singapore three times a week, and from Davao twice a week, making access to the offshore sites around Bunaken simple.

Domestic connections can be made via Garuda, or with any of the country's main ancillary carriers Merpati, Bouraq and Mandala; a plethora of new domestic carriers have begun operating, and with the increased competition prices have been dropping. Despite these air-

Overleaf:
Indonesian reefs are so rich that on a single fist-sized chunk one can find soft corals, sponges, hydroids, four species of algae, and five species of tunicates. Tulamben, Bali. *Photo by Gary Bell.*

Opposite:
Snorkeling on the reef flat off Bunaken Island. The common, and distinctive, blue sea stars are *Linkia laevigata.* *Photo by Mike Severns.*

24

Above: Though it often sits out in the open, the leaf scorpionfish (*Taenianotus triacanthus*), which not only looks like a leaf but also sways back and forth in the current, owes its survival to deception. Komodo, Indonesia.
Photo by Shaun Tierney.

lines' improvements over the last decade the reliability of domestic connections still leaves much to be desired. The further you travel from tourist centers, the greater the problems. The biggest problems are delayed or cancelled flights. Also, the aircraft serving some of the smaller islands are Twin Otters and Cessnas, and a diver may find himself stymied by 20 kg baggage limits.

That is not to say that everything falls foul—but travelers should be aware that business does not always run as smoothly as one would like, and some margin of time should be allowed for travel to and from the more remote parts of the archipelago. Patience, tolerance and a strong sense of humor are indispensable for travel in this country.

Once at the dive destination, there will be more innovative ways of travel. You can forget flashy cruisers—journeys to and from dive sites are often on local outriggers and simple fishing boats.

Diving Operations

The caliber of dive guides is certainly improving. In many of the well-visited locations like Bali and Manado, guides can take a guest directly to a spot to find a specific fish or coral. Many photographers have even begun toting laundry lists of bizarre and exotic critters they wish to photograph; and they rarely go home unfulfilled—the best guides locate the popular fish with an accuracy and speed that is truly startling.

What local guides lack in knowledge and organization, they make up for in charm. And a few have the rare combination of all three traits, which makes a dive with such a character thoroughly memorable.

Lack of professionalism is not usually a problem for well-trained and experienced divers, but beginners should take great care. It is far better to take a certification course before coming to Indonesia, although the larger operations do offer resort courses. But it is better to avoid those that are not recognized by international organizations such as CMAS, NAUI, PADI or SSI.

Generally, gear available in Indonesia is fairly basic, and is not always in tip-top condition. We recommend that divers take as much of their own gear and spare parts as possible, and rely as little as possible on rentals. If you do choose to rent, make careful equipment checks regularly.

Indonesia is not a place, either, to push the dive tables or argue with dive computers. There are decompression chambers on Bali, in Surabaya (east Java) and in Manado, and several private chambers on east Kalimantan (near Derawan and Sangalaki); but if you suffer a bend in a more remote area of the archipelago do not count on immediate emergency assistance. Live-aboards and operators in remote locations have emergency procedures in place (relying on private services—i.e. charter helicopters and planes), but even an extraction from an island in Komodo, for example, would be expensive, involve crucial timing and a lot of luck. It's better to err on the side of caution.

Generally the best practice is to dive conservatively (even to the point of extreme caution) and safely, and always to make a decompression stop on the ascent. The reefs are rich enough that you will never be bored spending a few extra minutes at the end of a dive exploring the shallows.

When and Where to Visit

Because of the size of the country, there is no recommended best season for diving—indeed, diving is possible year round. The main seasons for tourists are July and August, and the Christmas and New Year holidays.

The areas included in this dive guide all have compressors, equipment and other professional facilities for diving. Some areas offer the visitor a great place to holiday and have the added bonus of well-organized diving as a diversion. Others have great diving, but only modest accommodations. As mentioned earlier, there are a number of boats, luxury and otherwise, that ply the Indonesian waters, and these are generally fairly well-equipped.

El Niño created a wave of coral bleaching in Bali and other areas in 1998. The effect was heaviest in the shallow, protected reefs. In some sites the corals turned a ghastly, pale white. The top, living layer of polyps died; and green or brown algae quickly overwhelmed entire colonies, suffocating any polyps that may have survived—the result was not pretty. Some coral regeneration has begun, but these fragile ecosystems will require more time to recover. Always dive carefully, taking extra care to keep your fins and hands from affecting this precious resource even more.

— *Fiona Nichols*

Below: Glorious panoramas, with white sand beaches penned in by luscious coral reefs and verdant palm trees, are not an uncommon sight among Indonesia's 17,000-plus islands. Siladen, Sulawesi. *Photo by Shaun Tierney.*

10 min–1.5 hrs by
boat, depending
on location

5–25 meters

Variable, 0–2 knots

Good

Walls and coral
slopes

Good variety

Mantas; diving
in marine lake

SANGALAKI

INDONESIA

26

Derawan and Sangalaki

Mantas, Turtles and a Mysterious Lake

Because of their proximity to both Indonesia and Malaysia, the islands of Derawan and Sangalaki have long been the subject of a heated territorial dispute. But divers can all agree on one thing: the diving here is world-class, and features turtles on virtually every dive, snorkeling with mantas and perhaps the greatest pelagic site in all of Indonesia.

There are only two dive operators in the area—Derawan Dive Resort and the re-opened Sangalaki Dive Lodge. While the diving around Derawan is adequate to good, the resort has a top-notch house reef. Divers need only walk to the end of the wooden pier and step down the ladder to be immersed in a water wonderland.

At the base of the wooden pil-ings, which are swarmed with schooling baitfish, there is a wealth of reef fish, big and small. In five meters of water divers might find crocodilefish, juvenile boxfish, nudibranchs, ribbon eels and other more common angelfish and octopus. The reef slopes gently down to 20-plus meters, where it is common to see turtles, schools of humphead parrotfish and reef sharks.

Using the resort as a home base, guests travel by speedboat to various sites in the vicinity.

Sangalaki

Since Sangalaki opened for diving in April 1993 virtually every group to dive there has reported seeing

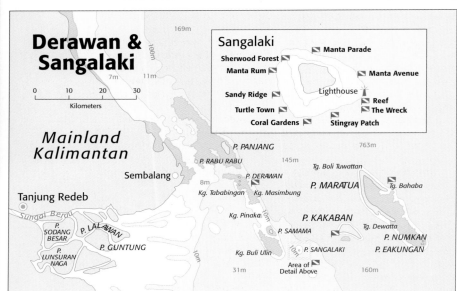

mantas in the rich planktonic waters. During the rainy season (November through March) the visibility is poor (5–8 meters), but there is plenty to see. As mantas tend to feed near the surface, and in light currents, divers need only descend a few meters underwater to enjoy the show; the rays are even accustomed to human presence.

The other dives at Sangalaki are worthwhile, as the corals are healthy, the currents are mild and the visibility is stellar. There are huge groupers and bountiful reef fish at a bommie near **Coral Gardens**. And **Stingray Patch** is famous for regular sightings of blue-spotted rays, eagle rays and, what else, mantas.

Green turtles live, breed and lay eggs on several of the small islands off the northeast coast of Kalimantan—Derawan and Sangalaki are the islands of choice. Lucky guests, beyond witnessing the tiny turtles hatch, might even see a tiger shark, which preys on grown turtles, patrol the reef's outer edge.

Kakaban Island

Less than an hour away by speedboat, Kakaban offers an excellent wall, which drops to 50 meters, pocked by caves and crevices and covered in an array of hard corals. The wall is thronged by surgeonfish, snappers, white tip sharks and grays. There is typically a mild to strong current here, but experienced divers should have no troubles. The **Blue Light Cave** is another excellent site. At low tide, guests swim over the top of the reef to a small hole that opens inside into a large cathedral.

But Kakaban lays claim to a much more unusual fame. A lake fills much of the central part of the island, slightly above sea level, and with a salt concentration about two-thirds that of the ocean. The lake holds a variety of marine life, including thousands of stingless jellyfish.

Other marine life observed includes tunicates, small, colonial

bivalves, nudibranchs, a land snake, pure white anemone-like animals, at least three species of holothurian sea cucumbers, sponges of two distinct growth forms and two kinds of crabs.

The lake is ringed by thickly encrusted mangrove roots, and the slopes at the lake edge are covered in lush vegetation. It is an easy, 10-minute walk to the lake's edge along a wide trail. Bring a snorkel, because lugging your scuba equipment is not an option.

Maratua

The horseshoe-shaped island of Maratua lays the furthest from the resorts—nearly two hours away by speedboat. Because of its secluded location, only one to two trips per week visit.

The best place to dive is at **The Channel** on the eastern rim, where divers can see pelagic fish in abundance. The channel's mouth is where the best action occurs. On an incoming or slack tide, it is swarmed by separate schools of chevron and yellowtail barracuda, gigantic, bus-sized groupers, schools of surgeons, trevally and tuna. Visibility is nearly always gin-clear.

Below the lip a vertical wall drops to 60-plus meters, where gray, white tip and black tip sharks school. If the current is running, it's best to sit at the edge to watch the show, then drift into the shallow lagoon.

— *David Espinosa/Kal Muller*

Above: Sangalaki's most popular denizen, the manta ray, is a frequent visitor to the island year round. *Photo by Bob Whorton.*

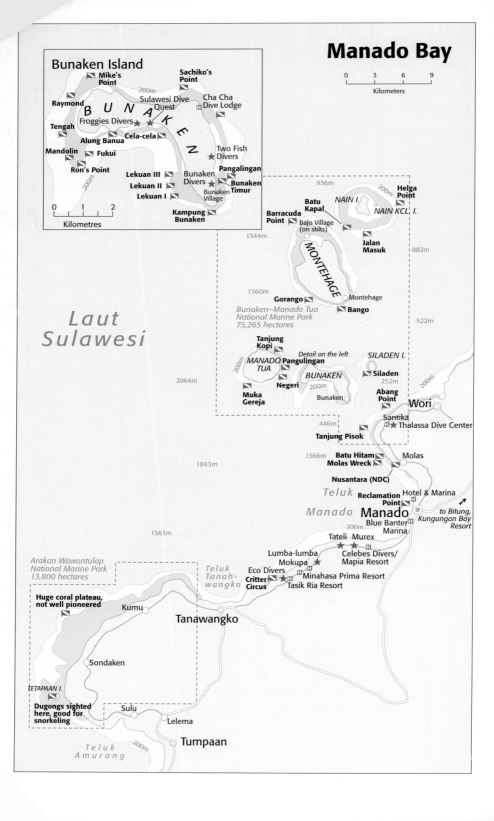

Manado Bay

0   3   6   9
Kilometres

Bunaken Island

Mike's Point
Sachiko's Point
Raymond
200m
Sulawesi Dive Quest
Cha Cha Dive Lodge
B U N A K E N
Froggies Divers
Tengah
Cela-cela
Alung Banua
Mandolin
Fukui
Ron's Point
200m
Two Fish Divers
Lekuan III
Pangalingan
Lekuan II
Bunaken Divers
Bunaken Timur
Lekuan I
Bunaken Village
Kampung Bunaken

0   1   2
Kilometres

936m

Helga Point

NAIN I.
200m
NAIN KCL. I.

Batu Kapal

Barracuda Point
Bajo Village (on stilts)

Jalan Masuk

1344m

882m

MONTEHAGE

1360m
Gorango
Bango
Montehage

522m

Laut Sulawesi

Bunaken–Manado Tua National Marine Park 75,265 hectares

2064m

Tanjung Kopi
MANADO TUA
Pangulingan
Detail on the left
SILADEN I.
Siladen
252m
BUNAKEN
200m
Negeri
Bunaken
Abang Point
Muka Gereja

Wori
Santika
Thalassa Dive Center

446m
Tanjung Pisok

1843m

1566m
Batu Hitam
Molas Wreck
Molas

Nusantara (NDC)

Teluk
Reclamation Point
Hotel & Marina

Manado Manado
Blue Banter Marina
to Bitung, Kungungan Bay Resort

1563m
Tateli Murex
Lumba-lumba
Mokupa
Celebes Divers/ Mapia Resort
200m

Arakan Wawontulap National Marine Park 13,800 hectares

Teluk Tanah-wangko
Eco Divers
Critter Circus
Minahasa Prima Resort
Tasik Ria Resort

Huge coral plateau, not well pioneered

Kumu

Tanawangko

Sondaken

TETAPAAN I.

Dugongs sighted here, good for snorkeling

Sulu
Lelema

Teluk Amurang
200m
Tumpaan

Sulawesi

World-class Walls and Outstanding Fish Life

15 min–1.5 hrs
by boat

Fair to very good,
12–25 meters

Usually gentle; at
some sites to 2
knots or more

Excellent condition
and variety, parti-
cularly soft corals

Steep coral walls

Good numbers and
excellent variety

Pristine walls; inter-
esting wreck; muck
sites; Wakatobi,
Indonesia's "best"
house reef

Divers have nothing but praise for the reefs surrounding the small islands in Manado Bay. These are sheer walls, covered with an incredible amount and variety of hard corals and invertebrate life. Visibility is usually very good—in the 20–30 meter range, sometimes even better—though periodic plankton-rich upwellings can reduce the visibility to 10–15 meters.

The reefs here are relatively untouched, with little damage by fishermen or divers. In 1989, thanks to the collective efforts of Dr. Hanny and Ineke Batuna, Loky Herlambang and Ricky Lasut, 75,265 hectares of area underwater around Bunaken, Manado Tua, Siladen, Montehage and Nain islands became a national marine reserve—Bunaken National Park.

North Sulawesi and the islands in the Bunaken group face the Sulawesi Sea, which plummets down to more than 6,000 meters. Nutrient-rich water from these depths sweeps across the reefs.

The variety of marine life here is excellent; the surfaces of the walls are crowded with hard and soft corals, whip corals, sponges and clinging filter-feeders like crinoids and basket stars.

Huge schools of pyramid butterflyfish, black triggerfish and clouds of anthias swarm around the reef edge and the upper part of the wall. Sharks, schools of barracuda, rays, moray eels, and sea snakes—particularly the black-and-grey-banded colubrine sea snake—are relatively common here.

The Bunaken–Manado Tua reserve features some 18 dive sites. Most are concentrated off the south and west coasts of Bunaken, a low, crescent-shaped coral island surrounded by a steep fringing reef. Adjacent to Manado Tua—Old Manado—is a volcano, a well-shaped cone reaching 822 meters. Three other islands complete the group: tiny Siladen, a stone's throw northeast of Bunaken; Montehage, the largest of the islands, north of Bunaken; and Nain, a tiny island north of Montehage surrounded by a large barrier reef.

Bunaken Island

Aside from the storm-damaged shallows along the north coast, the reef is good all the way around Bunaken, and the 6-km-long island features no less than 13 dive sites. Bunaken is the centerpiece of the reserve.

All the sites but one are similar in that they feature steep walls of coral with small caves buzzing with reef fish. Good coral growth usually extends down to 40–50 meters, and in the deeper parts of the wall one can see sharks, large rays and Napoleon wrasse.

The most popular sites in the park are along this spectacular three-pronged coral wall that can keep any diver enthralled for dive after dive after dive. Check out the turtles, Napoleon wrasse and sleepy white tip sharks. **Bunaken Timur** offers shelter from the occasional storms that come out of the west, so the coral gardens remain some of the most pristine in the park, though the fish density is much less than the other popular sites. **Sachiko's Point** offers good soft coral growth and, like any of the current-swept points around the island, ample shark and pelagic action. The entire west side of Bunaken is a fine 2-km stretch of wall that can see troublesome downcurrents on a falling tide. But on a rising tide it's a superb drift running in a northerly direction with plenty to behold: excellent coral growth along **Mandolin** as schools of fusiliers wash past you in waves, forests of whip corals along **Tengah** and extending into **Raymond**, which also boasts lovely soft corals. Common inhabitants include turtles, colubrine sea snakes, the occasional passing eagle ray, Napoleon wrasse, dog-tooth tuna or reef shark, and when the current is light enough to allow closer inspection along the wall,

numerous leaf scorpionfish, candy crabs and other macro riches. **Fukui** is the exception to the walls of Bunaken: a gentle slope offering fish life ranging from ghost pipefish to Napoleons, an impressive bed of garden eels, a collection of giant Tridacna clams that's a popular photo stop and a nearby sea mount that comes to within 10 meters of the surface, which is frequented by schools of batfish, midnight snappers, big-eyed jacks, giant trevally, and barracuda. Mola Mola, mantas and even thresher sharks have even been seen here.

Manado Tua

"Old Manado" is a dormant volcano jutting up just west of Bunaken. The two best sites are wall dives on the west coast: **Muka Gereja** and

Below: For an underwater paradise, look no further than Sulawesi's Bunaken National Park, where the reefs are healthy and the waters clear. *Photo by Scott Tuason.*

Negeri offer first-rate coral growth and macro life with plenty of caves and cracks to peer into, but don't expect any pelagic action. **Tanjung Kopi** is where to go for big fish, but the currents dictate that this site is not for beginners and can only be dived properly at slack tide. *Gorango* means "shark," and these can usually be seen here. The reef profile is a steep wall to about 40 meters.

Siladen, Montehage and Nain

These three islands see fewer divers than the main two islands but they do offer some fine dives. The west side of Siladen has an exquisite reef that starts right off the best beach in the park and has fine macro attractions. Montehage is a large, flat, mangrove-dominated island with a wide fringing reef flat that is mostly damaged. For big fish, **Barracuda Point** is a standout site, though a bit of a gamble. Divers here usually see almost nothing or have their best dives, observing the huge resident school of chevron barracuda, eagle and mobula rays, schools of jacks, trevally, bumphead parrotfish, and any of a variety of shark species including gray reef sharks and hammerheads. The furthest island in the park from Manado is Nain, located in a large lagoon surrounded by a barrier reef offering good hard coral growth in places. **Batu Kapal** is an interesting dive, but it's for the very experienced only.

Manado Bay

Though the coral growth can't compete with the splendor of Bunaken-Manado Tua, and the visibility is usually in the 8–15 meter range, Manado Bay has plenty to offer, making a fine break from wall diving. The most popular site is the **Molas Wreck**, an intact, steel-hulled, 60-meter merchant ship that sits upright on a sandy slope at 25–40 meters, with the bow and roof reaching up to 17 meters to greet divers descending the mooring line. After a tour of the ship, divers follow the slope up into the shallows, which, like the entire Molas coastline, offers critter-hunting equal or even better than Bunaken, with ribbon eels, cuttlefish, ghost pipefish and more. Following the bay, some resorts have interesting house reefs, with the reef off **Tasik Ria** hosting pygmy seahorses among its treasures.

Lembeh Straits

Over the last five years, no one site has truly come to exemplify the ocean's strange and bizarre outcasts quite like the Lembeh Straits. When the first resort opened its doors in the mid-90s on this sheltered stretch of water east of

Manado by car), servicing the boom of divers searching for muck. Though black sand sites like **Hairball** have brought most of Lembeh's fame, with 30-plus dive sites covering a wide spectrum of topography, from black sand slopes, verdant hard coral and soft coral gardens, bommies, walls, pinnacles, rubble, wrecks and mixtures of all of the above, boredom is never a problem. Indeed, when every dive presents an opportunity to discover a species new to science, as happens with regularity, one begins to realize how unique this famed stretch of water truly is.

To the North

Atop Sulawesi sits an island group offering a sort of diving contrasting with Bunaken to the west and Lembeh to the east. The best dives are a number of pinnacles that rise off the east coast of Bangka Island and in the Pulisan area. The prime attractions here are the unbelievably kaleidoscopic soft coral gardens. With the clouds of anthias and other reef fish varieties schooling about, huge morays, white tip reef sharks dozing under table corals, and great macro attractions, the area is a visual feast. Compared to Bunaken the currents are stronger, the visibility usually reduced and the water a bit cooler, but the excellent diving around Bangka is rapidly gaining international renown.

Further north, a string of islands form stepping-stones all the way to the Philippines. For liveaboard aficionados, the Sangihe-Talaud chain offers some spectacular scenery in clear waters. Diving on volcanic flows, pinnacles, pristine coral reefs, no crowds, the Sangihe area also harbors one of the very few sperm whale calving grounds on earth. With deep trenches to both sides of the island chain, the currents can be wicked, but for experienced divers the region offers extraordinary adventures.

Above: Tiny treasures like the diminutive pygmy seahorse (*Hippocampus bargibant*), only 15-20 mm in length, abound in Indonesia's bountiful waters—the trick is in finding them! Lembeh Straits, Sulawesi. *Photo by Scott Tuason.*

Manado, it was designed and marketed as a relaxing upscale retreat that also offered diving.

Under the auspices of renowned divemaster Larry Smith, the Kungkungan Bay Resort (KBR) quickly became the Mecca for macro photographers and marine biologists. As Larry and his team of highly trained guides developed more and more sites, featuring frogfish in all sizes and colors, a veritable rainbow of countless nudibranch species, innumerable eels, an astonishing variety of venomous fish species, cephalopods galore, mandarinfish by the dozens as well as myriad others, the frenzy to dive there reached astonishing heights. The resort nearly cornered the market on macro diving; and though PNG's Bob Halstead coined the term "muck" diving, the impossibly rich and diverse Lembeh Straits catapulted muck into the international limelight.

In recent years, operators from nearby Manado have descended upon Lembeh (1.5 hrs from

Central and South Sulawesi

Situated in gin-clear, millpond-calm Tomini Bay, the idyllic and alluring Togian Islands are distinguished by the simple fact that they feature all three major coral reef formations—fringing, barrier and atoll—within a small area and in a sheltered environment. This means that divers can marvel at exquisitely delicate coral growth, but only in areas where the rampant bomb fishing that has effectively destroyed much of these reefs can be avoided.

There are a number of dive operators in the area, mostly operating out of the backpacker center of Kadidiri. Other than an intact WWII plane wreck, the inner central region of the islands doesn't offer much, but with a good guide the outer areas do. Fine dives can be had on the volcanic cone of Una-Una to the northwest and the best diving is at the opposite end of the islands, offered by a single operator, the Italian-run Walea Dive Resort located near the southeastern tip of Walea Bahi. In that area, besides the pristine reefs off the beach (which owe their continued healthy existence to the protective actions of the resort), there are a number of nearby seamounts rising from the depths that offer superlatives dives in astounding visibility, featuring possible encounters with some charismatic megafauna rarely seen off the rest of Sulawesi—mantas and silvertip sharks.

Largely unexplored by divers, the rest of Sulawesi does have a few operators providing fine diving in a few outposts: Donggala, near Palu on the west coast, Luwuk, adjacent to the Banggai Island group, Ujung Pandang, and nearby Bira. Each of these places offers a different type of diving experience; all are worthy of attention, and over time more destinations are likely to be added. The potential is indeed there.

The Takabonerate Atoll, south of Makassar, is another relatively unexplored region. Tales of breathtaking walls and huge pelagics trickle in from the occasional charter, but only two operators, the *Felidae* and Baruna, operate sporadic trips to these potentially intriguing outer islands.

Acknowledged as the one of the world's top coral reef dive destinations, Wakatobi Dive Resort is located in the vast Tukang Besi National Marine Park to the east. With only 11 rooms, the resort is a model of eco-friendly diving set amidst a tropical paradise, and is gaining a strong following of underwater photographers who travel there for the spectacular wide-angle reef opportunities and excellent shallows right in front of the dive shop.

Wakatobi is blessed with unquestionably the best house reef in Indonesia, if not the world. Only steps from the beach bungalows, the wall plunges 30-plus meters, pocked by caverns and crevices, and covered in a profusion of healthy, untouched hard and soft corals. More than six species of seahorse have been found on this small stretch of reef. Underwater visibility on the wall, as well as at the more than 30 sites in the area, averages between 20–80 meters. On the other side of the newly built dock, in the shallow sand flats and seagrass beds divers enjoy regular sightings of blue-ringed octopus, Pegasus sea moths and a wealth of invertebrate life.

—*Bruce Moore/David Espinosa*

Above: Manado's house reefs are often treasure troves for the bizarre and colorful, like this free-swimming male ribbon eel. *Photo by Scott Tuason.*

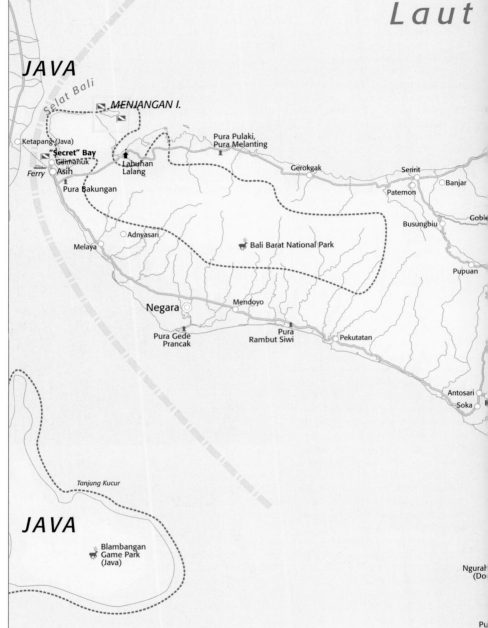

Laut

JAVA

Selat Bali

MENJANGAN I.

Ketapang (Java)
"Secret" Bay
Gilimanuk
Ferry
Asih
Pura Bakungan

Labuhan
Lalang

Pura Pulaki,
Pura Melanting

Gerokgak

Seririt

Patemon

Banjar

Busungbiu

Goble

Adnyasari

Bali Barat National Park

Pupuan

Melaya

Negara

Mendoyo

Pura Gede
Prancak

Pura
Rambut Siwi

Pekutatan

Antosari

Soka

Tanjung Kucur

JAVA

Blambangan
Game Park
(Java)

Ngurah
(Do

Pu

Samudra Hindia

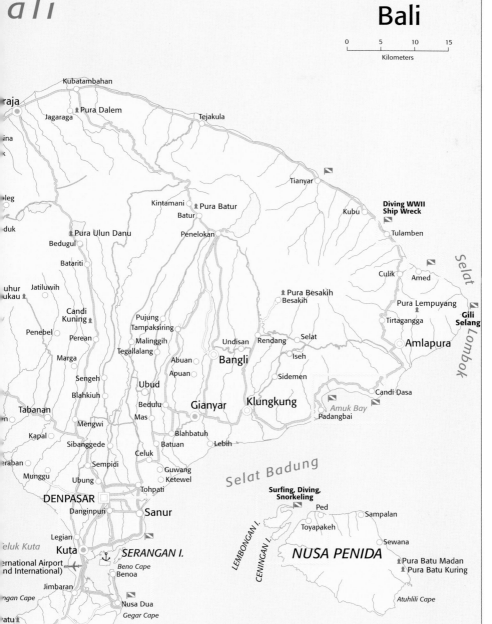

Bali

Kilometers
0   5   10   15

ali

Kubatambahan
raja
Jagaraga   🛕 Pura Dalem   Tejakula
ina
k
eleg   Kintamani 🛕 Pura Batur
duk   🛕 Pura Ulun Danu   Batur
Bedugul   Penelokan
        Batariti
uhur Jatiluwih
ukau   Candi
            Kuning 🛕   Pujung
Penebel   Tampaksiring
        Perean   Malinggih
Marga   Tegallalang   Abuan   Undisan Rendang Selat
        Sengeh   Apuan   Bangli
        Blahkiuh   Ubud
Tabanan   Bedulu   Gianyar   Klungkung
        Mengwi   Mas
    Kapal   Blahbatuh
        Sibanggede   Batuan   Lebih
eraban   Celuk
        Sempidi   Guwang
Munggu   Ubung   Ketewel
            Tohpati
DENPASAR
    Danginpuri   Sanur
        Legian
eluk Kuta
    Kuta   SERANGAN I.   Selat Badung
rnational Airport
nd International)   Beno Cape
        Benoa
    Jimbaran
ngan Cape   Nusa Dua
atu 🛕   Gegar Cape
Cape

Tianyar

Diving WWII
Ship Wreck
Kubu
        Tulamben

            Culik   Amed
            Selat Lombok

🛕 Pura Besakih
Besakih   Pura Lempuyang
            Tirtagangga   Gili
                    Selang
        Iseh   Amlapura

Sidemen

        Candi Dasa
Amuk Bay
Padangbai

LEMBONGAN I.   CENINGAN I.

Surfing, Diving,
Snorkeling
        Ped   Sampalan
    Toyapakeh
            Sewana
NUSA PENIDA
        🛕 Pura Batu Madan
        🛕 Pura Batu Kuring

        Atuhlili Cape

Beach; the ship is 30 meters offshore. Avoid midday—often crowds

Fair to good, 15 meters

None

Good growth on ship, fine growth on wall

Liberty shipwreck; wall; muck diving

Excellent variety, prolific

Full moon night dive

Tulamben

This is the Liberty Wreck Legend

At first sight, the little village of Tulamben is rather uninviting. Its beach is a rough spread of black sand, with small boulders and rubble cast here by nearby Gunung Agung's eruption in 1963. But people travel (in great numbers) to Tulamben to dive an extensive variety of sites, beginning, for most, with the wreck of the *Liberty*.

The wreck is the only site in Bali that can actually become crowded, as day-trippers from the south brave the three-hour drive just to do two dives. The volcanic rock is a bit hard on the feet, and the waves can be rough, but all inconveniences are soon forgotten on Bali's most famous site.

The Wreck

Just 30 meters from the beach the wreck lies on its starboard side, almost parallel to the shore. Parts of the superstructure are broken up, but the wreck is still large and impressive, stretching more than 100 meters along the steeply sloping black sand. On 11 January 1942, this ship was hit by torpedoes from a Japanese submarine, and was beached in Tulamben. She remained there for more than 20 years until the eruption of Agung pushed the ship off the beach to its current location.

The hull, which is encrusted in hard corals and covered in soft corals of purple, red and yellow, is broken into large chunks and laced with big holes, making it easy to peer in from the outside (penetrations should not be undertaken). The wreck is simply a wonderful place to dive, as there are hundreds of species of fish, and in great quantity. In recent years the large resident school of jacks has taken up tenancy on the wreck. Most of the medium-sized fish have become semi-tame, and will literally swarm a diver in the shallows. Smaller treasures, like nudibranchs and tiny cuttlefish can be found on the wreck itself and on the black sand that surrounds it. The *Liberty*

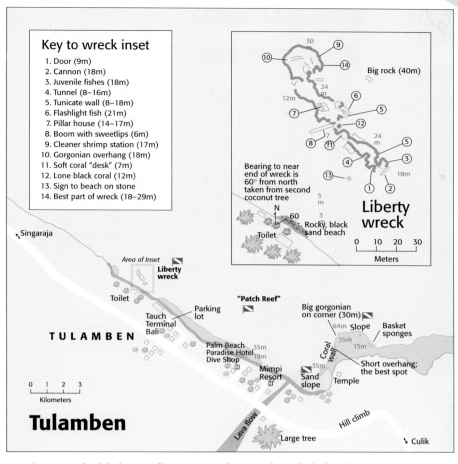

Key to wreck inset

1. Door (9m)
2. Cannon (18m)
3. Juvenile fishes (18m)
4. Tunnel (8–16m)
5. Tunicate wall (8–18m)
6. Flashlight fish (21m)
7. Pillar house (14–17m)
8. Boom with sweetlips (6m)
9. Cleaner shrimp station (17m)
10. Gorgonian overhang (18m)
11. Soft coral "desk" (7m)
12. Lone black coral (12m)
13. Sign to beach on stone
14. Best part of wreck (18–29m)

Bearing to near
end of wreck is
60° from north
taken from second
coconut tree

Big rock (40m)

**Liberty
wreck**

Rocky, black
sand beach

Toilet

0   10   20   30
Meters

Singaraja

Area of Inset
**Liberty
wreck**

Toilet

"Patch Reef"

Parking
lot

Big gorgonian
on corner (30m)

Basket
sponges

Tauch
Terminal
Bali

T U L A M B E N

Palm Beach
Paradise Hotel
Dive Shop

Mimpi
Resort

Sand
slope

Short overhang;
the best spot

Temple

64m Slope

35m 15m

0   1   2   3
Kilometers

Tulamben

Lava flow

Large tree

Hill climb

Culik

remains a wonderful place to dive, and it has recovered nicely from the El Niño bleaching, but with more divers visiting it now more than ever it is essential to be cautious.

Beyond the Wreck

Should you want to take a break from the wreck, there is a good coral wall beginning on the opposite end of the beach. Divers enter the **Drop-off** from a somewhat protected nook, swim down a small sand embankment and over to the wall, which drops from 5 meters to 60-plus.

The wall does not host huge numbers of fish but has a tremendous variety. The wall ends in a ridge 100 meters from the starting point, and becomes a steep slope.

In front of the Paradise Resort, many photographers find what is a delightfully rich little patch reef. **Paradise Reef** begins as patches of coral among cobbles, becomes a fully developed reef at about eight meters, and runs to black sand at 20 meters and below. This reef, which is the area's favored snorkeling spot, is dominated by hard corals, but there is a little bit of everything here.

Though less than 200 meters long, this reef, like the rest of the Tulamben sites, also supports a diverse fish population. Parrotfish, wrasse, snappers, angelfish, butterflyfish, to name but a few; there are also some rarities like ribbon eels, frogfish and colorful leaf scorpionfish. This reef, because of its proximity to the resorts, makes an excellent night dive.

— *David Espinosa/Kal Muller*

Opposite: Bali's most popular site, the *Liberty* shipwreck in Tulamben, has in recent years become the residence for, among other, more inquisitive fish, a large school of jacks. Tulamben, Bali. *Photo by Shaun Tierney.*

Nusa Penida

Abundant Pelagics and Some Fierce Currents

45 min–1.5 hrs
by boat

Good to great;
20+ meters

Moderate to very
strong. Currents are
unpredictable, often
fierce. Cold water

Very good variety
of hard corals;
excellent stand of
Dendronephthya

Drop-offs, steep
slopes

Excellent variety;
many pelagics

Large schools of
all kinds of fish;
very large hawksbill
turtles. Site also
hosts sharks, mantas
and even oceanic
sunfish

Nusa Penida, across the Badung Strait from Bali's southern tip, offers some of the best diving to be found anywhere. But conditions around Penida and its two smaller sister islands—Nusa Lembongan and Nusa Ceningan—can sometimes be difficult, with cold water and unpredictable currents reaching four or more knots. This is not a place for beginning divers.

Coral Walls and Pelagics

Most of the dive spots are around the channel between Nusa Penida and Nusa Ceningan. The standard reef profile here has a terrace at 8–12 meters, then a wall or steep slope to 25–30 meters. From there the bottom slopes gently to the seabed at 600 meters. Pinnacles and caves are often encountered. At 35–40 meters, long antipatharian wire corals are common, spiraling outward more than 8 meters. Pelagics are the main attraction, and you have a good chance to see jacks, mackerel and tunas. Reef sharks were once common, but are now likely to be found deeper. Mantas are frequently seen feeding at **Manta Point**. The most unusual

Lembongan
Point

Gunkan

Coral
outcrops

200m

50m

Big rock

Jungutbatu

Jackfish
Point

S.D.
(Grade School)

Ped

LEMBONGAN

Ceningan
Point

Toyapakeh

Binyaung

Lembongan

CENINGAN

Coral wall

Sebunibus

Ceningan wall

Gamat
Bay

Sakti

50m

Crystal Bay

Shark cave

NUSA PENIDA

0   1   2   3
Kilometers

Nusa Penida & Lembongan

pelagic visitor is undeniably the bizarre, two-meter-long mola mola, or ocean sunfish. During the late summer months, this mysterious, large flattened fish with elongated dorsal and ventral fins is spotted at several sites along Nusa Penida's north coast.

The most common dive spots are just south of the dock at Toyopakeh, or a bit further east, at **Ped** and **SD**, named for the *sekolah dasar,* or primary school, which sits on the beach. There are other dive spots down the northeast and southwest coasts of Penida, but these areas, swept by tricky currents, require an experienced dive guide and more time than is available in a single day to reach and dive. Overnight boats are available.

The currents sometimes flow quickly at both Ped and SD, but divers will marvel at the variety and numbers of fish, and the magnificent colors of the healthy hard and soft corals, colors that are accentuated by the stunning "gin-clear" visibility. Guests are typically dropped off in the rubble shallows, where they swim only a few meters before encountering the steep slope. Large schools of black triggerfish and unicornfish crowd the various bommies scattered across the slope. The topography does not vary at either site, so if the current is running—and it can often top 3 knots—divers can either duck into a cave or behind the large bommies to wait for stray buddies or divemasters! (Divers won't be the only ones to seek shelter, as often sweetlips, fusiliers and turtles can be seen resting in the lee of these bommies.)

Toyopakeh

One of the most commonly dived, and most popular dives in Nusa Penida is around the corner from SD, near the platform where the big Bali Hai boats tie up. While there are not enough superlatives to describe **Toyopakeh**, it is also without a doubt the most difficult site to dive, for the currents that rip through the strait here are fast and furious. (Warning: If dived at the wrong time, the currents can carry unwary divers out into the surrounding ocean.)

If judged correctly, these currents bring with them big schools of fish, sea turtles, occasionally mola molas and dozens of fusiliers and sweetlips that swarm the healthy, colorful pillars in various places. At rare periods of slack cur-

Below: A small white tip shark shelters in a cave off Nusa Penida's north coast. *Photo by Shaun Tierney.*

rent guests can make their way under the platform, where large jacks feed, or sit back in 5 meters and watch as thousands of smaller anthias and basslets play. If making only one dive on Nusa Penida, Toyopakeh is where you should go. But leave your camera with the macro lens behind, and bring reef hooks to hang onto dead corals…or get ready for the ride of your life!
— *Kal Muller/David Espinosa*

Above: Perched on the stem of a colorful sea pen, this small goby keeps a watchful eye for predators. *Photo by Shaun Tierney.*

Beach; 5 min by
small boat

Fair to good,
15–25 meters

Mild, up to 2 knots

Hard corals
good deep

Coastal reef; flats,
slope and wall

Excellent numbers,
superb variety

Density of fish on
the deep wall

Amed

Fish Lover's Heaven

Jemeluk Bay was hit hard by coral bleaching caused by El Niño in 1998, but some of the reef—including the shallows, which had become overgrown with brown-red algae—is already showing signs of recovery. The deeper sections fared better, and the gorgonians and corals on the outer reef below 15 meters were never hurt, and are still healthy and fantastic. Overall, what this reef lacks in coral coverage it more than makes up in the sheer numbers and variety of fish.

There are a couple operators here, but as access to phone lines in the north is still limited divers can only show up, book a dive and get wet (or alternatively book through an operator in Tulamben). The main, eastern reef off Cemeluk curves around a rock outcropping just east of town. A small *jukung* delivers divers out into the bay, where they drop in at a point just below a small temple on the hillside. A short coral flat—the one which was hit hard by coral bleaching—leads to a coral wall, which drops to 50 meters.

Schools of fish cascade down the wall, feeding in the mostly gentle current that sweeps around the point. The numbers of fishes are staggering—perhaps the best in Bali, with the exception of the sites to the east. And the diversity is a bonus, with hundreds of bannerfish, black snappers, pyramid butterflyfish and fusiliers, which swim in intricate designs off in the blue.

As the current picks up steam, it carries divers to a reef flat around the point. If the current gets too

Below: A gorgonian fan, swarming with basslets. Amed. *Photo by Takamasa Tonozuka.*

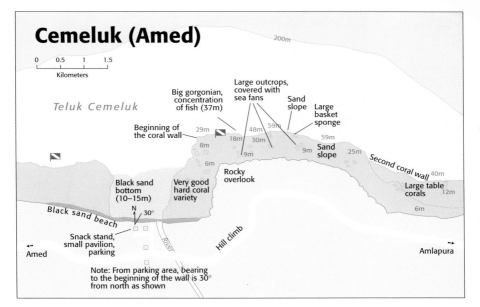

Cemeluk (Amed)

0   0.5   1   1.5
Kilometers

Teluk Cemeluk

Big gorgonian, concentration of fish (37m)

Large outcrops, covered with sea fans

Sand slope

Large basket sponge

Beginning of the coral wall   29m

48m   59m

8m   18m   30m

59m

9m   Sand slope

6m   9m   9m   Sand slope   25m

Second coral wall   40m

Black sand bottom (10–15m)

Very good hard coral variety

Rocky overlook

Large table corals   12m

6m

Black sand beach

N   30°

Snack stand, small pavilion, parking

River

Hill climb

← Amed

Amlapura →

Note: From parking area, bearing to the beginning of the wall is 30° from north as shown

strong, divers can take shelter behind the small patches of reef, large sea fans and big barrel sponges that are interspersed throughout this sandy slope. Barracuda, reef sharks, turtles and more butterflyfish swarm here.

The current typically dies out a little beyond this slope, and drops divers on a second, shallower wall. The corals here are mainly broken, but this is a popular spot for sighting humphead parrotfish and squid.

To the West

A deeper wall, and one that could typically be dived first, lies on the western rim of the small bay. Once again, *jukungs* motor around the corner to an area about 100 meters before the traditional salt works are seen on the beach. A blue-water descent can be avoided if guests drop in closer to shore, but this means more time swimming along a featureless sand flat, and less time spent at the wall.

A ridge begins forming at 40 meters, and soon turns into a wall, which gets progressively deeper as the current sweeps eastward. At the base of the wall, there are usually two or three white tip or gray sharks sleeping in the sand. While not as common, this is also where eagle rays and Napoleon wrasse have been spotted. The wall is covered in dozens of gorgonian fans, large and small, and it was on one of these smaller fans that guide Larry Smith saw two diminutive pygmy seahorses in 1998—at the time this was the furthest point west on Bali at which these magnificent little fish had been seen.

The wall continues on, getting steeper and steeper; but by this point most divers are up in the shallow flats, which feature small strands of hard and table corals. Angelfish and smaller groupers flit past, and in the cracks and crevices an occasional moray can be found.

Further to the west, beyond the first salt works, there is a prolific black sand slope, perfect for spotting muck critters and invertebrates. The gentle slope is littered with fish aggregation devices—typically wooden slats piled high or bundles of old tires—that attract white-eyed morays, crabs, lobsters and all types of colorful shrimps. With keen eyes and patience, if you comb the shallows you might be able to find Ambon scorpionfish, bizarre octopus and bobtail squid in the tiny patches of grass.

— *David Espinosa/David Pickell*

Menjangan

Clear Water and Walls off Bali's Westernmost Tip

30 min by boat from Labuan Lalang post

Very good to superb, 25–50 meters

Very slight

Very good numbers and variety; abundant soft corals

Walls, particularly rugged; wreck

Good number, only average variety

Fields of garden eels; steep walls

Menjangan Island lies just offshore from Bali's mountainous northwest tip. Because the island is in a protected position, currents and wind-generated waves are rarely a bother, and the reefs here offer fine, easy diving.

The reef flats of Menjangan, once famous for their sheer, uninterrupted growth of coral, were reduced to rubble by a crown-of-thorns starfish outbreak in 1997 and the El Niño warming of 1998. The reef wall is still rich, however, and the flats are coming back—with more variety, particularly in soft corals and gorgonians, than before.

The island is part of Bali Barat National Park, a protected reserve area that encompasses much of Bali's sparsely populated western end, some three hours from the popular resorts.

Craggy Vertical Walls

The coral walls around Menjangan are vertical, and drop 30–60 meters, to a sandy slope. The reef surface is rugged, and walls are cut by caves, grottoes, crevices and funnel-like chimneys. Gorgonian fans reach large sizes here, and huge barrel

Menjangan Island

0   0.3   0.6   0.9
Kilometers

277m

200m

124m

100m

⑤   ⑧   ⑥   86m

"Bat cave"

MENJANGAN I.

④

⑦   52m   ②

③   102m   ①

100m

160m   200m

1. Post II ranger hut; sand beach
2. Best diving route
3. Underwater cave (18m)
4. Post I ranger hut; sand beach
5. Anchor wreck (7m)
6. Sand slope
7. Underwater bay; nice overhang
8. Diving route; best for snorkelling

MENJANGAN

INDONESIA

42

sponges are very common.

The variety of fish here is somewhat inferior to Bali's other dive sites—but there are more schooling fishes here. Large batfish accompany divers, and barracuda, trevally and the occasional reef shark can be seen skimming the bottom of the wall.

Small boats ferry divers from the Nature Reserve dock at Labuhan Lalang to the dive sites, and a surface interval is spent onshore at either of the two posts. The edge of the reef terrace is between one and five meters, and in front of the southern shelter a V-shaped delta of sand points the way for snorkelers and divers.

The Northwest

Two of the best dives are on the island's northwest tip. The **Anchor Wreck** lies just off the reef edge in 40–50 meters, and is very close to one of the small docks and guard posts maintained by the park service. The wreck is coated with hard corals and gorgonian fans, and swarmed by snappers, sweetlips and wrasse. Because it lies on a deep sand slope, few guides would take recreational divers there; instead most stop at the beautifully encrusted anchor before heading off along the reef.

The point itself is a magnificent dive, popular with photographers for the vast fields of garden eels. Divers enter further eastward along the wall, gently finning (for there is rarely a current stronger than mild) towards the point. The reef is healthy here, with very little damage to the table corals and hard corals. Near the point, the wall becomes enveloped in large, purple gorgonian fans. Most divers choose to stay in the shallows here, where deserts of sand and extraordinarily healthy patch reefs extend southward.

— *Kal Muller/David Espinosa*

20–30 min by small outboard

Variable; poor to very good; 6–22 meters

Can be extremely strong—more than 5 knots and very tricky. Cold water

Excellent coverage and variety

Steep coral walls; underwater canyon

Abundant and varied

Tepekong's Canyon, good chance to see pelagics; Biaha's complex wall

Candi Dasa and Padangbai

Spectacular, Bone-chilling Dives on Offshore Reefs

Amuk Bay is 6 km across and located south of Bali's easternmost point. North of Padangbai is the Blue Lagoon, a treasure trove of marine life. Two sites—Tepekong and Mimpang—outside the bay, Biaha to the north, and Gili Selang on Bali's northeast tip also offer breathtaking diving.

The small islands of Mimpang, Tepekong and Biaha are surrounded by healthy, low-lying reefs, and are swept at times by torrential currents that bring in nutrients, accounting for the diversity. The upwelling of very cold water from the deep basin south of Bali brings with it some stunning marine life.

The currents from the Lombok Strait require care and respect as they create unpredictable water movements. But at these unprotected sites you'll find a vast number and great diversity of fish, abundant

Below: Hundreds of outrigger boats, like these descend every morning on Bali's east coast with the previous night's catch. *Photo by Shaun Tierney.*

sharks and frequent pelagic visitors set against a backdrop of craggy black walls with beautiful, healthy corals and often superb visibility.

You must have a guide who has a great deal of experience in the area. While the sites may be diveable, they are small, and if the current is too fast your dive may be finished in only 5 minutes.

The Blue Lagoon

Accessed by small *jukungs* from nearby Candi Dasa or Padangbai, sites here are worth the ride; while the topography is not spectacular the fish life is amazing. On any one dive expect huge Napoleon wrasse, several kinds of reef sharks, stonefish, moray and blue ribbon eels, nudibranchs, rays, squid and octopus and leaf scorpionfish in every hue.

This is a site used for courses and snorkelers because visibility in the protected bay is typically 15–20 meters.

Mimpang

Also known as Batu Tiga (three rocks), the site is part of a north-south ridge with the richer, south end (Shark Point) dropping into deeper water. Shark Point offers the best chance in Bali to see white tip sharks and, from August through October, the ocean sunfish (mola mola).

The topography of Mimpang is diverse, with sloping reefs, craggy rocks and walls—all covered in hard and soft corals and gorgoni-

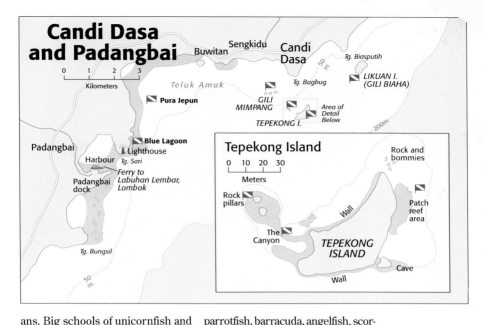

Candi Dasa and Padangbai

Buwitan • Sengkidu • Candi Dasa

Teluk Amuk

Pura Jepun

GILI MIMPANG

TEPEKONG I.

Tg. Biasputih

Tg. Bugbug

LIKUAN I. (GILI BIAHA)

Area of Detail Below

0 1 2 3 Kilometers

Padangbai

Blue Lagoon
Lighthouse
Harbour Tg. Sari
Ferry to
Padangbai Labuhan Lembar,
dock Lombok

Tg. Bungsil

50 m

Tepekong Island

0 10 20 30 Meters

Rock pillars

The Canyon

Wall

TEPEKONG ISLAND

Rock and bommies

Patch reef area

Cave

Wall

200m

---

ans. Big schools of unicornfish and snappers, many blue-spotted rays, Napoleon wrasse, morays, trumpetfish, bannerfish, butterflyfish and triggerfish swarm here.

Tepekong and The Canyon

This island offers some of Bali's most spectacular diving: steep walls, The Canyon, cold water and strong currents make this a site for experienced divers. Very good visibility.

Maximum depth at The Canyon is 40 meters, and if there is no current you can see the dramatic beauty of these stunning walls. In the usual swirling current, your view is somewhat obstructed by the schools of sweetlips, snapper and big-eyed trevally, bumphead parrotfish, unicornfish, batfish, groupers, sharks and other pelagics.

East Tepekong

Enter on the right and there is an excellent wall, which plunges to depths of 40-plus meters; to the left, there is a small coral reef (max depth: 24 meters) with hard, soft and table corals. The marine life is outstanding, with the occasional turtle, tuna,

parrotfish, barracuda, angelfish, scorpionfish and several species of triggerfish. Conditions are generally less difficult here than at The Canyon.

Biaha

This crescent-shaped rocky island is 4 km from Mimpang and Tepekong. Very few dive companies offer trips here, but the diving is superb—although both the surge and up/down currents can be very strong. Most of the awkward currents are on the northern slope.

There is a beautiful reef around the island, a rocky slope in the north, and a wall around in south, which has waves breaking from above. The inner area of the crescent (the east side) has a cave in which white tip sharks sleep.

Gili Selang

To the northeast, and more than an hour by boat, the island of Gili Selang features, like all of the exposed sites on the east coast, ripping currents (only for expert divers). However, take the plunge here and be rewarded with a healthy reef slope.

— *Annabel Thomas*

Chocolate-colored sand; lots of garbage

Excellent, for muck divers. Exotic and bizarre

Bobbitt worms, seahorses, frogfish and so much more!

Secret Bay (Gili Manuk)

Much Ado about Something

On an island as small as Bali, it's difficult to keep a secret. Therefore, it was no small feat that a local dive operator was able to keep the whereabouts of a particularly plentiful muck spot hidden for so long.

Gilimanuk Bay in northwest Bali is about 2 km across and very shallow, much of it less than 5 meters deep. A reef north of the bay's mouth makes the opening even narrower than it appears on a land map, and creates a channel that sweeps in and hooks around two islands in the bay's center. This strong flow (with speeds of up to 7 knots) through the strait is what makes the diving in Gilimanuk so interesting: The bay becomes a kind of refugium, a catch tank for larval fish and plankton.

This bay harbors a number of rare jewels for the macro-photographer, including odd gobies and dragonets, and such rarities as the juvenile Batavia batfish, a beauty with zebra stripes and ragged fins that seems to want to make itself look like a crinoid.

Macro Heaven is Mighty Muck

Gilimanuk is not a dive for everyone. Nowhere will you find a sounding of 15 meters, or rich stands of coral and abundant reef fish. Secret Bay is a specialty site for photographers, and for divers who are looking for something a little different.

Near the ferry terminal, Dive & Dive's operates a small, basic losmen-style resort for divers looking to diversify their diving experience.

Just steps from the open courtyard lies the entrance to some pretty 'spectacular' muck (oxymoron?).

I wasn't quite sure what to expect of my first dive at Secret Bay. The wall of fame in the dive center was eye opening, with pictures of multi-colored frogfish, juvenile batfish, seahorses and the bizarre Bobbitt worm; but reports I'd heard from diving friends were mixed.

The first thing that struck me was the water's temperature—I had been warned by friends that the waters in Secret Bay could be as cold as 22°C (some friends). Though the divemaster mentioned that the temperatures are in a constant state of flux, I was overdressed in a 5mm wetsuit.

I also wasn't prepared for the nondescript landscape—the sand in Tulamben or Amed is broken by strands of coral here and there, but in Secret Bay it is colorless and featureless, and no deeper than 9 meters. The mud-colored sand wasn't broken by so much as a coral head, though there were various bits and pieces of trash—empty cans and bottles, chip wrappers, strands of rope, entire trees, old anchors and chains and barrels.

It was on one of these rusted barrels that we uncovered our first significant find; for hiding on the inner lip of this rusted hulk the divemaster, Made, found a family of six, red ornate ghost pipefish! After the obligatory cries of surprise, we shot our pictures and moved on.

A few feet away hiding in a tin can was a curious little goby, being cleaned by a small, orange shrimp. Inches to the left a dwarf lionfish took refuge in an empty pipe. When I looked up Made was missing, off somewhere in the murk—visibility rarely tops 5 meters—hooting up a storm to indicate that he'd found yet another critter.

The rest of the dive was a blur of frantic activity, as my buddy and I bounced from place to place, as if in some large pinball machine, taking turns shooting the exotic fish Made turned up. After nearly two hours (at an average of 7 meters deep) I emerged, having seen Jan's pipefish, banded pipefish, mating cuttlefish, more ornate ghosties, bearded frogfish hiding amongst the branches of a dead tree and a spiny seahorse.

Five-Meter Worms and Mossy Snakes

If the day dive was special, I was in for a real treat that night. For when light turns to dark, the really bizarre critters make an appearance. With video in hand, I followed as Made swam furiously towards a predetermined site off in the distance. He halted, and pointed with a knowing look in his eye at a yellow disposable Gillette razor, stuck head up in the sand.

Just as rumors of a secret site in Bali had spread like wildfire, so too did the tall tales of one of its residents. According to some reports the Bobbitt worm grew up to twelve feet long, and lived in crevices deep in the ocean. Armed with vicious fangs with lightning speed it lashes out from its lair to devour unwary passersby… If that isn't the recipe for a great dive! For the entire day we pestered Made, begging that he show us this creature.

The Bobbitt worm wasn't a disappointment, though if he does grow up to 12 feet long the individual we saw had a ways to go. The razor was put in the sand not only to mark his burrow, but also to provide a means of comparison. This little guy sported jaws a half inch wide, and he could have only been a foot long. He was playful, though, making quick feints as I switched the strobes on and off, exposing a shiny, spiny underbelly that glowed in brilliant colors of yellow, green, blue and red.

The remainder of the dive was icing on the cake. We saw different frogfish, a mossy sea snake, two more Bobbitt worms and a finger dragonet. Two hours later we emerged from the water spent, but entirely satisfied: we never once ventured deeper than 6 meters, but expended all the air in our tanks and a 60-minute videotape.

— *David Espinosa/David Pickell*

Left: Mug shot of a finger dragonet (*Dactylopus dactylopus*). Secret Bay, Bali. *Photo by Scott Tuason.*

5–15 min by speedboat from live-aboard

15–50+ meters

Light, but swifter further east

Excellent variety and numbers

Walls, black sand slopes, pinnacles, submerged reefs

Excellent. Large variety of reef fish and muck critters

Mentjeng Wall, the world's best nudibranch site

INDONESIA

East of Bali

Island Hopping in Style

Often passed over because divers are more anxious to arrive in Komodo, the islands east of Bali are blessed with some world-class dives. Variety is the spice of life here, and live-aboards can now offer anything from black sand dives to vertiginous walls covered in hard and soft corals.

The **Gili Islands** off Lombok's west coast have become a favorite destination for backpackers, because of the flawless white sand beaches and non-demanding diving. Although coral rings the three islands, the diving isn't outstanding, as the ravages of fish bombing and El Niño have taken their toll. Still, there is some worthwhile diving on the deeper reefs, and quite an assortment of fish life that is ideal for less experienced divers. The gentle slopes, which are swept by mild currents, feature an assortment of reef fish including trevally, sharks, turtles and the more common angelfish and triggers.

Moyo Island gives divers their first taste of what can be expected in Komodo. Two submerged reefs off the island's west coast are swarmed by schools of fish, sharks and other pelagics. Though bombs have damaged the reef tops, the steep slopes of both reefs, which plummet to depths in excess of 80 meters, have survived and support a healthy variety of angelfish, bait-fish and groupers. The smaller reef to the north is rich in nudibranchs and exotic critters—hairy ornate ghost pipefish have been spotted in the mossy shallows. **Satonda**, a smaller island to the east provides another delightful half-day of diving. **Painter's Pleasure**, a healthy

shallow reef slope in front of the ranger station, is decorated in gorgonian fans of all sizes, coral whips, and home to twin-spot gobies, gaudy nudibranchs and dozens of mushroom corals, with the attendant pearly-white pipefish. The sand patch, also in front of the main beach, has stargazers, pipefish, leaf scorpionfish and bobtail squid for a very enjoyable night dive.

For a day diversion, bring some sturdy sandals and hike the short trail that leads to the crater's marine lake. And for a truly memorable show, sit back at dusk and watch as thousands of bats emerge from the island's southern trees, and fly to the mainland in search of food.

If Komodo is Indonesia's tastiest dive spot, then **Sangeang** is the flavor of the day. Because guests clamored for Komodo, live-aboards would push on, ignoring this lush, volcanic island for the adrenaline diving at Banta, two hours to the east. In 1999, on one of his famous hunches, guide Larry Smith directed his boat to the island's southernmost point and jumped in.

At the western edge of a small beach that serves as an itinerant fishing village lies one of the best muck sites in all of Indonesia. The currents at **Mentjeng Wall** can be tricky due to its exposed position, but there are spots to take shelter and visibility can be good.

The wall, which bottoms out at 15–20 meters, is covered in crinoids, sponges and sea whips, some of which host colonial anemone; and while there are ghost pipefish, frogfish and saron shrimp tucked away in the crevices, the real action is at the base of the wall, where anything from boxer crabs to robust ghost pipefish make their home. The black sand slope is also the most prolific nudibranch site in all of Indonesia, and guests make a game of counting the number of species found there on one dive (the current record is 34!).

Around the corner two more rich invertebrate sites round out the diving in the south. **Tikno's Reef** and **Black Magic** are so good, in fact that some operators—with the right group—might avoid Banta, in order to spend a full day at Sangeang.

At the mouth of the long bay that leads into **Bima**, Sumbawa, lie two sites that, although worlds apart continue to excite ardent divers. **Diversity** on the east side has two separate walls, one that drops to 20 meters and the other to 30 meters. Though it is unprotected during the months of December to March, visibility is quite good year round, and the ribbon eels, frogfish and good reef fish make it a splendid checkout dive for trips depart-ing from Bima. The top of the smaller wall might also be a manta cleaning station. **Copycat Copycat** on the other side of the channel is the quintessential muck dive, with visibility hovering at 5–7 meters. The small patch reef at 5 meters is covered in toon shells and spiny seahorses. The vast, featureless sand below the reef is punctuated by a single dead log at 15 meters, home to frogfish, pipefish, and marble-eyed morays. The real highlight, and the main reason to dive here is the presence of the elusive mimic octopus in the surrounding desert.

While few of the operators make the effort, the diving off southern Sumba is wild. With nothing but water between Sumba and Australia's northern shores, this place has become a haven for surfers; but several sites—including **Magic Mountain** and **Marlin Rock**—on the offshore reefs hold the promise of pelagic action. If the opportunity should arise, the local villages, throwbacks to a feudal time, merit a visit.

— *David Espinosa*

Below: Though its coloration may suggest otherwise, this bright yellow frogfish is indeed difficult to find, and a jewel for underwater photographers. *Photo by Shaun Tierney.*

Komodo

Dragons and Jurassic Gyroscopes

5–10 min by tender from live-board; 1 hr from Labuanbajo

Variable, from 2–50 meters

Can be extremely strong, up to 5 knots

Superb, with a good mix of hard and soft corals

Sloping reef and some walls

Excellent

Pioneer diving in many places. Encounters with a variety of large pelagics

Diving Komodo is like stepping on a Jurassic gyroscope—tilting and spinning at uncontrollable speeds. There are times when guests have been perched in a 2-knot current, holding on for dear life, mouthpieces vibrating, watching a *halimeda* ghost pipefish while their buddy gesticulates wildly, trying to gain their attention to point out a hovering manta ray. Dives like this are common—it is hard to know where to look and what to focus on. Welcome to Komodo!

Komodo, as well as the other islands between Sumbawa and Flores, belongs to another time and place. Rugged, dry, covered in scrub and borassus palms, it is just a few degrees south of the equator, and represents an arid anomaly in the lushness of the monsoon-fed islands of the Indonesian archipelago. But it is the perfect habitat for one of the world's most awesome animals—the Komodo dragon.

Biological Riches

The wild Komodo area offers just about every imaginable type of diving, from current-swept sea mounds patrolled by groups of sharks, tuna and other big fish to plunging walls, covered in impressive corals, to calm reefs alive with invertebrates and hundreds of colorful reef fishes. The water temperature varies from a chilly 22°C to 30°C bath water. Visibility ranges from a clear 25–30 meters to a dismal 3 meters, when clouds of tiny fish and plankton allow only macrophotography.

The variety of marine life in the Komodo area rivals the world's best. There are deep seas both north and south of the narrow straits running between the little islands, and strong currents and upwellings bring nutrients and plankton, keeping all the marine creatures well-fed.

While the Komodo area is well explored, due to its vastness there are new dive sites discovered every year. In general, there are two habitats and two seasons for diving Komodo—the winter for the cooler, temperate-water southern sites; and the summer for the warmer, tropical north. The main factor in enjoying diving Komodo is visibility, and the north is the more predictable in this regard.

Komodo is a unique region because it offers divers the choice of both tropical and temperate diving within the scant space of 10 kilometers. The volcanic thrusts and limestone uplifts combined with a half-meter differential between the South China Sea and the Indian Ocean have created a topography conducive to wild and unpredictable currents. Upwellings from the southern seas add to the unique mélange of planktonic life found here. Hence the unimaginable, prolific and dense marine-life that characterizes Komodo! If you can find shelter from the tempestuous currents, you'll discover an astounding plentitude of rare and unusual critters to photograph and to marvel at. That's what Komodo is all about—the rare, the unique, the special… and the colors are out of this world!

Opposite: Fishing boats anchoring at dawn; Komodo Island.
Photo by Clay Bryce.

Diving the South

South Komodo is arguably the best diving in the world, and the best time to dive there is from late October through early May. Then the sky is blue, seas are calm and there is enough of a breeze to cool sunburned bodies. Between November and January visibility (10–15 meters) is as good as it gets in such plankton-rich seas, and the soft coral, invertebrate life and fish are nothing short of spectacular. South Komodo is difficult to dive from May through September due to the southeast trade winds, which generate huge swells and howling winds. Due to the distance from Labuanbajo, land-based operators rarely visit this area.

The premier dive sites in the south are found in the horseshoe bay between Rinca and Nusa Kode. Divers are divided between **Cannibal Rock** and **Yellow Wall** as to which is their favorite site, as each has its own merit.

The **Yellow Wall** is actually two walls, one atop another, the second of which is an overhang that plunges 50 meters to the floor. The site is covered in yellow soft corals and is rich in invertebrate life—yellow pygmy seahorses, colonial blue tunicates, myriads of nudibranchs, and blue-ringed octopus. Yellow Wall faces west and the light is best from midday onwards.

Cannibal Rock is a more versatile site and can be dived from sunrise on through the night. The site, which is at the doorstep of a small promontory, is sloping, and features mini-walls, huge boulders with valleys, and giant terraces at 30-plus meters. There are two-meter red gorgonian fans that periodically—typically during cold water upwellings—host red pygmy seahorses and ghost pipefish; the rare lacey scorpionfish has been sighted nearby. The Rock is covered in sea apples, a rare and brightly colored—in hues of purple, green, blue, red and yellow—temperate sea cucumber, and a truly fascinating sight when its feeding tentacles are extended. There are also three species of venomous urchins found on the Rock, one of which hosts up to five different species of commensals. When the

Below (left):
Coleman shrimp (*Periclimenes colemani*) are one of four commensal organisms found on the toxic sea urchin. Komodo, Indonesia. *Photo by Shaun Tierney.*

Below (right):
This tiny swimming crab, barely 15 mm wide, lives in the colorful fronds of sea pens. *Photo by Shaun Tierney.*

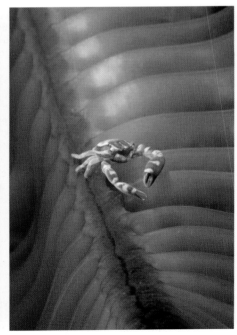

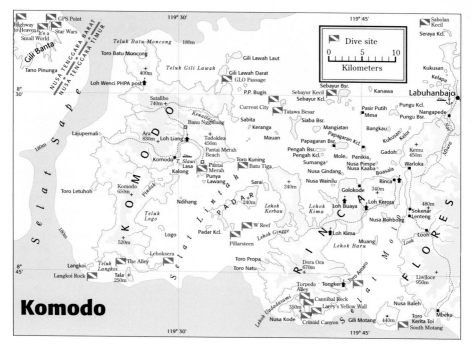

current runs, the fish school, and there have been regular sightings of mantas, large sharks and minke whales.

Other sites in Horseshoe Bay are **Crinoid Canyon**, **Boulders**, **Pipedream** and the newest discovery, **Torpedo Alley**, renowned for its torpedo rays and frogfish. Meter for meter, this bay has to be the richest and most varied in the world.

South Komodo has other distinctive dive sites off the islands of Padar and Tala. **Pillarsteen** is off south Padar, and is a topographer's dream with huge chunks of rock buckled into channels and canyons, caves, swim-throughs and chimneys. This dive is totally different from other diving in Komodo—it is fun and action-filled when the currents are running. **W Reef**, a few hundred meters to the north of Pillarsteen, is a series of four underwater pinnacles extending perpendicularly from the island to a depth of 30 meters. This structure is covered in pristine coral and regularly buzzed by mantas and schools of bumphead parrotfish. Off northwest Tala is **The Alley**, which fea-

tures large, lazing schools of manta rays November through March. **Langkoi Rock** is fully exposed, and so buffeted by strong current, which explains the regular presence of large pelagics. It is reputedly a mating site for gray sharks in April. **Lehoksera** is a high-voltage dive on the southeast tip. The dive begins mildly enough, with a gentle current that allows divers to get ready with reef hooks, gloves and other accoutrements. The current picks up faster and faster until divers reach a slot created by the main reef and a smaller pinnacle offshore. In the middle of this slot, there is a small bommie at 30 meters, which is buzzed by large groupers, turtles, sharks and schools of every fish imaginable. The current spits divers out onto another gently sloping reef, which is very rich in soft corals and hard coral formations.

Diving the North

Australians Ron and Valerie Taylor pioneered diving in Komodo, and the site they first discovered was

Pantai Merah, at the entrance to Slawi Bay, where the main ranger station and old dragon feeding area is located. **Val's Rock** (or **Pantai Merah**) extends from the surface down to 20-plus meters, and is richly adorned in all manner of colorful sea life. Pantai Merah represents a transition between tropical and temperate water habitats, north and south, and with its fabulous fish and corals is a good introduction to Komodo.

Considered by some as the best dive in the north, **GPS Point** is a submerged rock to the northwest of **Banta Island's** largest bay. This is one of the only sites where sharks are regularly found, and up to five species can be identified in a single dive. Invariably divers encounter strong currents here, which is why GPS Point is swarming with jacks, tuna and schools of barracuda and surgeonfish. Unfortunately this site has suffered depredation by long-line shark-fishermen and fish bombers. But on any given dive, be prepared to scan the gorgonian fans for pygmy seahorses and the deep blue for eagle rays and mantas.

If the currents are running too strong on GPS Point, operators have other options only minutes away. **Star Wars** is a gentle slope that bottoms out in a sandy floor at 30 meters. The currents, which can range from calm to raging, typically flow eastward, away from the shallow point. There are several gorgonian fans, which host the ubiquitous pygmy seahorse, invertebrates and sharks. The myriad smaller schooling fish like anthias, basslets and fusiliers that swim amongst each other look like they are playing out an outer space battle of epic proportions—hence the name. **Highway to Heaven** on the opposite point is a wild ride that must only be done on slack tide, or during gentle currents. A vertiginous wall extends around the point, and is covered in soft corals, fans and sea whips, and home to countless juvenile angelfish. But the highlight of the dive is the 40-meter-plus deep bommies, around which schools of snappers, two different species of barracuda, sharks and rays swarm. Continuing on to the backside, mantas and eagle rays play off in the blue. For end of the day muck dives with no current, **It's a Small World**, a sand slope fringed by a healthy reef, has resident stargazers, frogfish, leaf scorpionfish and a host of invertebrate life. It is no small reason why Banta is a must-stop for live-aboards visiting Komodo.

Sabolan Kecil, north of Labuanbajo, is a site regularly visited by land-based operators. To the east of the island are two sea mounds at 20 meters—a site called Shark Bank. The hard coral cover is minimal, but the soft corals and large gorgonians are excellent. The fish life, particularly sharks, makes this site well worth visiting. Work your way down the valley between the two mounds as you pause to view the pelagics.

Tatawa Kecil and **Batu Bolong** are two bare rocks are in

Below: The crinoid shrimp (*Periclimenes amboinensis*), or squat lobster, mimics the color of its host feather star. *Photo by Shaun Tierney.*

close proximity, and exposed to the full force of the currents that rage through the Linta Strait. On a high slack tide, when currents abate and the diving is less stressful, these are two more popular sites for land-based operators. Giant trevally, mantas and dugongs have been encountered here.

There are three great dives to the north of the island of **Gili Lawa**

Laut—**Crystal Rock, Castle Rock** and **Lighthouse**. All sites have good hard and soft coral cover, and swarms of schooling fish. Lighthouse has a "honey hole" on the point, which is home to schools of sweetlips and batfish. Mantas are frequently in evidence on the safety stop here.

— *David Espinosa/*
Cody Shwaiko

Weird Science

Over the course of the next few years Komodo will be a guinea pig, a testing site for a revolutionary type of marine science. American biologist Tom Goreau will be subjecting some parts of the underwater reef that have been bombed to a process known as coral regeneration.

A total of 20 solar panels will be erected on Punya Island, opposite Pantai Merah beach, and attached to a grid of wire-mesh fencing. This grid, which covers a total surface area of 100 meters square, will be laid directly over existing coral rubble produced by blast fishing. Broken and damaged pieces of coral will be affixed to the grid.

The mesh will be secured with boulders at appropriate distances to counteract the action of strong currents. A current of six volts will continually run through this grid in cables, encased in plastic pipes and buried in either sand or rubble to eliminate chafing and movement by current.

The electrical field generated by the grid accelerates mineral accretion on the exposed metal wires, promoting rapid growth of coral in the magnitude of several times normal growth rates. A varied selection of coral species will be recruited in an attempt to duplicate coral diversity typified on an ideal reef structure.

This coral reef regeneration program is called "jump-starting." Once the coral is deemed healthy and secure, the solar panels and cables can be moved to another site and the process, which is remarkably simple and inexpensive, will be repeated. To repeat the process, the additional cost incurred would be for wire mesh only, approximately US$100 per 100 square meters for materials. The cables and anodes could be re-used for repeated "jump-starts." If successful, the program could be expanded to other areas of the park, or virtually anywhere in the world where coral has suffered extensive damage.

Left: Putting its best face forward, this nudibranch (*Risbecia tryoni*) poses for a picture on a sand flat in Komodo.
Photo by Shaun Tierney.

5 min by speedboat from live-aboard;
1–2hrs from Kupang

5–50 meters

Varies up to 5 knots

Excellent

Walls, sloping reefs, pinnacles

Excellent

Pertamina Pier and Kal's Dream, as different as two sites can be

Alor

The East's Dream Destination

Alor is a small island that lies at the end of the Nusa Tenggara chain, north of West Timor. The dive locations that have been explored center around the three islands framed by Alor and Pantar: Buaya, Ternate and Pura. The diving here, with much of the topography dominated by steep walls, ledges and caves is world class. But Alor is in the middle of nowhere, and getting there takes some effort.

The remote location guarantees the type of diving that most only dream of. The fact that many of the best sites lay steps from fishing villages virtually ensures their protection. And Alor is beginning to attract the type of operators who can offer luxury and comfort. While there are no five-star resorts there is one land-based operator, and a few live-aboards ply these waters on a semi-regular basis.

Graeme and Donovan Whitford, a father-and-son team pioneered this magnificent group of islands in the early '90s. They operate what is currently the only land-based operation, and have developed many of the more than 40 sites that are dived today; this list begins, and for many divers ends, with Kal's Dream.

Dream Come True

I first experienced **Kal's Dream** in 1995, at the tender age of 18. At that time I was still a rank amateur, with only a handful of dives under my belt. Graeme's son, Donovan, took me under his wing, and for the first two days we experienced superlative dives at the **Arch**, where we were buzzed by eagle rays and sharks, the **Fish Bowl**, the **Boardroom** and **Cave Point**, where the steep walls covered in a profusion of colors dizzied me. These, however, were only a prelude to the real show.

On the morning of the third day, Donovan felt I was ready for the Dream, a small pinnacle that rises from the deep and sits in the middle of the strait.

I can still remember that dive as if it was yesterday. The Dream is marked by a vertiginous wall on the south side and a rather gentle slope on the north. We perched ourselves on a small outcropping on the north side at 30 meters, and watched the show unfold.

Numbers of gray sharks swam up from the abyssal depths, and began circling our roost. One particularly frisky shark passed a few times, getting nearer with each pass. Down in the depths bus-sized groupers slowly swam about, while schools of enormous tuna patrolled the reef top. The visibility was gin-clear, and we could see as barracuda swarmed a tip opposite our ledge.

Suddenly, a large, indistinguishable figure loomed from the dark. The ever-nearer and increasingly worrying gray shark quickly scattered, and before it disappeared back into the shadows I caught a brief glimpse of my patron saint and protector—a giant 3.5-meter hammerhead.

To this day not one dive on the Dream has equaled that first experience, but they come close. It is without a doubt a dive to dream about…

In and Around Alor

Because the Dream must be dived at slack tide (any other time would be insanity), operators there have looked to the many other walls and reefs in the area.

On Pulau Pura's southwest tip lies a marine anomaly that few divers have ever been able to comprehend. **Clownfish Alley** is an unremarkable slope, but what it lacks in topography it makes up in marine life. From 2 meters down to 30 meters, and for 1 km, every boulder and rock and pebble is covered in anemones.

Mandarin House is a new site in front of the north village on Pura. It is a rather unprepossessing, though healthy reef slope on which mandarinfish can be seen cavorting...during the day! If currents are minimal, at dusk divers can also gather there to witness the mating of these magnificent dragonets.

To the east of Mandarin House is one of Pura's healthiest reefwalls, the **Boardroom**, a "hidden" point near the local village. The wall, where several caves and overhangs give shelter to thousands of glassfish, begins just below the waterline, and drops to a sand slope at 50-plus meters. At these depths schooling jacks, snappers and fusiliers swim in the currents, which can gust up to two knots; if the current is running, divers can drift to either side of the point to finish the dive in peace. The wall is even topped by a large rock, home to nudibranchs, leaf scorpionfish and even the blue-ringed octopus.

Pertamina Pier is one of the new sites in Alor. Deep in the harbor, only minutes away from the town of Kalabahi, this black sand slope sits at the base of the old Pertamina Pier, and is home to fantastic muck critters—anything from seahorses to ghost pipefish, the wonderpuss (an unidentified species of octopus), juvenile batfish in the seagrass to the east and harlequin shrimp at various depths. Though the visibility is typically

poor, this is still an awesome dive! At night it only gets better, for stargazers, Pegasus sea moths and bizarre morays come out to play.

Though the various operators don't agree on the name, **Dead Chicken Run** is an amazing site. Near the road on the north edge of the narrow bay adjacent to three large trees there is a small cliff which extends 5 meters below the water. At dusk hundreds of flashlight fish pour out from a small crack in the wall, to disperse throughout the reef. After the light show, divers can wander about the silty, sandy slope below the wall, which on occasion has juvenile batfish, juvenile and adult frogfish, ghost pipefish, seahorses and other invertebrates.

— *David Espinosa*

Above: Alor's underwater marine life is some of the most amazing in Indonesia. Case in point: Clownfish Alley has nothing but clownfishes and host anemones as far as the eye can see.
Photo by Scott Tuason.

On live-aboard,
2–5 min; from land-
based operations, 1hr

Fair to excellent,
10–20 meters in
the off-season,
40 meters at best

Varies: weak to
very strong

Excellent
undamaged reefs

Vertical walls,
slopes

Excellent numbers
and superb variety

Pristine sheer walls
in Banda; wrecks
and untouched
reefs in Irian Jaya

The Northeast

Good if you can get there

Banda Sea

The islands of Maluku were the first in the archipelago to capture the imagination of European explorers. Not for their beauty, although these coconut-fringed islands with powder-white beaches and constant, lazy sunshine certainly fit most tourists' definition of paradise. The Europeans went to the Moluccas in search of one of the world's most coveted commodities—spices.

While the islands there are still sun-bleached and redolent of exotic spices like the clove, this is *also* one of those rare spots on earth where seemingly every dive location you drop in on abounds in fantastic life. If the current political state of affairs was not so volatile, divers would flock to this region.

The Banda Islands, rising from a depth of over 4,000 meters in the Banda Sea, are one of Indonesia's best diving destinations—if you can get there. The wounds from the political and religious turmoil that racked Ambon and Banda in 1999 still haven't healed, and much of the area is unofficially off-limits to travelers. But one or two live-aboards still ply these waters occasionally, because the diving is too good to ignore. Serious divers will enjoy diving in Banda as there is a choice of excellent muck locations and high-voltage pelagic sites, from the shallow lagoon between Banda Neira and Gunung Api to the vertical walls of Hatta, and countless other sites at Manuk, Ai and Koon (among many).

Still good after all these years

The *Pelagian*'s cruise director, Larry Smith, still has fond memories of these sites, as Banda was the first region he dived when he arrived in Indonesia from the Caribbean more than 10 years ago. Every time he plans the next, return trip, "romantic and adventurous images come into startling focus."

The Banda Sea is just one of those few places that divers only dream of adding to their logbooks. The variety and numbers of fish are both excellent, and the chances here are always good to see several big animals. The reefs are pristine, with little signs of fish bombing or other man-made damage. Currents can be tricky at times, but on a good live-aboard with a knowledgeable crew the risks should be negligible.

There is some good diving near Banda Neira at **Keraka** and **Sonegat**, and slightly further away at Lontar, and the two isles to the north—**Batu Kapal** and **Sjahrir**. But it is the islands off Banda Neira at which the best diving can be found.

Hatta Island (formerly Rosengain) is great because it offers a variety of fish in excellent numbers. The sheer wall at **Tanjung Besar** ends in white sand at 40 meters. The surface is honeycombed with small grottos and overhangs, covered in an unusual variety of soft corals that hang from the roofs of these crevices and caves. There is an abundance of moray eels and gorgonians, as well as angelfish, butterflyfish and more.

Together with Hatta, **Ai**, some 25 kilometers to the east of Banda Neira, offers some fantastic diving. Both the north and southwest coasts are ringed with flawless coral walls, rugged and full of caves harboring plenty of fish.

The southwest features a vertiginous wall that drops to more than 70 meters. Tube and barrel sponges and great quantities of soft corals of all hues can be found growing on a wide terrace on the west coast. The sheer drop-off, the number of caves and fissures and the overwhelming richness of life

here compares only to the very best sites in south Komodo and a few isolated islands in the Banda Sea.

Snakes, sharks and everything in between

The sites that continue to draw the most acclaim from guests are Gunung Api, Manuk, the "Twilight Zone" and Koon Island.

Both **Gunung Api** and **Manuk**, to the west and south of Banda Neira, respectively, feature sites with an impossible number of colubrine sea snakes that seem to thrive near the remote, active volcanoes. A typical dive will have upwards of a hundred of the curious snakes poking about in the various nooks and crannies of the reef.

The **Twilight Zone**, a dive with the highest concentration of muck critters in one area (and this coming from the man who "discovered" the Lembeh Straits), is unfortunately located in front of the small *kampung* (town) of Laha, on the west side of the long bay that cuts into the war-torn island of Ambon (so diving there might not be an option). In a spot that is no more than 75 meters long resides a "who's who" of strange and exotic fish and invertebrate life: giant, painted and clown frogfish, sea-

Above: Banda's Gunung Api is the one site in Indonesia where divers are guaranteed seeing large numbers of inquisitive, though relatively harmless banded sea snakes.
Photo by Robert Yin.

Opposite: In order to watch the coupling mandarinfish, divers must have a store of patience and a keen eye—these gaudy dragonets emerge only at dusk to cavort for a few minutes.
Photo by Scott Tuason.

horses of all shapes and sizes, Coleman shrimp, every imaginable color of leaf scorpionfish, *Rhinopias*... and that is not counting the bizarre life living in the sandy area next to the reef.

Finally, **Koon** in the sea's far east remains what Larry believes to be "the best fish place on earth," with schools of tuna, mackerel, fusiliers, jacks and a number of large and unafraid sharks. The site does not show the signs of overfishing or damage that has beset some of the other well-known dives in the region, and is as good today as it was 10 years ago.

Irian Jaya

For more than 10 years divers have been searching Indonesia for the perfect spot. My own logbook is filled with entries from Komodo, Alor, the Banda Sea and far-flung islands in between—and while those areas certainly have outstanding diving, there was always something missing: large numbers of fish!

A wild, virtually unexplored region of glacier-topped mountains, swamps and islands covered with vast areas of rainforest, Irian Jaya is Indonesia's easternmost province. Also called West Papua (or Papua Barat), it occupies the western half of New Guinea Island, which it shares with Papua New Guinea. Few roads exist on the island, due to the rugged terrain, and tourism is limited, with less than 1,000 visitors per year.

But the lack of human presence guarantees great diving! The reefs of the Raja Ampat Islands, off the northwest coast of Irian Jaya, are so full of schooling fish that divers sometimes can't see each other. And the diversity of Raja Ampat is mind-blowing. While Irian Jaya is rich in timber, minerals and valuable natural resources, marine scientists believe it might also be richest in something far more precious —the Raja Ampat Islands are now thought to sit in the most species-rich sea in the world! During a three-week survey in 2002, the Conservation International research team recorded 950 fish species, 450 coral species and over 600 mollusk species. They anticipate that over 1,100 fish species exist in the area. (Dr. Gerald Allen, one of the lead researchers for the team, reported 273 species on a single dive in Raja Ampat, his 30-year lifetime record fish count!)

Irian Jaya was a major battleground in WWII, and originally the vast numbers of wrecked aircraft and ships lured pioneer Max Ammer to the area. Max has operated the region's only permanent diving and eco-resort for 10 years. A tough, resourceful and personable Dutchman with family ties to Irian, he manages the logistics of spare parts, bad fuel, and relationships with local villagers and bureaucrats to provide superb diving. In addition, he supports research teams, spearheads conservation efforts and uses only local Papuan people to build and staff his operation, bringing much needed income and attention to the area.

Max's Irian Diving Eco-Resort is paradise, built in the local Papuan style, with houses perched on stilts beside a jetty, which crosses the lagoon at Kri Island, a one-hour boat ride from Jefman Field airport near Sorong. Beneath the houses guests can watch as small sharks, schools of fish, starfish and clumps of sargassum weed occupied by sargassum frogfish drift by. On most nights, everyone gathers at twilight on the jetty to watch the schools of fish and colorful hard corals fade in the light, to be overtaken by spectacular sunsets above the surrounding islands. By night, it is peaceful and dark. There are few lights, and no manmade noises to distract the senses. Only a moving school of flashlight fish competes with the stars for attention.

Each morning, guests awaken to the smell of local cooking and the sounds of exotic birds. On a non-diving day guests can visit a nearby island to see the red bird of paradise. Small kangaroos, cuscus and other endemic animals are sometimes kept as pets at the resort.

And the diving is good, too. **Cape Kri**, of Dr. Allen's record fish count, is 5 minutes from the jetty, and a superb introduction to the area. Near the point, huge schools of fish parade by—barracuda and pale or bluetail surgeonfish patrol the reef top, while below schools of trevally and fusiliers whiz past and encircle divers. Meanwhile, schools of snapper and batfish cruise slowly between the colorful soft corals and fans. Divers typically stay deep to avoid the current at the top of the reef, current that would suck the unwary into a whirlpool that leads down to 40 meters.

There are more than 50 excellent sites in the Raja Ampats, with many more waiting to be discovered. **Mike's Point**, named after Max's son, is a rock island that was blown apart in WWII. With the wake strong currents create around the island it is no wonder that the pilots thought this site was a ship! Schooling barracuda, surgeonfish, snapper and fusiliers hang in blue water or swirl in endless circles over the slope of green tubastrea coral trees, leather corals, red soft corals and sea fans. Hundreds of sweetlips gather in coral covered crevices below the wall. When there is no current, divers look for pygmy seahorses, nudibranchs, and small cowries with red mantles on the soft corals, golden sweepers and a large area covered with anemones and clownfish.

The other sites near the resort (5–20 minutes away by boat) are best dived during "prime time," when currents bring the biggest and brightest fish. **Sardine** and **Chicken Reef** (named so because of a diver afraid to find sharks) are dives with a large quantity fish—bannerfish, sailfin snappers, three species of barracuda, fusiliers and snappers, bumphead parrotfish, Moorish idols, trevally, batfish, rabbitfish, golden sweepers, goatfish, bream and unicornfish are common. On one dive I counted seven species of sweetlips. "Drop me in

Above: Surgeonfish swarm a healthy reef off Irian Jaya's Raja Ampat Islands. *Photo by Deborah Fugitt.*

where I came out!" is not an infrequent request. Tasseled wobbegong sharks frequent these sites along with white or black tip reef sharks.

For the best sites in the area, divers armed with sunscreen depart early in the morning to the islands further out. Day trips are made to **The Passage**, **Dayang**, or **Melissa's Garden**, and the 45–60 minute ride to these protected areas (with less current) is worth the effort. Raja Ampat boasts amazing natural scenery, rainforests fringed by powdery white sand beaches, incredible rock islands and deep lagoons which divers can visit between dives or explore on specially arranged expeditions.

There is still so much to discover in Irian Jaya, but exploration may take a while: because the area has escaped the blight of bomb and cyanide fishing that has affected other areas in Asia most divers are content to dive the excellent sites at their doorstep. Under Ammer's careful shepherding these sites should remain pristine for many years to come.

—*David Espinosa/ Deborah Fugitt*

Live-aboards
Diving Indonesia's Most Remote Sites

Though the wealth of dive resorts in Indonesia has taken the sport to new heights, to really experience the flavor of this colorful archipelago the best option for a serious diver is on a live-aboard. Live-aboards not only provide unlimited diving, but are also capable of operating in areas that are not readily accessible from land. Divers need only to worry about the diving, and can leave everyday details to the crew.

Diver safety becomes a matter of course as many operators rigidly adhere to international guidelines. There are many packages offered, with something to fit every budget. Look for an operator who offers fixed schedule departures as they are cheaper and can be pre-booked. Stand-by rates are sometimes available, especially in the off-season.

There are a number of factors to consider when choosing a live-aboard, depending on one's personal interest in diving. The current trend in scuba diving is increasingly towards greater involvement and understanding of marine animals. This interest usually manifests itself in U/W photography, which is within the means of many divers.

Indonesian live-aboards cater to this market, and offer a level of service unparalleled in the world: Cameras are gently lifted in and out of tenders, rinsed after use and generally pampered. The crew does everything but take the photo and change the film! Dive guides lead photographers around by the arm, spotting for animals—big and small—even to the point of having "addresses" on the territorial fish.

Sulawesi

Founded by Dr. and Mrs. Batuna in 1987, Murex has been operating live-aboard cruises since 1992, and is currently the only operator to visit the islands to the north and south of Manado. A lifetime seafarer and ship-builder, Dr. Batuna was one of the first persons to explore the underwater treasures of North Sulawesi in the late 1960s.

The MV *Serenade*, Murex's popular flagship, is the first live-aboard to ply the pristine waters of the Sangihe island chain, which offers world class diving, gin-clear visibility and abundant fish life accentuated by unimaginable coral gardens and reef walls. The *Serenade* handles 12 divers in six air-conditioned cabins, all with private bathroom.

Launched in 1998, the MS *Symphony* has three cabins for six divers. Both the *Serenade* and *Symphony* provide excellent service and serve authentic Manadonese cuisine. Either ship is available for charter to Sangihe, Lembeh Straits, Togian Islands—virtually anywhere; and Murex offers fixed departure cruises every Saturday.

East of Bali

The islands in and around Komodo are host to the largest number of live-aboards in Indonesia. But this large number doesn't mean crowded sites. In fact, the opposite exists: operators are in constant contact with one another, sharing observa-

Opposite: Snorkeling in Southeast Asian waters is a special treat. *Photo by Jones/Shimlock.*

tions about where the big fish are and making sure that their boats aren't anchored in the same locations at the same time.

The big franchise boats (Peter Hughes and *Aggressor*) were notably absent in Komodo until 2002, when Peter Hughes' *Komodo Dancer* began operations. With the *Dancer* there are now more than a dozen boats from which to choose—anything from bargain basement boats to luxury liners.

Baruna has one of the longest running live-aboard dive operation in Indonesia, and differs from other operators in that the boats are steel-hulled. The *Baruna Explorer* and the *Baruna Adventurer* were constructed overseas in the 1960s and re-fitted in Indonesia in the 1990s. The cabins are compact but comfortable, and big enough to suit their mainly German clientele.

Below: A journey on Kararu's traditional *phinisi* schooner is a must for divers looking to sample a bit more of Indonesia's nautical culture and history. Sangeang Island, Komodo. *Photo by Wolfgang Poelzer.*

wooden *phinisi* schooner combines hundreds of years of building tradition, modern facilities and state of the art dive equipment to form the quintessential live-aboard experience.

Hand carved from teak wood from the keel to the tip of the mast this unique ship offers ample space on its three decks, while indoors the exquisite teak wood and hand crafted furnishings surround you in local culture. The vessel has 12, fully air-conditioned cabins each with hot shower and toilet.

However, it is the service that distinguishes this boat. Specializing in marine life habitat, the multilingual divemasters/owners Lisa Crosby, Sascha Dambach and Antony Rhodes are experts in the region. Suitable for the avid photographer, Kararu Dive Voyages knows best the underwater treasures and secret areas known only to those intimately familiar with the region. Beyond Komodo, Kararu offers trips to Sulawesi, Alor and Irian Jaya.

Grand Komodo Tours pioneered live-aboards in Komodo, and were responsible for most of the dive sites discovered in the South. The company is Indonesian-run, and uses traditional 25-meter wooden boats, with basic below-deck double-bunked cabins, and simple shared toilets and showers on deck. The success of foreign operators and ships has spurred Grand Komodo into the luxury end of the market where they compete with two new vessels—*Tarata* and *Temu Kira*—for the attached bath, A/C standard rooms requested by most Western divers. Shortcomings in food quality and divemasters are more than made up for by the savings in cost. Grand Komodo puts live-aboard diving within the reach of every diver.

Baruna pioneered live-aboard diving to destinations east of Bali, and has regularly scheduled trips on the Bali-Lombok-Sumbawa-Komodo-Sumba run. Baruna is a well-run Indonesian operation that offers a quality package at a reasonable price.

Kararu Dive Voyages may be a relative newcomer on the live-aboard scene, but experience and dedication are certainly here in abundance. Sailing from Bali and diving the islands of Lombok, Sumbawa and the Komodo National Park, the 38-meter, fully-equipped

The *Komodo Dancer* is the newest addition to the fleet of ships that cruise to Komodo, beginning operations in March 2002. A 30-meter wooden phinisi ship built in 2001 it operates as a Peter Hughes franchise. The *Dancer* offers two custom-built fiberglass tenders, dual Bauer compressors, airbanks, nitrox, E6 processing, and eight double cabins. For increased safety, navigation includes flat-screen computer with itinerary, maps and detailed descriptions and photos of each dive site, including a CD-Rom disk with maps and tide charts.

There are ships, and then there are *ships*. The *Pelagian* is the undisputed queen of the live-aboard fleet in Indonesia. This classic design, steel-hulled vessel was built as a Lloyds-classed private yacht in 1965, and has been painstakingly restored in Thailand by owner/captain Matt Hedrick.

The *Pelagian* is a world unto itself, the QEII of the live-aboard world—it oozes luxury, comfort and the highest level of professionalism. The facilities are staggering: two custom-built rigid-inflatable tenders with twin 50hp four-stroke outboards, depth sounder, console steering, and individual seating where your BCD and tank stay permanently, and are filled noiselessly after every dive. Nitrox is also available. On the *Pelagian*, quiet is the word—you could be sitting next to the outboards and not be aware they are on!

Inside is an E6 developer, computers for editing digital video, computers for sending and receiving emails, camera tables and battery chargers. There are hot water rinse showers on deck.

The owner also hired the best divemaster in Indonesia, if not the world—the affable, knowledgeable and eagle-eyed Larry Smith. This man knows more about diving in Indonesia than all operators put together, and with a wealth of stories is an entertaining companion on any trip. The staff are friendly and quietly efficient, and the food is superb—American chef Patrick, who lived for years in Thailand, turns out marvelous Western and Asian cuisine. The candle-lit, outdoor BBQs under the stars on the aft-deck are particularly memorable. In fact, everything is so perfect it is hard to believe you're on a dive boat and not a private yacht.

The *Pindito* is the longest serving live-aboard in Indonesia. Built in Borneo by Swiss owner/operator Edi Frommenwiler in 1992, it has been in continuous service ever since. Edi pioneered diving in the Banda Sea, moving to the Sorong region of Irian Jaya when Ambon disintegrated into communal violence. Political turmoil has occasioned yet another move to safer haven—Bali—where the *Pindito* has added professionalism and a wealth of experience to dive operators on the Bali-Komodo run. Despite fantastic diving in Komodo, Edi's heart is elsewhere, and he is anxious to return to Irian Jaya, where he will be for four months a year starting in 2002.

The *Pindito* operates most efficiently, but the dive schedule is flexible in the face of unforeseen cir-

cumstances: poor weather, lost baggage, political strife, etc. The *Pindito* now offers three dives per day plus night dives.

A trip on the *Pindito* is one of the most memorable and enjoyable you will ever take. This wooden ship looks and feels great and is solid as can be humanly made. The meals are healthy and delicious, and the dining room atmosphere convivial. Beer, rum and whiskey are included in the package. The crew is cheerful and unobtrusive.

— *David Espinosa/ Cody Shwaiko*

Above: After a long, satisfying day of diving, guests on board the *Pelagian* can retire to the deluxe stateroom to relive the best moments in style. *Photo by Barry Kulick.*

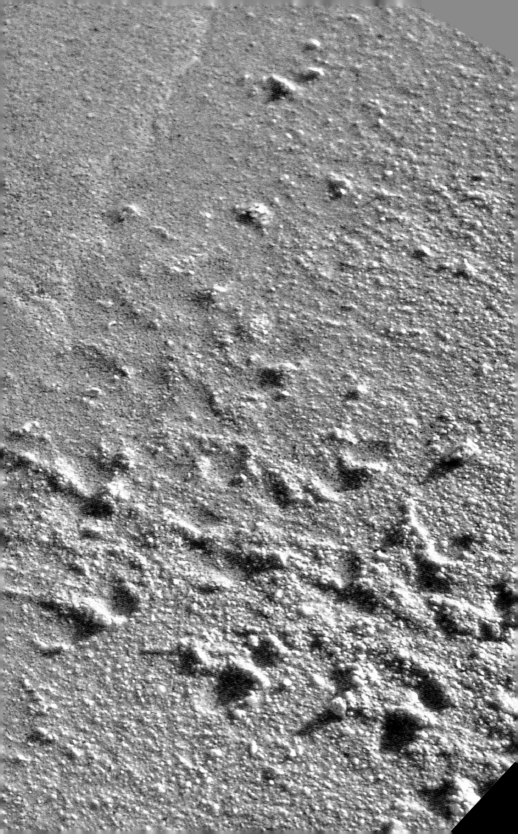

Diving in Malaysia
Where Rainforest Meets Reef

Twenty years ago, those adventurous travelers who made their way to Malaysia were rewarded with a rich culture and a lifestyle that had changed little over the centuries. Occasionally they snorkeled the island coral reefs and even more occasionally they dived the offshore waters. The attractions that the country advertised overseas were, however, largely on *terra firma*. But much of that has changed, especially in the last 10 years. Scuba professionals have set up operations in a number of places in the country, and now offer a good variety of services and dive options. With the help of some individuals in the private sector, the tourism arm of the government has made a very conscious effort to attract overseas visitors to Malaysia's marine attractions. With considerable success.

Malaysia lies entirely within the tropics and is divided into two main geographical areas. Peninsular Malaysia joins, on its northern boundary, Thailand and on its southern shore, the Republic of Singapore through a causeway linking the two countries. Some 650 km away, on the huge island of Borneo, lie two more Malaysian states, the vast states of Sabah and Sarawak, separated by the independently ruled Sultanate of Brunei. The two states on Borneo complete the 13 states of Malaysia, ruled under a federal system from Kuala Lumpur on the Malay peninsula.

Like many of its Asian neighbors, Malaysia has made tremendous economic progress in the last decade resulting in a large growth in population and a huge increase in urban development, both on a commercial and domestic level.

The capital, Kuala Lumpur, has expanded both laterally and skyward, while Johor Bahru, the country's second largest town and Singapore's nearest neighbor, has similarly grown in size and population. Shopping malls, office buildings and international class hotels now decorate these skylines that once carried a silhouette of palm trees and thatched roofs.

Malaysia has two distinctive seasons, dividing the country climatically, though the temperatures at sea level do not vary radically with either season. You can expect a high that rarely exceeds 31°C on the coast, and a low that rarely drops below 22°C. Of course, in the highland areas temperatures are quite different. While the northeast monsoon lashes the eastern shores, dumping heavy rain from November to late February, the western parts of the country—and that includes the dive sites around Langkawi—enjoy drier, sunny tropical weather. Conversely, when the southwest monsoon picks up from May to October, it is time for the East Coast dive sites, and those in Borneo, to enjoy sunny dry days—and the western shores get their torrential downpours.

Of the 18.6 million inhabitants in the 13 states comprising Malaysia, 8 percent are ethnically Indian, 31 percent are of Chinese origin while the majority, approximately 60 percent, are pure Malays and aborigines.

The Malays, a Muslim population, have always been fishermen

Overleaf: A green turtle hatchling reaches the surf, still to face many predators. The best places in Malaysia for sea turtle watchers are Sipadan Island and Terengganu. *Photo by Jones/Shimlock.*

Opposite: Nazri's Beach on idyllic Tioman—often regarded as one of the ten most beautiful islands in the world. *Photo by Jack Jackson.*

though perhaps not sailors. They know their coastal waters and have fished them for centuries. Unfortunately with a growing population to feed, an active tourism industry and a worldwide interest in tropical fish for aquaria, their fishing techniques became more radical in the sixties and seventies. Dynamite and cyanide might bring more fish into their nets, but it also killed and maimed many more, and did irreparable damage to the country's coral reefs.

Creation of Marine Parks

In the mid-seventies, Sabah gazetted one of the first marine parks in the country, the Tunku Abdul Rahman Park. Then in the eighties, answering a call from concerned environmentalists and divers, four further marine reserves were gazetted to protect the fauna and flora off Peninsular Malaysia's coasts. These included Pulau Payar in Kedah and the three areas off the East Coast of Malaysia. These last three marine parks together cover thousands of square kilometers of water and embrace some of the most picturesque islands and coral reefs anywhere, among them Redang, Tenggol, Kapas, Rawa, Tioman and Aur. It was no accident that Tioman was chosen as one of the sites for filming part of the movie, *South Pacific*—an island that breathed the ingredients of a tropical paradise.

All the East Coast islands are reefed with coral and host a marine ecology which enthralls snorkelers and provides plenty of interest for divers. In addition, outer islands are sufficiently far away from the effects of the mainland and deep enough into the South China Sea to boast a variety of large pelagics.

These islands and the shores of the East Coast generally are also, interestingly, one of the main breeding grounds for leatherback, green and hawksbill turtles. Traditionally turtle eggs have been collected in Malaysia as they are believed, in some instances, to have aphrodisiacal qualities. This, and the killing of turtles for their flesh, has led to a huge decline in numbers. In an effort to conserve these harmless creatures, wardens and volunteers search nightly during the summer laying season for nests containing turtle eggs, incubating them in the safety of government hatcheries and releasing the young turtles into the sea. Similar schemes to ensure turtle survival operate on the three islands comprising Turtle Island Park off Sandakan, on the tiny isle of Sipadan, Sabah, and on Pulau Besar, near Malacca, off the West Coast of Peninsular Malaysia.

Locating Malaysia's Coral Reefs

On Peninsular Malaysia's East Coast, the best coral reefs are to be

Below: If you see a cloud of juvenile fish or small cardinalfish like this one, look closely as there will probably be a frogfish lurking somewhere on the outcrop.
Photo by Jones/Shimlock.

found in the nine islands that comprise Pulau Redang, until recently inhabited only by a number of fisherfolk. Its natural beauty has inevitably caught the eye of developers who have created a golf course on the island and will soon open hotel facilities where scuba diving will be one of the main attractions. Fine corals too, are to be found at fairly shallow depths around the two Perhentian islands and at Lang Tengah.

To the south, Pulau Tenggol has good coral formations in excellent condition and the only real wall diving in Peninsular Malaysia, while Kapas, with its exquisite white sandy beaches, offers shallow and pretty coral reefs.

Tioman, despite its beauty, is not the best place for corals; overfishing, dynamite fishing and human influence have done much to destroy the nearby corals. Offshore, and on submerged reefs, the conditions are better. However, because it is served by a small airport with daily flights to and from Kuala Lumpur and Singapore, and excellent sea connections, it proves a very popular resort for holidaymakers and divers, particularly over weekends. In the southern waters of the East Coast lies the small island of Aur, which boasts good corals and some fine diving. With its proximity to Singapore, it too attracts plenty of weekend divers from the republic.

Although the formation of marine parks has helped limit the damage caused by illegal fishing, it can do nothing to prevent the runoff from the peninsula itself (deforestation has not been kind to the rivers and offshore waters)—which has had disastrous effects on the mangrove swamps as well as on inshore corals.

The best areas for coral on the west side of the country are around the three islands that form the Pulau Payar Marine Park, just south of Langkawi. With the creation of a new Australian-style platform in the Park, snorkelers and divers now have easy access to the reef. And even though the visibility is not as good as that on the East Coast, divers report that there is good coral and marine life.

In Borneo, the situation is far better. With the gazetting of Tunku Abdul Rahman Park over 20 years ago, the reefs around the five small islands off Kota Kinabalu's shore have benefited enormously from the park's protection. Visibility is not always as clear as it might be, but the shallow reefs are a major attraction to holidaymakers in the area. Snorkeling and diving facilities are available to visitors.

But the best reefs lie, without a doubt, at Sipadan, a small mushroom-shaped island rising from the ocean floor, situated some 25 km off the coast from Tawau. The reefs are in excellent condition, with a rating amongst the best in Asia and when the waters are not filled with plankton, the visibility can be good. There are, however, now three dive operations on the island, a figure which some conservationists fear will be the island's downfall.

New to the diving fraternity as a dive destination is Layang-Layang, some 240 km north of Kota Kinabalu. Because of its remoteness, the reefs are in fine condition and provide divers with some fabulous encounters not only with reef life but with large pelagics.

Live-aboards

In the last few years, divers have found that live-aboard dive boats offer an excellent alternative to land-based diving in Malaysia. Divers can also enjoy Sipadan and the Kunak group of islands, north of Sipadan, from the comfort of a live-aboard dive boat. Lastly, many dive trips to Malaysia, in particular those to the islands off the East Coast, can also be organized from neighboring Singapore.

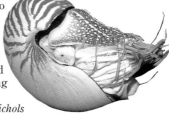

— *Fiona Nichols*

Photo by Roger Steene

Sipadan

Memorable Diving from an Oceanic Isle East of Borneo

2–15 min by boat

Variable,
10–22 meters

Light, occasionally
more

Generally good
variety

Slopes and walls,
cave

Generally good
numbers of big
fish at best sites

Hammerheads;
Turtle Cavern;
turtles galore

The diving is always good at Sipadan and, sometimes, it can be superb. Good-sized pelagics generally represent Sipadan's main attraction to divers. While nothing is guaranteed, it's likely that a week's diving will be highlighted by one or more of the following: a hoard of 50 hammerheads sharks, leopard sharks, barracudas in shoals of several hundred, a rumbling herd of many bumphead parrotfish, a manta or two, and perhaps a half-dozen whitetip sharks.

Reef fish are present in fair numbers and variety and perhaps most impressive are the quantities of medium-sized fish—between 25 and 40 cm—in relatively shallow waters. This is especially the case for groups of up to a dozen harlequin sweetlips, but also snappers, emperors, triggerfishes, longfin batfish and a couple of species of unicornfishes.

Macro-lens wielders and those with acute powers of observation could spot an unusual crinoid, shrimp and tiny fish combination, all matching the host's coloration. Or a golden-spotted shrimp on a very flattened carpet anemone. Some divers have found a patch of relatively tame spotted garden eels, elsewhere requiring the patience of Job to photograph outside of their burrow. Sharp eyes can also reveal a pink sailfin leaf-fish or a scorpionfish, and nudibranchs.

It has been said that the reefs of Sipadan are less colorful than elsewhere in Southeast Asia. This is possibly due to the restricted visibility in the shallows (often of pea-soup quality) but also to far less aggregations of fairy basslets and other small fry. However, sponges are there in various shapes, especially enormous barrel sponges.

We find the dive spots live up to their names: White Tip Avenue, Turtle Patch, Staghorn Crest, Lobster Lair, Hanging Gardens (for soft corals).

But Sipadan also has problems. Visibility is seldom great—our dives often averaged 10 to 15 meters. There are also too many divers for the ecosystem. Three spartan but adequate resorts can accommodate about 100 people, three times the number generally agreed as optimum. These numbers also swell on weekends.

South Point On one trip we saw a school of 50 hammerhead sharks at South Point; a solid wall of barracudas stretching over 10 meters high, almost motionless in the current and relatively undisturbed by the gazes of fellow divers, and several dozen bumphead parrotfish in a herd, lazing just under the surface in dappled sunlight. These highlights require a touch of luck. But on every one of our 18 dives we saw green turtles—up to a dozen in a single dive—along with reef whitetip sharks and, always, a fair variety of reef fishes.

Barracuda Point There is one good reason to dive this spot—barracuda. Time after time they turn up in their hundreds, a shoal that turns the water into a glinting wall of fish. There are also sharks, accompanying every dive along with a shoal of bumphead parrotfish.

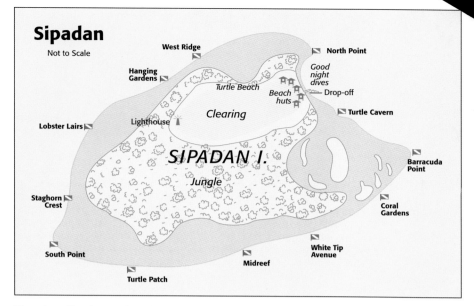

Sipadan
Not to Scale

West Ridge

North Point

Hanging Gardens

Good night dives

Turtle Beach

Beach huts

Drop-off

Clearing

Turtle Cavern

Lobster Lairs

Lighthouse

SIPADAN I.

Barracuda Point

Jungle

Staghorn Crest

Coral Gardens

South Point

White Tip Avenue

Midreef

Turtle Patch

Hanging Gardens Coral lovers love this beautiful dive spot just minutes from the resort. The soft corals hang like dripping wax from candles in a profusion of colors that can hardly be matched elsewhere. We have rarely had good visibility here (diving in the morning without sunlight is not the best) but the beauty of the sights compensates.

Turtles While you tend to become blasé about green turtles, this is the one guaranteed highlight on Sipadan. It is claimed that these waters have the largest turtle population found anywhere. And most of these gentle giants, used to humans, even allow physical contact, though this is rightly discouraged. Just swimming close to one is thrillin. Or watching them tearing and chewing a chunk of soft coral. And almost nothing disturbs a mating pair, not even other males climbing on top, hoping to get in on the action.

Turtle Cavern offers the unusual, if macabre. This cavern, which turns into a cave, holds lots of turtle skeletons along with that of a dolphin. Just so you don't join the skeletons, cavern-diver certification is required. Borneo Divers offers the PADI speciality course on Sipadan. (This takes 4 days but you can still get one normal boat dive a day while the course lasts.)

Entrance to the cavern passes through a wide opening: buoyancy control has to be strict or clouds of sediment get stirred up, taking hours to settle. Heading back towards the entrance, schooling fish often make a good parting shot, framed by the cavern entrance.

Turtle Facts

A large population of green turtles (*Chelonia mydas*) call Sipadan home. Their name comes not so much from their overall color, an olive-brown, as from their greenish fat. We saw some of these turtles on every dive, with an occasional individual close to the species' maximum size: 140 kg and a carapace length of over 1 meter. Indeed turtles are one of the main reasons for Sipadan's popularity.

The animals are almost exclusively vegetarian, feeding on sea grasses, algae, occasionally sponges and soft corals. While they are protected on Sipadan, elsewhere the green turtles are killed for their meat, hide and oil. Here their eggs are collected for local sale. Of course, egg collecting can also lead to a decrease in the numbers of the species as it has been calculated that it takes between 500 and 5,000 eggs to produce a single surviving adult turtle.

But it's a lucrative business. The three families with traditional turtle egg gathering rights on Sipadan have earned a handsome living. Sea turtle eggs sell for 20 cents each in Sabah. Turtles take their time copulating and because of this, some believe the eggs can increase male potency, especially if the first three of any batch are eaten raw.

Aside from the big chaps, schooling fish are below average, with only two species of fusiliers relatively abundant. An exception to this general rule is at Barracuda and South Point, where we sometimes drifted down through four good-sized schools. Anemones and their guest-fish can be spotted on almost every dive, along with hefty-size, solitary barracuda (usually in the shallows), and an occasional imperturbable crocodilefish, alias longsnout flathead. Moorish idols, often in pairs, usually accompany every dive.

Diving Basics

Sipadan diving is not for everyone. Currents are often present and shift during the course of a dive. At Barracuda Point, in particular, there is often 2 knots of current, heading away from the reef and downward. There are relatively easy dive spots, but we found the most interesting were also the ones with the strongest current: Barracuda and South Point.

All the resorts offer unlimited beach diving. The north wall drop-off next to the pier is only a few meters in front of the Borneo Divers' resort. Only night diving is allowed here.

Sipadan is largely boat diving. Suiting up on the resorts' premises, divers get on their boats in full gear for the two or three daily dives. It's a short ride to the various spots,

usually 10 minutes or less, but the surface can be choppy to or from the entry point. To avoid reef damage, the boats do not anchor but the boatmen will follow the divers conscientiously.

Sipadan Island lies not far, but in splendid isolation, from the continental shelf. While it's only some 12 km to Mabul Island on the edge of the shallow Sigitan reefs, the ocean plunges to almost 1,000 meters before rising abruptly.

The 15-hectare island, with its lush vegetation and white sand beaches, is but the tip of a marine outcrop. To walk the surrounding beach takes around 30 minutes, and there is much nature to observe along the shore and on land.

Three resorts are currently crowded on the island's northwest shore, spread behind a wooden pier. Just a few meters to the west of the jetty, where the reeftop extends less than 10 meters from the shore, the turquoise waters abruptly turn dark blue at the edge of a vertical wall. Elsewhere the shallow reef extends as an irregular fringe, over 500 meters off South Point. A dozen-odd dive spots dot the edge of the reef, all above vertical walls.

The discovery of Sipadan only goes back to 1984. While on a commercial job on a nearby grounded ship, Borneo Divers checked out the island, and liked very much what they saw. After obtaining all the necessary permits, the outfit started bringing clients here in 1985. Divers were initially put up in tents. Now the accommodation has been upgraded to a very comfortable dive resort, and two competing resorts have recently been established on Sipadan.

The island received a boost at international level when Jacques Cousteau spent several weeks here to shoot his film, *Ghost of the Sea Turtles*. While Cousteau claimed the discovery of Turtle Cavern, he and his team were allegedly taken there by Borneo Divers, who had already surveyed the site.

— *Kal Muller*

Opposite: The Borneo Divers' longhouse—accommodation for divers on Sipadan Island. *Photo by Jones/Shimlock.*

Layang-Layang and Kota Kinabalu

Diving off Sabah's Northwest Coast

Two world-class possibilities exist for diving from the East Malaysian state of Sabah on the island of Borneo. About 300 km northwest of Kota Kinabalu (KK), in the midst of the South China Sea, lies the Layang-Layang Atoll, part of the group of atolls that make up the controversial Borneo Banks. A small man-made island supports a military base, a 17-room resort, and the air-strip used to get visitors to and from the island. The remainder of the atoll lies underwater, with the exception of rocks that are exposed at low tide. The reefs drop in walls on all sides to depths of up to 2,000 meters. However, there are some good, shallow reefs for repeat dives.

Below: Sea fans *(Melithaea sp.)* feed on plankton and thrive in exposed locations where the currents supply them with food. *Photo by Jones/Shimlock.*

A Gathering of Pelagics

Layang-Layang's diving season is from March until September. It is, above all, famous for schooling hammerhead sharks, and they are there in abundance until July, but as the water warms up the sharks go deeper. The best diving is found around the northeastern end of the atoll, followed closely by the southwestern end.

The eastern point of the atoll is called Dog Tooth Lair, and in addition to the tuna that the site is named after, this seems to be the spot for hammerheads. Normally swimming at depths of 40 meters or more, we once encountered a school of sharks in the 10-meter-deep waters of the coral gardens. Schools of barracuda populate the reef and wall; a huge school of jacks hang out at 10 to 15 meters, and manta rays are also frequent visitors here.

The Gorgonian Forest is a continuation of the wall at Dog Tooth Lair, so it is not uncommon to see schooling hammerheads on this dive either. But this site is famous for its sea fans. From 20 meters down, the wall is covered in multi-colored sea fans of impressive size—great for wide angle photography. Navigator Lane is next along the wall, and here the sea fans give way to an impressive display of soft corals. The site was visited by hammerheads during our dives, and invariably there were gray and whitetip sharks circling around off the wall. Tuna cruise up and down the drop-off in search of any

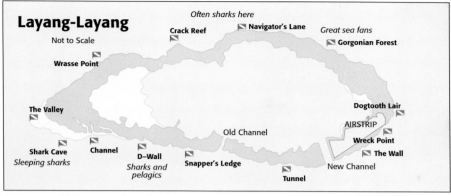

unwary reef fish among the schools along the wall.

At the southwestern end of the atoll is a site called D-Wall, a wall so impressive because it is so sheer and so deep. Even at 50 meters there seems to be no end to its vertical drop. The wall is festooned with colorful soft corals that entice the diver deeper. On one dive, while photographing soft corals at some 35 meters, a school of 40 hammerheads swam by. Although not sighted as often in this area, they are here! Whitetips, tuna and clouds of reef fishes populate the wall to make a great dive site.

At the end of D-Wall is a site aptly named Shark Cave, for at 20 to 25 meters there is a deep cave extending under the reef where a group of whitetips can often be found sleeping. Here we found 10 sharks piled up like logs on the left side of the cave and a school of about 50 snappers hanging around the entrance on the right side of the cave. Down current, the reef is flatter with rolling terrain. This area is generally swept by currents, and consequently is often favored by large fishes.

Abdul Rahman Tunku

If sharks are not your idea of fun diving, KK has an alternative. Twenty minutes by boat from the center of KK, capital of Sabah, lie five islands that make up the Tunku Abdul Rahman Park, offering secluded beaches and reefs just

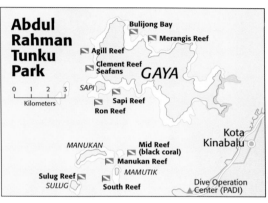

offshore, which are perfect for snorkeling and diving.

Mid Reef near Manukan Island is a good site. The reef is generally round and slopes off on all sides from 5 to 20 meters. The top of the reef has good hard corals. Dropping down to 15 to 29 meters you encounter a garden of black coral trees. A small school of yellowfinned barracuda are present on most dives, and juvenile leopard sharks can often be seen here on night dives.

Clement Reef, closer to Sapi Island, is also a sloping reef that ranges from 12 to 18 meters, with the exception of a small finger that juts out from the reef and reaches 25 meters in depth. This finger is covered with sea fans, sponges and soft coral, attracting schools of snappers and abundant reef fish. In February and March whale sharks migrate through the area and are sometimes seen by divers.

— *Bob Bowdey*

5–15 min by boat

Good,
10–25 meters

Light to moderate

Excellent condition

Walls and reef crests

Good numbers
and variety of
big pelagics

Hammerhead sharks,
dogtooth tuna,
mantas, turtles

Terengganu

The Best Diving from Peninsular Malaysia

From its northern borders near the small coastal town of Besut to the sandy shores of Kemaman in the south, the Malaysian East Coast state of Terengganu boasts some 225 km of nearly uninterrupted coastline and a score or so offshore islands, many of which offer excellent coral reefs that form part of a marine park.

The state of Terengganu is a traditional Muslim one with a pretty capital town, Kuala Terengganu, at the mouth of the river. Fishing, palm oil and agriculture were the mainstay of the economy. When oil was discovered offshore, the fortunes of this state changed radically, and it has become one of the wealthiest in the federation. And now tourism is beginning to play a major role in the state's economy, for its beaches and offshore islands have been discovered by sun lovers and divers. Indeed, a fabulous new golf club and hotel has taken shape on Redang, while a hotel has recently been built on Lang Tengah, and among the marine recreational options, snorkeling and diving are being given priority.

Access to these tropical isles is from the capital, Terengganu, or alternatively, from the small coastal towns of Kuala Besut, Marang and Dungun.

The Perhentian Islands

The two islands of Perhentian lie at the furthest extremity of Terengganu, some 14 nautical miles offshore, and are accessible by bumboat from Kuala Besut. Perhentian Kecil (the smaller island) has few facilities for tourists, so most stay on the larger island, Perhentian Besar, with its beautiful white sandy beaches, which has accommodation in the form of huts for holidaymakers and divers.

In the dry season (April to September), diving from Perhentian can be excellent, and the waters on the South China Sea side of the island are quite clear. The reefs are generally fairly shallow, although they extend deeper on the northern sides of the islands. There are some hard corals though not that many, plenty of beautiful soft corals and some impressive gorgonians on the outer reefs.

On a good dive you can expect to come across schools of trevallies, jacks, glasseyes and rainbow runners. There are some blacktip sharks in the area. Visibility here averages 12 meters, though it can fall. Among the pelagics often encountered around the Susu Dara group of isles just northwest of Perhentian—probably the best dive location—are whale sharks, but mantas, sailfish, barracudas and large groupers are also common.

Lang Tengah

Some 8 to 9 nautical miles (15 km) south of Perhentian lies the 120-ha island, Pulau Lang Tengah, another good spot for diving. A new resort has been built here with an emphasis on diving, snorkeling and watersports, and more and more good dive sites are being identified around the island.

Opposite: *Nemanthus annamensis,* the gorgonian wrapper or whip coral anemone, on a gorgonian. *Photo by Jones/Shimlock.*

By bumboat from coastal towns and from island resorts

Fair, 8–20 meters

Usually negligible to light

Good condition, fine variety in most places

Usually coral gardens

Schools, reef fish, pelagics

Whale sharks, manta rays; wall at Tenggol

Because of the surrounding deep waters and its isolation, Lang Tengah has good corals, both hard and soft, hosting a proliferation of marine life. Six good dive sites have been identified in the area including one with prolific *Dendronephthya* and another of table corals. On a regular 15-meter dive, you should find schools of jacks and trevallies, yellowtails and rainbow runners. Late afternoon is a particularly good time for diving. A resident blacktip shark is often sighted near the resort while two large groupers have established a home practically at the resort door. Occasionally, bumphead parrotfish come into the reef in front of the resort. For macro-photographers there are some great nudibranchs. The best time to dive here is in the dry season, from April to October.

Redang

The premier dive spot on the East Coast, Redang comprises nine islands. It is accessible from all the coastal towns mentioned earlier, or on the fast boat from Tanjong Marang, operated by the new resort itself. Once home to a few fishing families, it is now one of the country's newest tourist destinations. Its powdery white, sandy beaches and excellent coral reefs are a powerful magnet, and divers who want to explore the nearby reefs and islands further afield should book for at least 5 days to do the area justice.

The reefs around Redang have suffered the minimum of damage over the years because of their relative distance from the mainland.

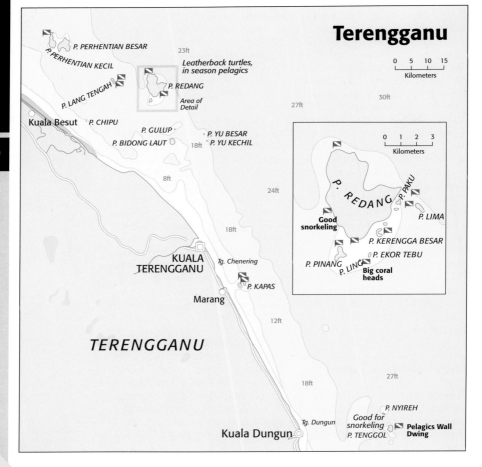

Consequently the reefs offer a fine variety of both hard and soft corals, which host a wealth of marine life.

Around the southeastern end of the main island there are some small offshore isles, Kerengga Kechil and Kerengga Besar, Pulau Ekor Tebu, and the large rock known as Ling. The reefs here are shallow in depth and you'll encounter a veritable forest of mushroom corals on the southwestern tip of Kerengga Besar. A huge area of *Porites,* rising over 5 meters from the seabed, is a favorite dive site around Ling, while staghorn corals are also predominant. The main island has some good shallow patches of coral—ideal for snorkeling or a repeat dive—which drop to deeper levels on the east coast.

The instructors and divemasters operating from Redang Island Resort have identified some eight good sites for diving, amongst which the reefs off the northeastern part of the main island and around Pulau Paku Besar and Pulau Paku Kecil come up a repeat favorite. A bit further eastwards, Pulau Lima has deep coral reefs, while the reefs around Pulau Pinang are very shallow and suffer from the run-off from the river Redang.

So what are the highlights? In season (April to November, before the monsoons arrive) you can expect to see plenty of schools of fish: jacks, golden trevallies, groupers, coral trouts, snappers and barracudas. The macro-photographers should keep their eyes open for Spanish dancers—pink, purple and orange delights. The seabed is the place to find stingrays (there are plenty), while pelagic highlights inevitably include whale sharks, manta rays and the occasional tiger and hammerhead sharks.

Another highlight of diving in Redang is an encounter with turtles. Huge lumbering leatherbacks often lay their eggs in the beaches of the islands, and can be spotted swimming offshore. It's worth looking out for them at night, too, when they come ashore to nest. As mentioned elsewhere, turtles are a protected species in Asia and any encounter is a truly fascinating experience.

Although the diving is good throughout the summer months, it can be especially good early November and again sometimes in late April. Visibility averages 10 to 15 meters and it can occasionally clear to 18 meters.

Kapas

Accessible from Kuala Dungun, the beautiful island of Kapas is known for its white, sandy beaches rather more than for its diving. However, it does have pretty corals in the shallows and this appeals particularly to snorkelers. The reef shelves gradually from 3 to 12 meters but it is symptomatic of the reef's condition that you'll find plenty of sea urchins! Look out for clownfish and their host anemones, small nudibranchs, damsels and sergeant-majors.

Tenggol

The island of Tenggol is situated further south from Redang and some 12 nautical miles offshore. It comprises one main island with a beautiful sandy beach of fine white sand and two small isles. On the western side of the island lies a sheltered bay.

However, the big attraction at Tenggol is wall diving, for the island has steep rocky cliffs on the eastern, South China Sea side of the island, which drop dramatically to the seabed. In addition, there are some pristine coral formations and a number of submerged rocks with excellent coral growth on them. Diving at Tenggol goes down to 48 meters, to the seabed, and divers who are more interested in fish than in corals and tunicates will find bumphead parrotfish, lizardfish, large schools of jacks, some whitetip sharks, and an occasional whale shark and manta ray. The rarely seen ghost pipefish is also known to make its home here.

—*Fiona Nichols*

Tioman and Aur

Playground for Divers and Holidaymakers

From the very first glimpse of its white sandy beaches, azure waters and often mist shrouded mountains, the island of Tioman exerts an almost mystical pull. Nearly 50 years ago it delighted film-goers, and it continues to delight romantics today. Tioman has become renowned as a great place to holiday. Indeed, during the late April to September season, visitors arrive

Above: A coral grouper, *Cephalopholis miniata*. This fish, a common inhabitant of caves and ledges, preys on small fishes and crustaceans. The younger specimens are more brightly colored.
Photo by Jones/Shimlock.

from Kuala Lumpur, Johor and Singapore—so book in advance.

But Tioman is not a divers' paradise, but a paradise in which divers can dabble in their favorite sport. The once pristine corals have suffered through illicit dynamite fishing, run-offs from the rivers and the effects of being a popular resort.

In 1985, however, the waters around Tioman were designated part of a large marine park where sustainable fishing is permitted but dynamiting, cyanide poisoning and spear fishing are outlawed. Similarly, the islands off the coast of Johor—Rawa, Tinggi, Besar and

Sibu and Aur—were put under protection.

Although the visibility is usually in the region of 8 or 9 meters, it can very occasionally reach 30 meters. On an average dive, you'll meet schools of jacks, trevallies, coral trout, pufferfishes, a few stingrays and a number of moray eels. The crown-of-thorns starfish, which has done much damage to the reef, seems to be less prolific nowadays. We've heard stories about meeting a dozen hammerheads on one dive, but such sightings are uncommon. There are sharks—blacktip, nurse and even a whale shark from time to time. We have seen mantas on many trips and even the occasional sailfish.

There are some five or six favorite dive spots around Tioman, most of which can be accessed in less than an hour by the regular, converted fishing boats.

Some 15 minutes from the main resort, Magician Rock is the place for whale sharks and mantas when they pass. Schooling fish hang out here. There are plenty of fans for the photographers. Off the east coast, Juara is a good spot to see barracudas, snappers, stingrays, and to enjoy the hard corals. There is a submerged pinnacle here that attracts plenty of fish. Off the northeast, Sri Buat is renowned for its beautiful hard corals and some exceptionally tall soft corals.

Adjacent islands with good coral include Labas and Tulai. Check out the Napoleon wrasses at Tulai (it has a beautiful beach, too), and look out for the schools of trevally and barracuda. There are

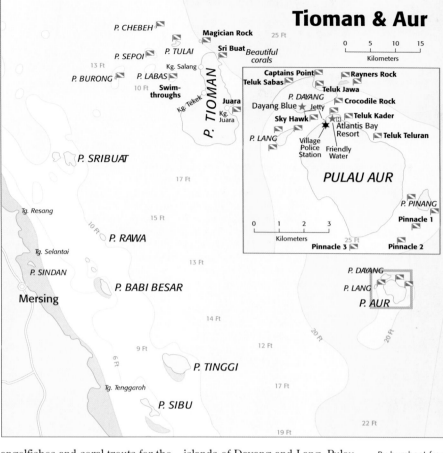

Tioman & Aur

P. CHEBEH
Magician Rock   25 Ft
P. SEPOI   P. TULAI   Sri Buat Beautiful
13 Ft   Kg. Salang   corals
P. BURONG   P. LABAS
10 Ft   Swim-
throughs
Captains Point   Rayners Rock
Teluk Sabas
Teluk Jawa
P. DAYANG   Crocodile Rock
Dayang Blue ★ Jetty
Juara   Sky Hawk   Teluk Kader
Kg.   ★ Atlantis Bay
Juara   Resort   Teluk Teluran
P. LANG   Village   Friendly
Police   Water
Station

PULAU AUR

P. SRIBUAT

P. PINANG
Pinnacle 1
0   1   2   3
Kilometers   25 Ft
Pinnacle 3   Pinnacle 2

17 Ft

Tg. Resang
15 Ft
10 Ft
P. RAWA
Tg. Selantai
P. SINDAN   13 Ft
Mersing   P. BABI BESAR

P. DAYANG
P. LANG
P. AUR

14 Ft

20 Ft   20 Ft
9 Ft   12 Ft
P. TINGGI
Tg. Tenggaroh   17 Ft
P. SIBU
22 Ft
19 Ft

angelfishes and coral trouts for the keen eyed. Labas is also a favorite due to its rock formations and swim-throughs.

Tiger Reef has two huge pinnacles where there are schools of yellowtails, angelfishes and snappers. Nurse sharks are often sighted here. There are also some impressive sea fans and lovely soft corals. Diving is also excellent on the Jubilee Shoals, some 80 minutes by speedboat—it's pioneer diving on a virgin shoal—but only for those with GPS facilities.

Pulau Aur

This small island, located 65 km from the Malaysian coast, is home to an active fishing community. Together with the neighboring islands of Dayang and Lang, Pulau Aur is a great favorite with divers, as the distance from the mainland has ensured its corals remain in good condition while its relative remoteness contributes to a better-than-average visibility for this part of the coast. Bungalows on Pulau Dayang and Aur offer accommodation. Access is usually via the town of Mersing.

Expect to find trevallies, sweet-lips, coral trout, wrasses, plenty of parrotfishes, anemones and a wide variety of nudibranchs. Night diving in the main bay is also fun. Further from the shelter of the island, currents can be strong, especially on the surface, but as a compensation there are more large fish, and sighting a whale shark or even a hammerhead is possible.

—*Fiona Nichols*

By bumboat from Tioman or live-aboard boats from Mersing and Singapore

Fair, average of 9 meters; Aur averages 12 meters

Variable

Fair in Tioman; good in Aur

Coral gardens

Good numbers, fair variety

Whale sharks, mantas; beautiful beaches

Langkawi

Diving the Marine Reserve at Pulau Payar

Below: The anemonefish *Amphiprion perideraion* in the magnificent anemone, *Heteractis magnifica*. The larger fish of an anemo-nefish pair is the female. *Photo by R.C. Anderson.*

This marine park encompasses four islands, Pulau Payar, Pulau Kaca, Pulau Lembu and Pulau Segantang, and is located 19 nautical miles south of the island of Langkawi, and 40 nautical miles north of Penang. The park's pride lies in its wide variety of habitats and the largest number of coral species in the country, including the most colorful soft corals.

The Marine Park was conceived to protect the natural marine wealth, while specific zones have been marked for research and educational activities, as well as for recreation.

Coral Garden At the southwestern tip of Pulau Payar, this site offers a scenic dive with multi-colored soft corals, mainly *Dendronephthya*. The panorama is one with steep gullies and crevices which hide plenty of jacks, titan triggers, moray eels, blue-ringed angelfishes, lionfishes, porcupinefishes and many barrel sponges. Don't expect gin-clear visibility—it's around 10 meters usually, but can extend up to 16 to 20 meters.

Grouper Farm Named for the large number of groupers which dwell here, this nearby site also

Boat from Kuah to marine platform, 50 min

Fair, 2–10 meters

Negligible

Best variety in Malaysia

Coral gardens, artificial reef

Fair variety

Ease of access; great for snorkelers

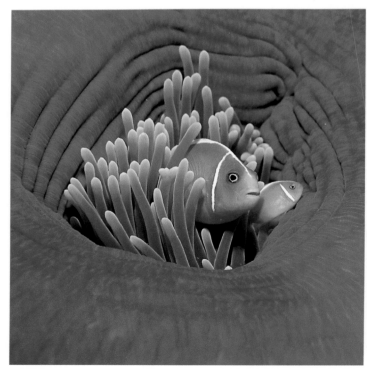

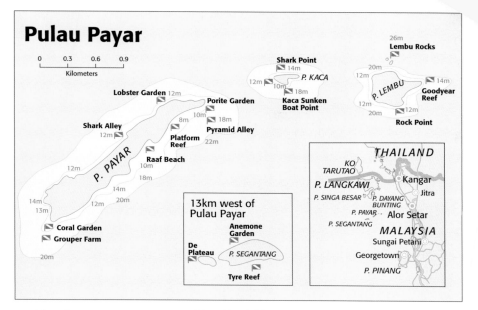

Pulau Payar

0   0.3   0.6   0.9
Kilometers

Shark Point
14m
12m
10m P. KACA
18m
Lobster Garden 12m
Porite Garden
Kaca Sunken
Boat Point

Lembu Rocks
26m
20m
12m
P. LEMBU
14m
Goodyear
Reef
12m
20m
12m
Rock Point

Shark Alley
12m
8m
10m 18m
Pyramid Alley
Platform
Reef
22m
Raaf Beach
10m
12m
18m
14m
12m 20m
14m
13m
Coral Garden
Grouper Farm
20m

THAILAND
KO
TARUTAO
Kangar
P. LANGKAWI
P. SINGA BESAR P. DAYANG
BUNTING
Jitra
P. PAYAR Alor Setar
P. SEGANTANG
MALAYSIA
Sungai Petani
Georgetown
P. PINANG

13km west of
Pulau Payar

Anemone
Garden
De
Plateau P. SEGANTANG

Tyre Reef

---

provides a home to mangrove snappers (*Lutjanus argentinaculatus*) and barracudas. Visibility, unfortunately, is usually very poor and only reaches 10 meters on a good day. However, the groupers are worth coming to see.

Sriwana Beach At the southeastern side of Pulau Payar, in front of the newly installed reef platform, a coral reef at a depth of between 6 and 8 meters is a great place for a snorkeler or diver to explore coral. Look out for the staghorns (*Acropora nobilis, formosa,* and *florida*), brain and *Montipora* corals. There are also sponges, anemones with their associated anemonefishes, jacks, black-tipped fusiliers, groupers and Moorish idols. Keep an eye open too for young blacktip sharks; the fish life here is prolific.

Kaca Sunken Boats Point An artificial reef has been created off the southern tip of Pulau Kaca by the sinking of confiscated fishing boats. These have proved a haven for fish life. Japanese jacks, lionfishes, mangrove snappers *(Lutjanus argentimaculatus)* and giant groupers are all frequently encountered, while you'll also come across ramose *Murex* shells.

Tyre Reef The steep vertical walls at Tyre Reef extend down to 20 meters before sloping down gently to a sandy bottom depth of 26 meters. Fish life is plentiful with large shoals of barracudas, sergeant-majors, red snappers, mangrove snappers, jacks and Javan rabbitfish. Sea fans, black corals, wire and whip corals are common in the deeper waters.

Anemone Garden Sea anemones cover the surface of most of the rocks and boulders on the northern side of the island. Large *Murex* shells, helmet shells, spiny lobsters and moray eels are all common.

Langkawi Coral Langkawi Coral operates a 25-meter, high-speed catamaran designed to carry 162 passengers to Pulau Payar on a daily basis. The cruise takes 50 minutes. On arrival, the catamaran moors at a large reef platform. The platform's underwater observatory, glass-bottom boats and snorkeling equipment allow visitors of all ages, even non-swimmers, a close-up look at the marine life.

All dives are led by qualified BSAC instructors. Resort dives for beginners are also available.

— *Danny Lim*

Diving in the Philippines

Hundreds of Sites and a Well-developed Dive Industry

As a diving destination, the Philippines is hard to beat. Walls, drop-offs, coral reefs, wrecks, submerged islands and lagoons abound. Divers can choose from a staggering array of locations, both easily accessible and hard to reach. Choices range from off-the-beach resort diving to dive safaris and exploration dives from boats. Among these options are a variety of live-aboard boats and other vessels which visit not only the popular and well-known sites, such as the Sulu Sea and the Visayas, but also the untouched, remote locations.

Whether you're a humble scuba enthusiast with a limited budget or a wealthy aquanaut with a taste for the luxurious, the Philippines can accommodate your every whim at a price to suit your pocket.

Scuba Potential

Since the early 1960s, when scuba diving first started to gain popularity, entrepreneurs were quick to realize the potential of a country with 7,107 islands (counted at high tide), each with its own unique coral and reef formations.

Anilao in Batangas Province, to the south of Manila, became the very first dive center in the country, and probably one of the first in Asia. Since those distant days, diving has caught on in a big way. Resorts all over the country have invested in diving equipment, and there are scuba diving instructors and divemasters everywhere.

In fact, the Philippines is an outstanding place to learn diving or to upgrade your certification level. A typical Open Water Course costs between US$200 and $300 in most places, and can be taught in languages as varied as English, French, German, Italian, Hebrew, Swedish, Japanese, or various Chinese dialects, by multi-lingual instructors of many nationalities who have made the Philippines their home. You'll find international certification agencies such as PADI, NAUI, SSI, ADSI and CMAS are well established here, and there are three resident PADI course directors running PADI Instructor Development Courses frequently throughout the year. These are usually in La Union, Anilao, Puerto Galera, Boracay and the Visayas.

Diving is most commonly done from native *banca* boats, motorized outrigger canoes which can vary in size from 6 to over 25 meters. As a general rule, the smaller the boat, the less stable it is likely to be. Care should be taken when stowing gear and selecting a place to sit, as the balance can be critical, especially in smaller *bancas*. The driest part of such a *banca* is usually right in the front, beneath the plywood covering the bow. Stow items you want to keep dry there. Let the *bancero*, or boatman, take charge of this and try not to make any sudden movements. Inform the boatman when you are about to enter the water or get back on board after a dive, as he may have to provide counterweight to avoid capsizing. Another useful tip is to arrange the price for your trip before leaving and pay when you get back. There are, sadly, uncommon but verifiable stories

Overleaf: A rhizostome jellyfish, maybe family *Thystanostoma*. The fish visible above the jellyfish's bell is a juvenile jack, which uses the jelly's stinging tentacles for protection. *Photo by Lynn Funkhouser.*

Opposite: A diver, eager for the ultimate wide-angle shot, peers at a marvelously colored feather star. Balicasag Island, Philippines. *Photo by Scott Tuason.*

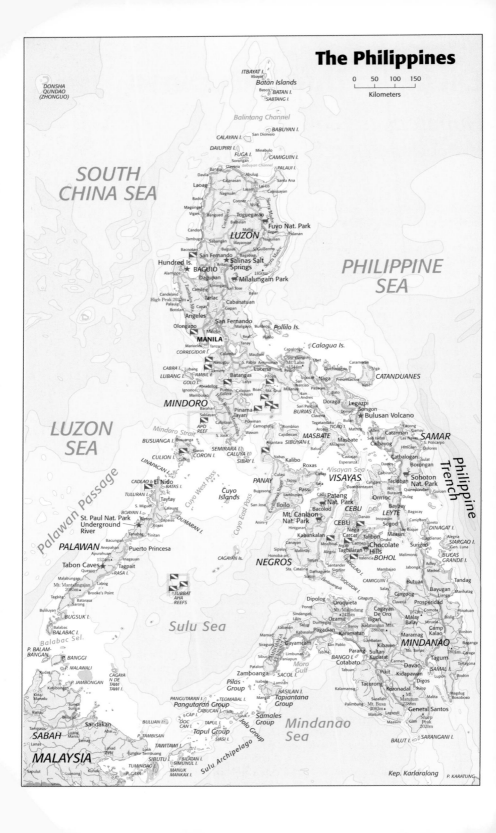

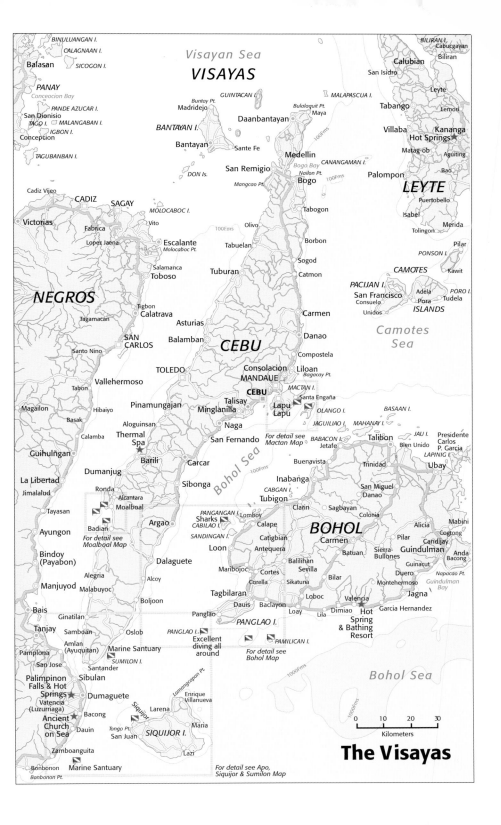

The Visayas

VISAYAS

Visayan Sea

BINULUANGAN I.
CALAGNAAN I.
Balasan
SICOGON I.
PANAY
Conceocion Bay
PANDE AZUCAR I.
San Dionisio
TAGO I. MALANGABAN I.
IGBON I.
Concepcion
TAGUBANBAN I.

GUINTACAN I.
Buntay Pt.
Madridejo
Daanbantayan
BANTAYAN I.
Bantayan
Sante Fe
San Remigio
DON Is.
Mangcao Pt.

MALAPASCUA I.
Bulalaquit Pt.
Maya
Medellin
Boga Bay
CANANGAMAN I.
Nailon Pt.
Bogo

Calubian
San Isidro
Tabango
Villaba
Matag-ob
Palompon

BILIRAN I.
Cabucgayan
Biliran
Leyte
Lemori
Kananga
Hot Springs
Aguiting
Bao
LEYTE
Puertobello

Cadiz Viejo
CADIZ
SAGAY
MOLOCABOC I.
Victorias
Vito
Fabrica
Lopez Jaena
Escalante
Molocaboc Pt.
Salamanca
Toboso

Olivo
Tabuelan
Tuburan

Tabogon
Borbon
Sogod
Catmon

Isabel
Tolingon
Merida
Pilar
PONSON I.
CAMOTES
Kawit
PACIJAN I.
San Francisco
Consuelo
Unidos

Adela
Pora
ISLANDS
PORO I.
Tudela

NEGROS
Tagamacan
Santo Nino
Tigbon
Calatrava
Asturias
Balamban
SAN
CARLOS

CEBU
Carmen
Danao
Compostela

Camotes
Sea

Magailon
Tabon
Basak
Hibaiyo
TOLEDO
Vallehermoso
Pinamungajan
Aloguinsan
Calamba
Thermal
Spa
Barili
Guihulngan
Dumanjug

Consolacion
MANDAUE
CEBU
Talisay
Minglanilla
Naga
San Fernando
MACTAN I.
Lapu
Lapu
Santa Engaña
OLANGO I.
JAGUILIAO I.
Liloan
Bagacay Pt.

BASAAN I.
MAHANAY I.

For detail see
Mactan Map

Talibon
BABACON I.
Jetafe
Bien Unido
JAU I.
Presidente
Carlos
P. Garcia
LAPINIG I.
Ubay

La Libertad
Jimalalud
Tayasan
Ayungon
Badian
Bindoy
(Payabon)
Manjuyod
Alegria
Malabuyoc
Ronda
Alcantara
Moalboal
For detail see
Moalboal Map
Argao
Loon
Dalaguete
Alcoy
Maribojoc

Ronda
Carcar
Sibonga

Bohol Sea

Inabanga
CABGAN I.
Tubigon
PANGANGAN I.
Sharks
CABILAO I.
SANDINGAN I.
Calape
Catigbian
Antequera
Balilihan
Cortes
Sevilla
Corella
Sikatuna

Clarin
Lomboy
Sagbayan
Colonia
BOHOL
Carmen
Batuan
Bilar

San Miguel
Danao

Trinidad
Buenavista

Sierra-
Bullones
Duero
Montehermoso

Alicia
Pilar
Candijay
Guindulman
Guinacut
Napacao Pt.
Guindulman
Bay
Jagna

Mabini
Cogtong
Anda
Bacong

Bais
Ginatilan
Tanjay
Samboan
Amlan
Pamplona
(Ayuquitan)
Marine Santuary
San Jose
SUMILON I.
Santander
Palimpinon
Falls & Hot
Springs
Sibulan
Vatencia
(Luzurriaga)
Ancient
Church
on Sea
Dauin

Boljoon
Tagbilaran
Dauis
Panglao
PANGLAO I.
Panglao
Excellent
diving all
around
PAMILICAN I.

Baclayon
Loay
Loboc
Lila
Dimiao
Hot
Spring
& Bathing
Resort

Valencia
Garcia Hernandez

Bacong
Larena
Tongo Pt.
San Juan
Maria
SIQUIJOR I.
Lazi

For detail see
Bohol Map

Bohol Sea

Zamboanguita
Bonbonon
Marine Santuary
Bonbonon Pt.

For detail see Apo,
Siquijor & Sumilon Map

0   10   20   30
Kilometers

The Visayas

of divers who have paid up front and then been left to fend for themselves once they are in the water.

If the *banca* has no steps to get back on board, another useful tip is to take a length of rope, tie one end to the outrigger close to where it joins with the hull and tie a stirrup, or loop, at the other end at about water level. Then, by placing a foot in the stirrup and standing up, you can avoid the embarrassment of struggling to get back in the boat, otherwise accomplished by pulling oneself up by the arms.

Protecting the Seas

Spear fishing and the collection of corals and shells is illegal in the Philippines, but that doesn't seem to worry the many fishermen and gatherers who make their living from the sea. Dynamite fishing is still widely practiced and the damage is horrendous in some places. Sodium cyanide and other poisons are sometimes used to stun fish for collection for the aquarium and live food fish trade, a practice that burns dead patches into the coral and invertebrate cover. Then there is *Muro Ami* fishing, where teams of swimmers bounce rocks, tied to string with streamers attached, across entire reefs to drive the fish into a net at one end. This practice strips a reef of its fish and destroys the coral at the same time—yet another major factor in the continuing degradation of the Philippines' estimated 27,022 sq km of coral reef at the 10-fathom level.

While various attempts have been made to cope with the problem, local politicians and influential supporters in many areas have effectively negated any serious effort to stop the devastation. The coast guard suffers from a lack of vessels and other resources: this means that policing of marine sanctuaries and other likely targets of the *dynamiteros* is a haphazard and arbitrary affair. In a country in which millions rely on the fishing industry for their livelihood, it is ironic that the fishermen themselves, through the harmful techniques they employ, are the main culprits behind the continually declining fish stocks which they so vocally complain about.

The scuba diving industry in the Philippines has always been at the forefront of the struggle to protect the magnificent resources nature has bestowed on the Filipinos. In Anilao, for example, there is a long history of co-operation with the coast guard, and an ongoing, aggressive, pro-environment sentiment among the large scuba diving community there. In Puerto Galera, the industry has developed in harmony with the local population who can see the benefits that tourism has brought to their little corner of paradise. As with Anilao, there are some superb sites around the area because of this concern.

In the Visayas, the story is the same. On Mactan Island, there can be no doubt that the presence of so many scuba diving operations over the years has considerably slowed down the ravages of illegal fishing. Sites that are frequently visited by divers—and there are a lot of divers in the water every day around the island—are perceived as too risky by most illegal fishermen. While there are areas bombed out beyond hope, there are also some incredible spots just waiting to be discovered, and no shortage of knowledgeable guides to take them there.

Around Bohol, especially at Panglao and Balicasag islands, the locals seem to have held their marine resources in higher regard than some others, because they are precious jewels in the crown of Visayan diving. Apo Island, to the south of Cebu and east of Negros, is another outstanding, pristine site not to be missed.

Obviously, the remoteness of a location can be its salvation, though some *Muro Ami* vessels are quite seaworthy and can stay at sea for long periods, over 6 months if necessary. The Sibuyan Sea, to the northeast of Boracay and southeast of Marinduque Island, is largely unexplored by divers. Banton Island and the wreck of the *Maestre de Campo*, two popular Sibuyan Sea sites, are now regularly accessed from Boracay and Puerto Galera, and returning divers praise them with gushing superlatives. Other, remoter sites which have been visited by "frontier divers," often on live-aboard vessels on transition runs, are reported as either fantastic or devastated, with few assessments of anything in between.

Professionalism in the Industry

The Philippine Commission on Sports Scuba Diving (PCSSD) was formed in 1987 to promote the development of the sport, oversee the conservation of the country's marine resources and to register and license dive establishments and professionals in the industry. This regulatory body has done a lot to improve and develop scuba diving.

Numerous dive establishments and diving professionals in the Philippines are registered with the PCSSD. Air from registered dive centers is tested twice annually, and licensees are required to conform to an ethical and environmental code. It is always a good idea to check that a dive center is registered with the PCSSD as it may say a lot about the integrity of the operation. The PCSSD works closely with the industry to promote the country as a diving destination, and visitors are always welcome at their office in the Department of Tourism Building in Manila. The PCSSD also maintains a recompression chamber in Cebu.

In the private sector, most of the popular dive areas have attempted to organise an association of local dive operators. DITO Philippines (Dive Industry Trade Organisation of the Philippines) was set up in 1999 to act as a focal point for interested parties such as media groups, trade show organisers and travel and industry professionals. The Haribon Foundation is another effective environmental group working with divers, as is Mario Elumba's *Scubasurero* project at Anilao. *Scubasurero* is a play on the Tagalog word for a garbage collector, a *Basurero*, and that's what participating divers do: pick up plastic bags and other garbage strewn over affected reefs.

Prices for all Pockets

But don't be put off by tales of dynamite and plastic bags. A visiting scuba diver is not short of superb destinations from which to choose. For most, deciding which area to choose will be based on financial considerations and the amenities on offer. From a US$500 a night resort to a US$6 hut on the beach, the choice is yours. In the US$20 to $40 range, the possibilities are almost

Below: Specimens of an unidentified species of porcelain crab. The pattern is similar to *Neopetrolisthes maculatus*. *Photo by Gerald Allen.*

endless. These days, most dive centers have good equipment, many offering niceties such as rental of dive computers and underwater videos, and are run by professional, competent businessmen.

Various consultants and specialized tour operators, such as Whitetip Divers and Dive Buddies, both located in Manila, can give valuable tips on most areas as well as up-to-the-minute information on weather and dive conditions around the islands, advice on travel, accommodation, amenities, night life, dining and other points of interest.

—Heneage Mitchell

La Union
Calm Waters and Pleasant Beaches

Opposite: Blotched hawkfish *(Cirrhitichthys aprinus)*. *Photo by Mike Severns.*

Only a 5-hour bus ride from Manila, La Union was one of the first beach resorts to be developed in the Philippines. The US Air Force had around 150 men stationed at Wallace Air Station until 1992, many of whom learned scuba diving in the warm, clear waters of La Union's Lingayen Gulf.

Unfortunately, indiscriminate dynamiting and other illegal fishing techniques have wreaked havoc over the years on the once prolific inner reefs. Nonetheless, there are enough interesting sites in the usually calm and gentle waters of the gulf to justify several days of lingering around to enjoy both the diving and the beaches of Bauang, Paringao and San Fernando.

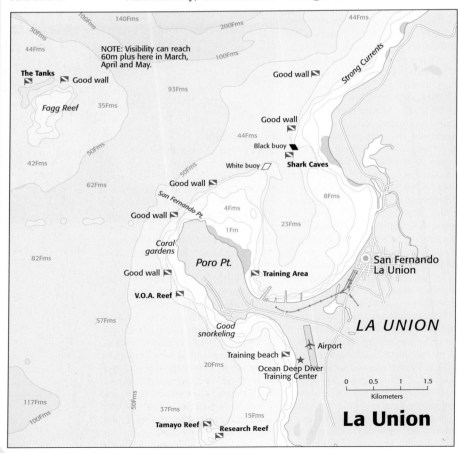

NOTE: Visibility can reach 60m plus here in March, April and May.

The Tanks

Good wall

Fagg Reef

Good wall

Strong Currents

Good wall

Good wall

Black buoy

White buoy

Shark Caves

Good wall

Good wall

San Fernando Pt.

Coral gardens

Good wall

Poro Pt.

Training Area

San Fernando La Union

V.O.A. Reef

LA UNION

Good snorkeling

Airport

Training beach

Ocean Deep Diver Training Center

Tamayo Reef

Research Reef

La Union

0   0.5   1   1.5
Kilometers

140Fms
200Fms
44Fms
50Fms
100Fms
44Fms
100Fms
93Fms
35Fms
42Fms
50Fms
44Fms
62Fms
50Fms
8Fms
4Fms
23Fms
1Fm
82Fms
57Fms
117Fms
100Fms
50Fms
37Fms
15Fms
20Fms

The Tanks

This is the most famous dive in the gulf. Resting 39 meters down on a ledge protruding from the almost vertical western wall of Fagg Reef, a mile or more off Poro Point, these three World War II-vintage M10 tanks are now home to a variety of marine life, including a 65-kg moray eel. It's best to check if he is at home before sticking your head into the turret of the middle tank.

Currents can be tricky this far out, but it is usually possible to come up from this deep dive and drift across the top of the reef while decompressing and still see plenty of interesting stuff. I have come across pelagic whitetip and whale sharks on the wall at Fagg, as well as wrasses, dorados, the occasional Spanish mackerel, king barracuda and leopard rays. There used to be plenty of hawksbill turtles, but sadly they are rare now.

The caves on Research Reef are another popular dive, with an average depth of around 15 meters. A series of easily penetrable tunnels and canyons rather than actual caves, expect to see lobsters (usually young), parrotfishes and lionfishes, as well as almost any kind of other tropical reef fishes, though usually small and timid, at this site. It's an excellent site for a night dive.

Voice of America Reef

In the next cove to the north, you'll find VOA Reef, so named because of the half-million watt Voice of America transmitting station which still occupies a large section of Poro Point. From the white, coral sand at 6 meters to the bottom of the wall at 22 meters, VOA is a delightful, easy dive. In common with the other local sites, there is a profusion of table, basket, staghorn, brain, star, flower and finger corals, together with a wide variety of soft corals and anemones. La Union makes up in shell life for what it lacks in fish,

and following trails in the sand will usually lead to something interesting. There are eggshell, map and tiger cowries all over the place, as well as green turbans, a variety of augers, cones (be careful!) and *Murex*. There is generally more fish life—groupers, parrotfishes, squirrelfishes, snappers and lionfishes— at the southern, deeper end of the wall, but visibility is less here.

Visibility in the Lingayen Gulf is unusually good year round. In peak season (March to June), it can get to over 60 meters. In the middle of the rainy season (from June to December) it rarely falls below 7 meters, and is often better at many sites. The Gulf is protected from all but the worst weather by the Cordillera mountain range to the east, and is well north of the usual typhoon tracks, and so enjoys mild weather year round.

— *Heneage Mitchell*

Bañca boats, 20–90 min

Good, 20–50 meters in season

Usually negligible

Damaged but pretty in certain places

Rocky: crevices, caves and corals

Skittish, fair variety, small numbers

M10-1A World War II tanks; caves

Subic Bay

A Choice of Wrecks in a Perfect Natural Harbor

Just a few hours northwest of Manila are the newly discovered corals and wreck sites of duty-free Subic Bay. During the years the US Navy held sway over the perfect natural harbor in the bay, diving and fishing were off-limits in many areas. Now that they are gone, new sites are being discovered almost weekly. Visibility can reach over 40 meters in the bay, though it is usually between 5 and 15 meters. There is virtually no current and the water is almost always calm enough for diving.

Probably the most accessible wreck, and the most interesting one

Below: Close-up of the hull of the *El Capitan* wreck, Subic Bay.
Photo by Jack Jackson.

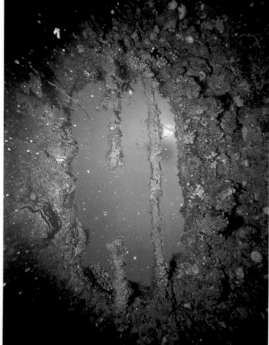

to dive on, is the battleship USS *New York*. Built in 1891, the ship saw service in the Philippine American War, the Chinese Revolution and World War I. Decommissioned in 1931, she rode at anchor in Subic Bay for the next 10 years until she was scuttled by retreating US forces to prevent her massive 17-inch cannons from falling into Japanese hands. She lies on her port side in 27 meters of water between the Alava Pier and the runway at Cubi Point, and is home to a variety of marine life, including barracuda, lionfishes, spotted sweetlips, groupers, lobsters and spotted rays. The cannons are still intact and the photo opportunities are outstanding.

A Sunken Freighter

Not to be missed is the *El Capitan*. Lying on its port side, the stern is in only 5 meters of water while the bow rests at 20 meters. A small freighter, the *El Capitan* is safely penetrable. The accommodation area is now taken up by a wide variety of tropical fishes; look out for glasseyes, wrasses, tangs, gobies, spotted sweetlips, lobsters, crabs and clownfishes. Visibility is usually between 5 and 20 meters, depending on the tide.

There are several other wrecks visited regularly by local dive centers, including the *Oryoku Maru*, an outbound passenger ship carrying over 1,600 prisoners of war when it was attacked and sunk 400 meters off Alava Pier. Despite having been flattened by US Navy demolition

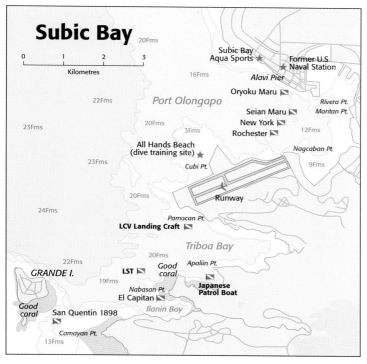

Subic Bay

(map labels: 20Fms, 16Fms, 22Fms, 23Fms, 20Fms, 24Fms, 22Fms, 19Fms, 13Fms, Subic Bay Aqua Sports, Former U.S. Naval Station, Alavi Pier, Oryoku Maru, Port Olongapo, Rivera Pt., Maritan Pt., Seian Maru, New York, Rochester, 12Fms, 3Fms, Nagcaban Pt., All Hands Beach (dive training site), Cubi Pt., 9Fms, Runway, Pamocan Pt., LCV Landing Craft, Triboa Bay, Apaliin Pt., GRANDE I., LST, Good coral, Nabasan Pt., Japanese Patrol Boat, El Capitan, Good coral, San Quentin 1898, Ilanin Bay, Camayan Pt.)

divers for navigational safety reasons, this is still a good dive with plenty to see, including a resident shoal of barracuda patrolling the site overhead.

Good Coral and a Spanish Galleon

Coral reef fanatics are also well served in Subic. Apart from the ever popular sites at nearby Grande Island, a former R&R centre for US servicemen, several new sites in pristine condition have recently been discovered. These include sites such as the coral gardens off Nabasan Point in Triboa Bay. Their healthy condition is due to the fact that they have been protected from fishing and divers for many years. Expect to find outstanding examples of brain, table and star corals, as well as a profusion of crinoids, sponges and crustaceans.

Brian Homan, who has been discovering wrecks around the Philippines for over 15 years now, conducts regular explorations and excursions of the region aboard his replica of a Spanish Galleon, *La Gallega*. Plunging into the waters of Subic Bay from this outstanding and unusual vessel is an experience in itself. As there is probably no-one around with better local knowledge than Brian, divers are strongly recommended to check out his operation.

Subic is now a duty-free port and is a good place to buy diving equipment: remember to take your passport. You should also try to visit the recompression chamber on the former base, still maintained and operated by a team of well-trained and dedicated professionals. This chamber is one of three available to careless sport divers and ignorant, hose-diving fishermen who resort to recompression all too often to save their lives after diving accidents. Complete diver training is offered at several centers from Olongapo to Barrio Barretto, a popular, laid-back beach resort area a few miles to the north of the city of Olongapo.

— *Heneage Mitchell*

Banca boats, 5–60 min

Usually fair, 10–25 meters

Usually none

Fair variety in places

Sand, mud bottom, some corals

Good variety, prolific in places

Excellent wreck diving

Nasugbu

Easily Accessible from the Capital

A few hours' drive by bus to the south of the capital of Manila, in the province of Batangas, is the sleepy little coastal town of Nasugbu. Facing onto the waters of the South China Sea, this region has long, volcanic sand beaches and no shortage of good diving.

Fortune Island

Perhaps the most famous dive sites around here are at Fortune Island, a small, privately owned resort island a few miles out to sea west of the town itself. Except for the Bat Cave, the visibility here is usually

 By boat,
10–60 min

 Depending on site,
5–50 m

 Can be strong in places

 Good variety,
prolific in places

 Walls, drop-offs

Good variety

 Fortune Island,
walls and caves

excellent, reaching 50 meters and even more.

On one particular site, the Blue Holes, there are large groupers, sweetlips and parrotfishes everywhere, as well as angelfishes, puffers, wrasses, gobies, butterflyfishes and damselfishes—to name but a few. Squid and cuttlefish are also common. The corals and other reef organisms are prolific and diverse—you'll find gorgonians and barrel sponges, vast slabs of star coral with plume worms all over them, and anemones galore. There are three sink holes which converge into an open cavern, and a coral overhang at 28 meters. Hawksbill turtles and shoals of leatherjackets frequent the area, plus several species of pelagics.

Also at Fortune Island are the remains of an old freighter lying in 20 meters or so of water. Not much is left now except box sections, but the wreck is very penetrable and excellent for photography. Beware: there are large scorpionfishes and lionfishes all over the place.

The Bat Cave is also a popular site, another 20-meter dive which leads to a semi-submerged cave with bats hanging around inside. Cuttlefish breed here, and there are abundant soft corals around.

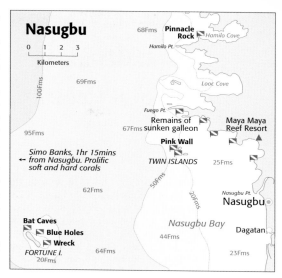

Sumo Bank

Several miles further out, this is another excellent local dive. Among other features is an abundance of cauliflower-shaped corals which cover the sandy bottom. Whitetips and other sharks roam these waters, and a wide variety of tropical reef fish make their homes here. The corals, soft and hard, are prolific, and the area is well suited for the more experienced diver.

Closer inshore are Twin Islands, really two large rocks jutting up out of the sea. There are several good dives here, the Pink Wall being our favorite. An almost sheer drop-off starting at 8 meters, the wall is covered by thousands of soft, pink corals. There are lots of small tropical fish here all the time and a few turtles sometimes. Visibility doesn't usually exceed 20 meters, but the diving is always memorable.

Sunken Booty

At Fuego Point, almost directly north of Twin Islands, a boulder-strewn bottom hides artefacts from a long ago sunken galleon. The remains of the anchor, rope and chain can still be seen. The fish life is not impressive, but lots of small tropicals are swimming around. Visibility is seldom much above 15 meters but the drop-off, which goes past 30 meters, usually enjoys better visibility—between 12 and 25 meters—and is draped with colorful gorgonians, and other hard and soft corals. Tuna and other pelagics cruise the waters, and there are plenty of small tropical reef fish to enjoy.

The dive sites around Nasugbu are not visited as frequently as one might expect, given its proximity to Manila. However, the PADI dive center at the popular Maya Maya Reef Resort is an excellent place to discover what many of the local divers have been missing for all these years.

— *Heneage Mitchell*

Opposite: The red-banded wrasse (*Cheilinus fasciatus*) is a popular fish among divers because it often allows close approach. *Photo by Robert Yin.*

Anilao

Birthplace of Philippine Scuba

A two-and-a-half-hour drive through the lush Southern Luzon countryside from Manila, Anilao can justifiably claim to be the birthplace of scuba diving in the Philippines.

In the mid 1960s, Dr. Tim Sevilla transplanted an entire coral reef onto a large rock formation a short distance off shore from his Dive 7000 resort. At the time, the conventional thinking about coral reef growth regarded transplanting a coral reef to be futile, but Dr. Sevilla proved them wrong. And to this day, Cathedral Rock is a much visited site, a vibrant, colorful dive with a profusion of small reef fish, soft and hard corals and even a small underwater shrine.

The shrine is in the form of a cross, and was blessed by the Pope and placed at about 40 ft (13 meters) between two coral carpeted pinnacles in 1982 by Lt. General Fidel V. Ramos, who would later become the President of the Philippines.

Anilao has remained at the forefront of the scuba industry since then, and is still an excellent place for snorkelers, novices and experienced aquanauts alike.

However, don't expect to find much beachfront along the rugged Balayan Bay coastline—you don't come to Anilao to laze around on beaches—trips here are definitely focused on water sports, and scuba diving in particular.

Photographers inevitably have a field day here, and professionals come in time and time again from around the world to shoot the area's diverse sites. The macro-photographer will enjoy the legendary photo opportunities this dive destination affords while wide-angle enthusiasts won't be disappointed either.

Unfortunately, the pressures of an ever increasing population has put a lot of stress on the local ecosystem, typical of many premier dive destinations elsewhere. Being "just round the corner" from a major port, Batangas City located at the mouth of Batangas Bay, Balayan Bay has not escaped the negative effects of shipping and constant water movement.

The many thousands of Filipino divers who trained and still dive regularly in Anilao have long been on the cutting edge of the social,

Below: This cross at Cathedral Rock was laid by President Fidel Ramos and blessed by Pope John Paul II. *Photo by Jack Jackson.*

Anilao

0 1 2 3
Kilometres

344m

Dalig Pt.

Locloc

LUZON

Locloc Pt.

San Andres

Janao Bay

Galung Pt.

Santa Maria

Mainaga

Biluga Pt.

Mato Pt.

Anilao

Mabini

Cathedral Rock  Solo

Talaga

Pungo Pt.

340m

CALUMPAN PENINSULA

Bagalangit

Masaging

Batangas Bay

Bagalangit Pt.

300m

294m

100m

Beatrice Rock

Sombrero I.

Dilao Pt.

Bajura

Kirby's Reef

Nagiba

Mainit

Sepoc Pt.

Mainit

300m

Sepoc wall

Daralout

CABAN I.

Cazador Pt.

391m

Maricaban

Bethlehem

Maricaban Strait

Soft Corals

Mapating
Excellent macro
photography

Tingloy

Talahib

Gamao Pt.

Burijar Pt.

Gamao

Devil's Point *Masasa Pt.*

MARICABAN I.

BONITO I.

Nelson's Rock
Hot Springs

Gorda Pt.

Pisa

521m

Papaya Pt.

MALAJIBOMANOC I.

environmental and political issues affecting all marine areas of the Philippines from Mactan to Marinduque. Dynamite and other illegal fishing techniques, collection of corals and shells, overfishing and pollution: these are just some of the harmful influences that have put immense pressure on the environment. Action is being taken against such practices at many levels and by a increasing number of people throughout the islands.

Anilao has led the way in programs such as the *Scubasurero* (a play on the Tagalog word for a garbage collector) clean-up operation and has attracted wide interest from such prestigious organizations as the Haribon Foundation and the PADI AWARE Program. This is not to say that diving around Anilao is any way deficient: far from it. But it is important to recognize Anilao's importance to the development and to the future of scuba diving in the Philippines. The fact that the local diving continues to attract many thousands is testament to the continuing struggle between the ecologically aware locals and the diving community on one hand, and the forces of industrialization and the unending demands for resources, on the other.

Anilao is still, and plans on continuing to be, an extremely popular year-round destination, and there is certainly no shortage of excellent diving available here. Most of the better sites are not actually in Balayan Bay but around the islands of Sombrero and Maricaban, each located a short *banca* boat ride to the south of Anilao.

Banca boats,
10–60 min

Usually fair,
10–40 meters

Can be stiff
in places

Prolific and varied

Walls, drop-offs

Prolific in places

Outstanding macro-
photography

Sombrero Island

Uninhabited, this island has a delightful beach which is often used as a picnic spot between dives. The diving is good all the way round the island but perhaps the best site is Beatrice Rock, just off the northern point. From depths of 6 meters down to 25 meters, there are plenty of good hard corals. Currents are often strong, which encourages pelagics to visit the site. Several species of ray can be found here, including the occasional eagle ray, as well as rainbow runners and yellowtails. Look out for another small statue placed here at a depth of around 13 meters.

At nearby Bajura, east of Sombrero and north of Caban Island, the reef is over 1 km long and descends from 12 meters to around 37 meters. There are lots of caves and overhangs, often providing a temporary home to sleeping sharks. The drop-offs and walls here are covered in a profusion of table, staghorn, mushroom and other hard corals, as well as a wide variety of crinoids and gorgonians. The prolific fish life is impressively diverse, with plenty of parrotfishes, butterflyfishes, triggerfishes, wrasses, lionfishes, scorpionfishes, plenty of moray eels, aggregations of sweetlips, the occasional octopus, some angelfishes, a few batfishes, schools of surgeons and snappers, and from time to time, eagle rays and whitetip sharks. However, you should take care here as the currents are unpredictable and can be strong, but as this is an excellent dive you shouldn't be dissuaded by this possibility.

At Mapating, off the northwest shore of Maricaban, the reef has excellent soft corals and small fish in depths of only 3 to 12 meters. As with most sites around Anilao, the macro-photography here is outstanding: the wide variety of nudibranchs are an ever-popular subject. Then there is a big, long wall starting at 18 meters which drops off to over 60 meters. Another shelf at 20 meters has some good hard corals and provides temporary shelter to the occasional nurse and cat sharks. Schools of snappers and surgeons often swim by when the current is running, as do some very large southern rays and whitetip sharks. For those divers who are

Below: Juvenile striped eel catfish, *Plotosus lineatus*. As juveniles, these fish gather into large schools, actually more like wriggling *balls*. Their dorsal and pectoral spines are venomous, a fact perhaps advertised by their contrasty coloration and busy movements. *Photo by Jones/Shimlock.*

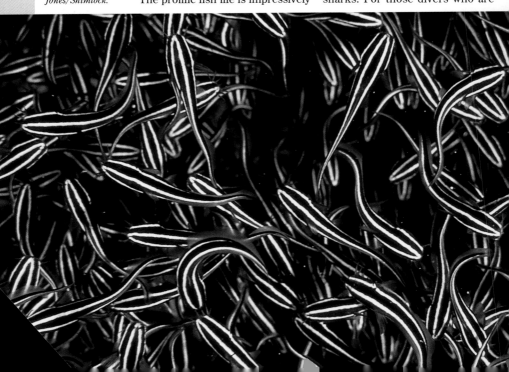

qualified to make a really deep dive, there is a huge cave here between 37 and 43 meters.

Pinnacles and Points

To the southeast at Devil's Point there is a large, submerged rock between 6 and 12 meters with pleasant corals and lots of small fish. The rock formations are picturesque but, again, watch out for the current.

At Mainit, which means "hot" in Tagalog, there is a rocky, ridged slope with a good selection of hard and soft corals on it. At 18 meters you'll find a submerged pinnacle while there's also a shark cave at 6 meters. Generally the site hosts an abundance of small reef fish. Currents can be awkward and strong, but they also produce a few pelagics when they are running so it's usually worth the effort. Afterwards, check out the hot springs on the beach.

Just off Layaglang Point on the northeastern tip of Caban Island is Kirby's, a pinnacle which goes down to 28 meters. There's a small wall with morays, lionfishes

as well as lots of colorful crinoids.

Between Culebra and Malajibomanoc (which means "chicken feather" in Tagalog) islands is Nelson's Rock, which tops out at 16 meters and drops down to a depth of over 30 meters. The pinnacle is carpeted, most of the time, by a profusion of blooming coral polyps, and large gorgonians, while the water is usually a haze with lots of damsel fishes. You'll also see caves that often host sharks, some stingrays, and a few pelagics when the current is running.

A little to the east are the Hot Springs—a very unusual dive site affording the opportunity to try out a neat trick. At 21 meters, hot volcanic gas bubbles out of holes in the seabed, and you can place an egg to cook on one of the holes while you swim off into a fairytale landscape of multi-hued pastels, bright greens and vivid yellows. Because the water is warm, the visibility here is always good. Walking fishes (the frogfish or anglerfish) are common in one spot, and sharks and rays can frequently be seen at this site. When you are ready to ascend, don't forget to collect your egg—it should be hard boiled by the end of your dive.

It is hard to include all the favorite dive sites in and around Anilao—this choice is inevitably very subjective. Suffice to say that Anilao has plenty to offer divers of all levels.

— *Heneage Mitchell*

Above: Soft coral goby *Pleurosicya* (maybe *boldinghi*) on *Dendronephthya* soft coral. *Photo by Gary Bell.*

Verde Island
A Fabulous Wall and Good Corals

Below: At Verde Island Wall, sea fans and anemones billow in the constantly moving water. Depicted here is a crinoid on a sea fan. *Photo by Jones/Shimlock.*

This is a favorite dive spot for regulars in the Puerto Galera and Anilao area. Situated in the aptly named Verde Island Passage between southern Batangas on the mainland of Luzon, and the northeastern tip of Mindoro, Verde has one of the best wall dives north of Palawan. There are also several beaches which divers use to picnic on between dives: please make sure you clean up afterwards!

Currents can be a problem here, but they do create some interesting drift dives. The island's west coast has gentle drop-offs starting from the shore and sloping down to abyssal depths. There used to be the remains of the keel of a Spanish galleon sitting in a few meters just off the beach. History relates that the galleon had just left Manila bound for Spain with a cargo of silks and spices from China when it ran aground. No-one was killed, but the incensed crew and passengers immediately constructed a gallows and hanged the unfortunate navigator. The keel has now been raised and preserved in the National Museum. However, the ardent treasure hunter can still sift the sand where the galleon sank and come across a few ballast stones or, even better, fragments of pottery or an ancient musket ball.

Jumping into the sea anywhere off this west coast will put a diver onto the gentle slopes of the fringing reef, which is criss-crossed with gullies and ravines. The current usually provides a free ride, but care should still be taken. There are lots of soft and hard corals here, but not so many reef fish around because most of these lurk in the gullies out of the current. It is worth investigating the various patches of sand with coral heads blooming out of them, as they are home to anemones and clownfishes, spotted rays, as well as a variety of crustaceans.

The Verde Island Wall

But it is the Verde Island Wall which attracts most divers to the

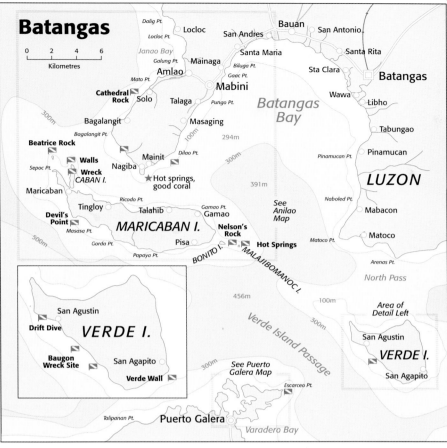

Batangas

0 2 4 6
Kilometres

Dalig Pt.
Locloc Pt.
Locloc
San Andres
Bauan
San Antonio
Janao Bay
Galung Pt.
Santa Maria
Santa Rita
Mainaga
Biluga Pt.
Sta Clara
Amlao
Gaac Pt.
Mato Pt.
Mabini
Batangas
Cathedral
Rock   Solo
Talaga
Pungo Pt.
Wawa
Libho
Bagalangit
Masaging
Batangas
Bay
Tabungao
Bagalangit Pt.
294m
Beatrice Rock
Dilao Pt.
Pinamucan Pt.
Pinamucan
Walls
Mainit
Sepoc Pt.
Nagiba
Wreck
CABAN I.
300m
391m
LUZON
Maricaban
Ricodo Pt.
Hot springs,
good coral
Tingloy
Talahib
Gamao Pt.
Gamao
Naboled Pt.
Mabacon
Devil's
Point
See
Anilao
Map
Masasa Pt.
Nelson's
Rock
MARICABAN I.
500m
Gorda Pt.
Pisa
Matoco Pt.
Matoco
Papaya Pt.
Hot Springs
BONITO I.
MALAJIBOMANOC I.
Arenas Pt.
North Pass
456m
100m
San Agustin
Area of
Detail Left
Drift Dive
VERDE I.
300m
San Agustin
Baugon
Wreck Site
San Agapito
VERDE I.
Verde Wall
San Agapito
Verde Island Passage
See Puerto
Galera Map
300m
Escarceo Pt.
Talipanan Pt.
Puerto Galera
Varadero Bay

island. Easily identifiable by the rocks sticking out of the water off the southeastern tip of the island, the wall descends from the surface almost straight down to seemingly unfathomed depths. Around the corner from the drop-in point, the wall curves in a bit, which allows divers to collect themselves in calm waters before starting to explore the surroundings.

There are vast slabs of star corals draped all along the wall, as well as giant gorgonians and large, cascading soft corals. Sea fans and anemones billow in the constantly moving water, and you can't help but be amazed by the impossibly diverse colors that meet the eye everywhere.

The first time I visited Verde, I encountered two large Napoleon wrasses who casually swam up and inspected our party. On other dives, we have seen mantas, eagle rays, whitetip and blacktip sharks. Schools of jacks and tuna are not uncommon, and there are plenty of sweetlips, batfishes, wrasses, emperors, surgeons, soldiers and tangs everywhere.

You must take care to control buoyancy and watch the depths on this particular dive. As the reef starts at the surface, safety stops can be made while still on the wall. Watch for schools of curious unicornfishes coming in close to check out decompressing divers. Serious photographers should bring two cameras: one for the larger animals and one with a macro lens to capture the nudibranchs which are generally plentiful around here.

— *Heneage Mitchell*

By boat,
30 min–3 hrs

Usually good,
15–40 meters

Very strong
in places

Prolific, colorful
and good variety

Walls, drop-offs

Often prolific
and good variety

Pristine wall,
excellent corals
and fish

Puerto Galera

Diving from a Popular Holiday Resort

The discovery of an ancient inter-island trading vessel laden with Chinese Dragon Jars and other ceramic goodies in the picturesque Batangas Channel of Puerto Galera was the precursor to the incredible growth of the scuba diving industry that thrives there today.

Local dive operators lay claim to 25 excellent dive sites within an hour of whichever of the many coves or beaches you may be staying at locally. Usually, there is fine snorkeling just offshore. At press time, there were 16 dive centers doing business in the area, with more on the way.

A place of outstanding natural beauty, Puerto Galera's underwater delights are some of the most popular diving sites in the country.

Probably the most famous dive hereabouts is the Shark Caves off

Escarceo Point. Prone to treacherous currents (one local veteran has been swept away into the Verde Passage twice now, fortunately surviving to tell the tale), this is not a dive for the timid or the inexperienced. The divemaster assesses the current and the divers descending to 18 meters. This is often a drift dive. You swim over a ledge to a patch of sand, and there, under the ledge, you can usually spot a few whitetip sharks, often with large grouper and other big fish. A little deeper and there is another, narrower cave which also accommodates sleeping sharks. This cave is popular with photographers as one can get really close to the sharks, but it is quite deep (28 meters), so bottom time is limited.

Ascending from here to around 12 meters you'll find the Pink Wall,

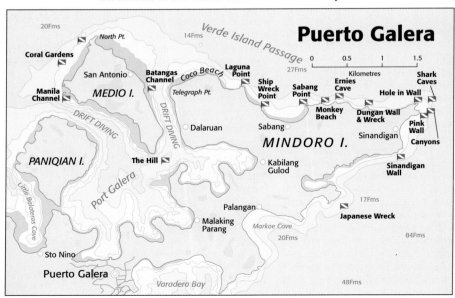

so named for the profusion of soft Cauliflower corals that have created an impressive overhang. A great spot for photography, and a popular night dive.

The Canyons

The Canyons is probably the most visited dive site in Puerto Galera, especially popular with Technical divers. Usually starting at the Hole in the Wall, a natural hole that's large enough to pass through one at a time, divers swim along a wall and then into a series of canyons. These are encrusted with all sorts of soft and hard corals, sponges, sea fans and feather stars. The sea is alive with morays, lionfish, sweetlips, jacks, tuna and frequently whitetip sharks. If you're lucky, you may even catch a glimpse of Barnacle Bill, a hawksbill turtle who often hangs around here. The dive ends at an old anchor covered with soft corals and small sea fans, home to two large lionfish.

Sabang Point is another site worth visiting. A booming coral reef starting at seven meters and descending to 18 to 20 meters, the reef is covered with feather stars, pot sponges, sea whips and sea pens. At one point there is a beautiful wall covered with different corals and home to morays, multicolored nudibranchs and fluorescent blue triggerfish.

Eight kilometers to the west of the town of Puerto Galera proper, past the secluded White Beach and out from Talipanan Beach is another reef for the serious diver, with strong currents, pelagic fish and stunning corals of all kinds. This reef, being a little further away from the majority of dive sites, is visited less often, but is none the worse for that either. Dorado and spanish mackerel have been spotted here, as well as tuna and other pelagics. Expect to find humphead wrasse, parrotfish, sweetlips, angelfish, lionfish and the peculiar crocodilefish, which, though difficult to spot, is quite common around Puerto.

Visibility in the area can reach 35 meters, but is typically 20 meters or less, depending on the site and the season. As mentioned earlier, currents can be very tricky, even on some seemingly innocuous shallower dives, so always plan to go with a professional dive guide or you could end up in trouble. Puerto is increasingly being visited by passing live-aboard boats, and is also a jump off point for regular live-aboard trips to Apo Reef, Coron Bay and the Sibuyan Sea. Trips are usually arranged at short notice.

Local dive operators own an interesting variety of vessels between them, from MV *Tabibuga,* a very seaworthy 70 ft (18 meter) steel boat sleeping up to 14 divers to large *bancas*, custom dive boats, yachts, catamarans, v-hulls and converted local wooden fishing boats. Ocean kayaks are available for rent, popular with snorkelers.

An active dive store owner's association works hard to ensure visiting divers have healthy reefs to dive on. They provide mooring buoys at popular dive sites and promote environmental and infrastructure projects. Six artificial reefs have been created since 1996 by sinking derelict vessels in the area. This professional attitude to safety and service that has developed over the years explains why so many divers just keep coming back to Puerto Galera.

— *Heneage Mitchell*

Above: The nudibranch *Chromodoris magnifica* and the yellow sea cucumbers *Cholochirus robustus* in front of soft corals and a red sponge. *Photo by Jack Jackson.*

Banca and custom dive boats, 10–30 min

Usually fair, 10–30 meters

Very strong in places

Prolific, colorful and good variety

Walls and coral gardens

Often prolific, good variety

Shark caves, coral gardens

Sibuyan Sea

Outstanding Sights in the Tablas Straits

A short flight or a five-hour bus and ferry ride south of Manila finds you in Marinduque. Famous for its Moriones festival, Marinduque and environs are far more rewarding to the diver for the profusion of outstanding underwater sites.

Wreck divers, wall divers, reef divers, cavern divers and photographers are well catered for, and many experienced divers who have visited some of the outlying islands in the Tablas Straits reckon them to be superior to anything they have seen anywhere, including the Red Sea, the Great Barrier Reef and the Sulu Sea too. High praise indeed.

To get to the choicest spots, it is necessary to plan full day trips and dive safaris of several days. Trips usually originate from Puerto Galera or Boracay. There are 11 main diving areas adjacent to Marinduque, from Natanco in the northwest to the Maestre de Campo Islands to the southwest and Banton Island to the southeast. Each has something special about it, and has more than one dive site to recommend it.

Natanco and Balanan

Natanco is noted for its walls and drift diving. On one section we found an unbelievable coral structure, white, like a huge avalanche of snow stretching for several meters, at another wall we came upon a huge shoal of tuna at 20 meters. We also found some great gorgonians and big groupers.

At Balanan, the Japanese torpedo boat is not a dive for amateurs.

This small (35-meter-long) casualty of World War II is sitting upright with a badly smashed bow in 36 to 40 meters of water. The visibility can be a problem sometimes, and averages around 10 meters. The prop is missing, but there's still a multi-barrelled gun on the deck and, to our horror, several depth charges still in their racks.

Elephante Island

Elephante Island, a private resort, is home to the other dive shop servicing Marinduque. Catering mostly to Japanese package tourists, there are a couple of good dives here. To the north, there is a wall off the beach with a fairly stiff current, (3 knots or more at times). The bottom of the wall is deep, we reached 40 meters at one point and it still kept going. Large gorgonians adorn the face. A little further south, there's an area with more of that incredible white coral, this time flatter and resembling a snow covered field. There are a lot of colorful fish here, and photo opportunities abound. Unfortunately, sometimes the resort guests think it's fun to buzz slow-moving boats following divers on jet skis.

Balthazar

At Balthazar, to the west, there is a cave you can enter at 20 meters and exit at 28 meters. There are lots of stonefish everywhere, so be careful. The gorgonians are particularly beautiful here, too. A little to the

Opposite: A pair of divers glide over a pristine reef covered in an array of soft and hard corals. *Photo by Scott Tuason.*

Live-aboard boats, 1–5-day trips

Good, 10–50 meters in season

Can be strong in places

Outstanding variety and prolific

Walls and drop-offs

Many species, great numbers and all sizes

Pristine diving, superb corals and fish, wrecks

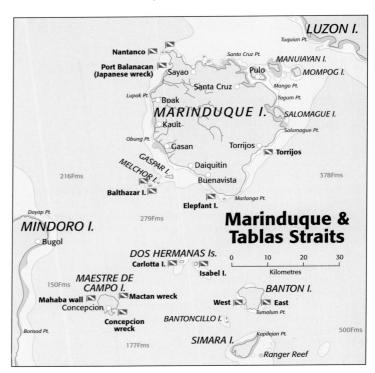

Map labels: LUZON I., Tuquian Pt., Nantanco, Port Balanacan (Japanese wreck), Sayao, Santa Cruz Pt., MANUIAYAN I., Pulo, MOMPOG I., Santa Cruz, Mango Pt., Lupak Pt., Boak, Tagum Pt., MARINDUQUE I., SALOMAGUE I., Kauit, Salomague Pt., Obung Pt., Gasan, Torrijos, Torrijos, Daiquitin, 216Fms, GASPAR I., MELCHOR I., Buenavista, 378Fms, Balthazar I., Marlanga Pt., Elepfant I., Dayap Pt., 279Fms, MINDORO I., Marinduque & Tablas Straits, Bugol, DOS HERMANAS Is., 0 10 20 30, Carlotta I., Isabel I., Kilometres, MAESTRE DE CAMPO I., 150Fms, BANTON I., Mahaba wall, Mactan wreck, Concepcion, West, East, Concepcion wreck, BANTONCILLO I., Tumalum Pt., Bonsod Pt., 177Fms, SIMARA I., Kapilejan Pt., 500Fms, Ranger Reef

south is a great night dive with prolific corals and plentiful fish life and an army of spiny lobsters.

Further south and west again, at Maestre de Campo, there are several excellent dives, including the MV *Mactan,* a ferry boat which went down 20 years or so ago. In good condition, she lies north to south on a sandy slope from 25 to 55 meters. The bow is to the south. Sweetlips, grouper, barracuda and a lot of lionfish and clouds of small tropicals have made this wreck their home.

At Port Concepcion, there are two Japanese wrecks in the harbour. A little scratching around in the muddy bottom usually rewards the searcher with bottles and other relics. The visibility is not so good, careful finning is the order of the day on these sites.

There are also the remains of World War II planes dotted around the place, and there is also good coral diving on the west side of the island.

At Isabella in Dos Hermanos to the east, there is a maze of crevices and lots of corals and reef fish. The area is often visited by local hookah fishermen, however, and the fish are skittish. A little to the west there is an excellent night dive area.

At Torrijos, on the east side of Marinduque, there's a shallow (15 meters) dive with cracks, fissures and canyons everywhere full of interesting things to explore, and a wall with large gorgonians, colorful sponges and lots of big fish. Expect to see tuna, barracuda, grouper, sweetlips, shoals of tropical reef fish of all shapes and sizes and Tridacna clams. The current is not usually too bad here.

Banton

Further south and east again finds the island of Banton. The inhabitants of Banton process copra, and many of the younger Islanders have found work abroad, apparently remitting sufficient funds to maintain their families comfortably. Perhaps that's the reason the locals don't fish the surrounding reefs, and that's the reason the reef fish are so abundant and frisky around the island. The west side has areas of stunning coral encrustation, hard and soft corals of all kinds everywhere, with pennant butterflies, huge grouper, snapper and sweetlips darting in and out of the holes and cracks in the reef. Several species of shark and ray are sometimes seen, as are dolphins, which are very common all around the surrounding Sibuyan Sea.

The North-West wall, easily found by the graffiti 'Class of '93' scrawled above it, is simply awesome, one of the best wall dives you will find anywhere.

The weather can kick up on this exposed westerly side, making it a site you should plan to visit during the relatively benign months of March, April and May.

On the west coast of Banton, the story is pretty much the same, pretty, white sand coves, some with fantastic, unspoiled diving in coral gardens which reach 20 meters.

The Slab, a block of rock in a few meters of water about a third of the way south along the west shoreline, has an interesting cave that stretches into the darkness and is penetrable for several meters. Visibility often exceeds 35 meters here during season (December to June), and the profusion of pelagic and reef fish of all sizes is simply staggering.

Sibuyan Sea

The Sibuyan Sea, which stretches south and east of here, is almost completely unexplored by divers. Due to its remoteness and inaccessibility, it is only now that a few intrepid operators are beginning to open up this frontier. Some areas which have been visited over the last few years are reported to be heavily devastated by illegal fishing techniques. Others are spoken of in awe by the few divers lucky enough to have reached them. These days, several dive operators such as La Laguna Beach Club of Puerto Galera arranging custom trips for small groups who want to dive this virgin territory, and some of them are surprisingly reasonably priced.

One last point to make about Marinduque is that, up to now, scuba instruction is not easily available.
— *Heneage Mitchell*

Below: Though the current will toss this anemone about, the pink clownfish is determined to keep his home safe from any menace. Balicasag Island, Philippines. *Photo by Scott Tuason.*

Boracay

Stunning Beaches with First-class Dive Sites Nearby

The fabulous, powdery white sand beaches of Boracay have been famous for quite a few years as some of the world's best. Yet despite the island's popularity, scuba diving was slow to catch on. Today there are at least 12 dive centers doing good business around this small island, making it an excellent place to learn scuba. Courses range from Discover Diving to PADI Master Instructor.

Several dive outfits operate safaris to hard-to-reach locations such as the Sibuyan Sea, Tablas, Romblon and to Semirara Island, as well as to the west coast of Panay and the outlying reefs and islands.

Closer to Boracay, there are some first-class dive sites catering to divers of all levels, and some good, easily accessible snorkeling.

Friday's Rock, close to the west shore and at a depth of between 10 and 18 meters, is a favorite dive site. Here you will find a variety of soft and hard corals, butterflyfishes, wrasses, tangs, damselfishes, snappers and stingrays, and big scorpionfishes and lionfishes. Most divemasters can take you to a fish feeding station where the fish swarm around divers.

A little to the northwest of Friday's Rock there are two dive sites

 By boat,
10 min–1.5 hrs

 Usually good,
7–25 meters

 Strong in
some areas

 Good variety and
quite prolific

 Walls and
coral gardens

 Prolific in places,
good variety

 Easy access,
awesome walls

named Punta Bonga 1 and 2. One is shallower, a drop-off to 24 meters, and the other starts at 30 meters and goes down to 50 meters. On the shallower dive, the top of the reef is covered with soft corals. Trigger-fishes, groupers and angelfishes are commonly seen. Diving on the deeper wall, you'll find large gor-gonians of all colors and big sting-rays. There are plenty of sizeable sweetlips and tuna about, and occa-sional barracuda and sharks.

Crocodile Island

Southeast of Boracay, Crocodile Island (named for its shape, not any resident reptile) is another popular site, but one with current as it is right in the channel between Boracay and Panay. The bottom of the wall is around 24 meters at its deepest, the top of the reef is about 10 meters. You'll find just about everything here: sweetlips, trigger-fishes, wrasses, butterflyfishes and snappers. There are a few banded sea snakes too—we've seen some over 2 meters long—but no-one has been bitten by one. Look out too for the pretty blue gorgonians.

Another excellent dive close by is Laurel Island. Currents can get very strong here, but it is these cur-rents which encourage the corals to open up their fantastic yellow and orange polyps to feed on micro-scopic elements, festooning the walls of an 8-meter-long tunnel at the tip of the island. There are also big sponges and large gorgonians.

At the northern end of Boracay is Yapak, a deep wall starting around 30 meters and descending beyond 60 meters depth. Currents are often tricky here and the water is usually rough, but for experi-enced divers and lovers of big ani-mals, this is the best Boracay has to offer. Covered with a profusion of soft corals, there are also some outstanding gorgonian fans hang-ing off the wall. Snappers, sweet-lips, surgeons, pennants and rain-bow runners are all plentiful as are barracudas, whitetip and gray reef

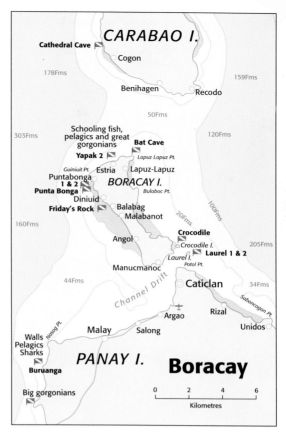

sharks. Occasionally a hammer-head will fin by. Manta rays have also been spotted from time to time. This is not a dive for beginners.

To the north, nearby Carabao Island has some fairly good spots. Cathedral Cave, a wide-mouthed cave at around 28 meters, is our par-ticular favorite for its plentiful groupers and colorful soldierfishes.

Neighboring Panay

To the southwest of Boracay, the west coast of Panay has some excel-lent sites. At Buruanga, off Nasog Point, Black Rock and Dog Drift, the walls and drop-offs start at around 10 meters and then go down to 40 meters. A variety of hard and soft corals are home to snappers, sweet-lips and big triggerfishes. Keep an eye open for large pelagics.

— *Heneage Mitchell*

Left: Beaked butter-flyfish *(Chelmon ros-tratus)*. Butterfly-fishes display a remarkable array of color patterns and are a favorite of underwater photographers. *Photo by Mike Severns.*

THE PHILIPPINES

Mactan

A Popular Resort with Fair Diving

Looking a little unprepossessing from the air, the island of Mactan, 45 minutes from the heart of Cebu, comes alive underwater. Visited by thousands of divers every year, Mactan's east coast has several good dive sites along its walls. The Hilutangan Channel, which separates Mactan from adjacent Olango Island, is extremely deep and, as a consequence, one can hope to see several species of large animals on a lucky diving day. Although visibility can exceed 30 meters it usually averages around 18 meters, and divers should note that currents are a factor to be reckoned with.

Dive off the Resorts

The Tambuli Fish Feeding Station, just off the 5-star resort of the same name, is an excellent opportunity to get to know many smaller species of fish which abound in the warm and generally clear waters off Mactan Island. Photographers will appreciate this dive, as literally hundreds of fish swarm all around proffered bread or other snacks which dive guides bring along. Tambuli recently sank a small light aircraft off shore which has already attracted a great number of residents.

Local boats,
10 min–1.5 hrs,
also live-aboards

Often excellent,
10–50 meters

Can be stiff
in places

Good variety,
pristine in places

Walls and
drop-offs

Good variety,
good shells

Fans, gorgonians
and pelagics

The soft corals off Mar y Cielo Resort are another interesting dive, a gentle slope covered with elephant ear coral and barrel sponges.

Although a little deep with an entrance at 26 meters, the Marigondon cave is another popular dive well worth making the effort to visit. The cave stretches inward for about 45 meters and comes to end at a depth of 25 meters where there is a small grotto, home to dozens of flashlight fish. These fish have adapted to life in the dark by developing a neat patch of bio-luminescence under each eye. Divers poke their heads into the narrow opening and turn off their torches to be rewarded with a wonderful light show as the fish dart around and hundreds of eyes appear to be winking back out of the dark recesses.

Good Walls

Just to the south of the cave on Marigondon Reef, there is a wall starting at 12 meters and descending to around 45 meters. Its attraction is that the face is covered in a wide variety of colorful sponges, soft corals, brain corals and gorgonians, a feature that characterizes most dives off Mactan. Not to be missed here is a sizeable colony of garden eels. There is usually a fair current—most dives are drift dives.

To the north is Pang Pang, another wall dive popular for night dives. Lucky divers see whale sharks, and sometimes manta rays.

The wall just off Kon Tiki Resort is another fine site. A short swim from the resort finds one on a gently sloping coral covered rocky seabed at 5 meters. This soon gives way to an impressive drop-off, festooned with fan corals, sea stars, feather stars and myriad crinoids. Barracuda and solitary whale sharks can also been seen.

Olango Island

Across the Channel at Olango Island, there are a couple of sites of interest, including Santa Rosa. A white sand bottom with a profusion of soft corals leads to a steep drop-off at 15 meters. This bottoms out around 50 meters where big grouper can be seen in the small caves which are dotted about.

Also at Olango is Baring, just off the northwestern tip of the island. A sloping, sandy bottom starting at around 15 meters with several small caves, this area is

Below: Mactan's east coast has several good dive sites along its walls. *Photo by Ashley Boyd.*

home to a number of large fish. Sharks can also be seen.

Mactan is a major jump-off point for divers wanting to visit the outstanding, remoter dive sites around the Visayas, such as Cabilao, Panglao and Apo Island. Most dive centers on the island organize dive safaris, lasting from a couple of days up to a week or more aboard a variety of boats.

— *Heneage Mitchell*

Above: The broad-armed cuttlefish, *Sepia latimanus,* is the largest cuttlefish found in Southeast Asian waters. It can reach a half-meter in length. *Photo by Ashley Boyd.*

North Cebu

A Less Crowded Alternative to the Southern Resorts

Below: *Goniopora djiboutiensis* looks superficially like a soft coral, but the stalked tentacles of the colony are attached to a typical hard coral skeleton. *Goniopora* is most common in turbid waters of coastal reefs and lagoons. *Photo by Mike Severns.*

Due to the somewhat sparse diving infrastructure in this area, most of the coastal dive sites visited regularly by divers in the north of Cebu tend to be close to the town of Sogod, on the east coast, which has two resorts offering scuba rentals and guides.

However, all is not lost for visitors and divers staying elsewhere on the island of Cebu. Some of the Mactan-based dive operators, in the central part of the island of Cebu, head north regularly, usually to visit Capitancillo, Gato and Calangaman islands.

Capitancillo Island

Capitancillo Island has a mushroom-shaped wall on its south side with outstanding coral formations and impressive gorgonian fans. Large manta rays are occasionally seen roaming around the teeming waters of the reef, and you can also hope to see shoals of yellowfin tuna and large groupers. The bottom is deep here—you still can't see it when you are down at 45 meters—so care should be taken at all time to monitor depths.

Local boats, 10 min–1.5 hrs, also live-aboards

Often excellent, 10–50 meters

Can be stiff in places

Good variety, pristine in places

Walls and drop-offs

Good variety, good shells

Fans, gorgonians and pelagics

As a diversion after diving, you'll find an old lighthouse on top of this small rocky island. It is worth the climb for its view.

North of Capitancillo lies Calangaman, another dive site visited by the adventurous few who enjoy diving on so-called "virgin" dive sites. Both sites are within relatively easy striking distance and visited often by divers from Club Pacific, a Sogod-based resort.

Quatro Island is another location frequented by northern Cebu divers, who rave about its caves and reef formations. The hard and soft corals are outstanding here, and snorkelers favor the place as there is plenty to see—even in only 1 or 2 meters of water. There are actually four different reefs at this site, with walls descending to 150 meters, but don't even consider trying to get near the bottom of the wall. Best to remember that although there is a recompression chamber in Cebu City, it is far away.

At Kimod Reef, another one of those sunken islands, you are quite likely to run into a wide variety of pelagic life, including several different species of shark, as well as eagle and manta rays.

Gato Island

Another popular spot. Between November and May it's a good area for whitetips and other reef sharks. Here you'll find plenty of soft corals, gorgonians of all colors, sponges and hard corals. Gato Cave, actually a tunnel underneath the island, is also frequented by sharks and banded sea snakes. It is not for the faint-hearted, but definitely a must for the thrill-seeker. Currents are usually a bit stronger here than at the previous locations mentioned, so expect drift diving.

Malapascua Island is the latest site to be developed by dive operators in the region (there are three currently on the island). It has become so popular because on adjacent Monad Shoal a group of thresher sharks has taken up

residence. These rare, shy creatures can usually be found swimming off the seamount. They cruise in a triangular pattern, swimming in circles at each corner of the route.

Divers can get quite close to these creatures but should avoid getting in the way of the sharks as this could upset their swimming patterns and may drive them away.

Closer to Sogod, there are a number of inshore sites that are

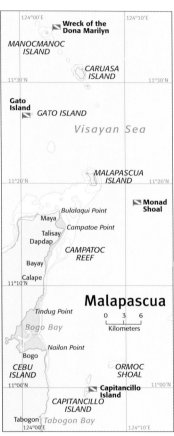

worth a look. Dive boats typically anchor in 3 to 12 meters. There is a series of lagoons with sheer drop-offs going down to a maximum of 40 meters then it slopes gently to several hundred meters. All kinds of soft corals, sponges, nudibranchs and other invertebrates flourish in these waters. Chances are you will encounter dolphins and hawksbill turtles, and discover shells.

—Heneage Mitchell

Boat or tricycle

5–35 meters

Sometimes strong

Dense, prolific,
untouched

Seamounts and
walls

Prolific pelagics

Whale sharks,
mantas, stunning
walls

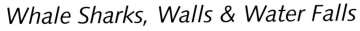

THE PHILIPPINES

Southern Leyte
Whale Sharks, Walls & Water Falls

Southern Leyte is a new destination just recently opening up to visiting divers. Although the diving facilities are not perhaps as impressive as they are in some other parts of the country, the diving certainly is. Topside, the topography is equally intense, with waterfalls and pristine primary forest coverage abounding.

Whale sharks are a major attraction here, but there are plenty of other things to see on the sites so far discovered.

Most of the sites are in Sogod Bay, a popular whale-watching area with several species of whales regularly spotted by tour boats operating from resorts along Cebu's east coast and Leyte's west coast. Southern Leyte is distinct from Cebu as it is another island and home to a different ethnic group.

Limasawa Island is a six-kilometer-long land mass with a fringing reef offering walls and drift dives along its length. The island is known as the site of the first Christian mass held in the Far East, but is more recently becoming famous for its underwater attractions: virginal coral gardens visited by large pelagics such as barracuda, mackerel, tuna and jacks.

Max Climax wall is found to the north of Limasawa, just off the coast of Lungsodaan, Padre Burgos. Many crevices along the wall provide shelter for angelfish, snapper, sweetlips, grouper and Napoleon wrasse, as well as a host of smaller tropical fish. Turtles are often seen nosing around and pelagics that regularly visit include several species of sharks, barracuda,

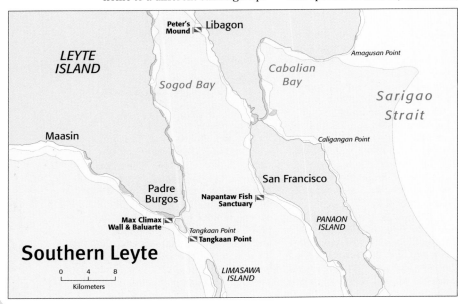

tuna, and eagle rays. Tangkaan Point, to the south of Max Climax, is home to a number of dive sites on the various reefs dotted around the area, many of which have been declared marine sanctuaries by the local communities. It is here that the odds of spotting a whale shark are the highest, sightings are regularly reported. Mantas are also common visitors, as are whitetip and blacktip sharks. Other shark species can sometimes be seen here too. The reefs are varied, from flat to rugged, some with gentle slopes, some with steep walls. Barrel sponges are prolific in some areas, notably at the site named Barrel Sponge Garden, which also features large table corals as well as a good variety of hard and soft corals and sponges and tunicates. Nearby Turtle Rock is a likely place to spot green turtles as well as batfish, eagle rays, and grouper. The corals at this site tend towards whips, gorgonians, table and brain, with plenty of soft corals and sponges filling in the gaps.

Napantaw Fish Sanctuary, also known as Rio's Wall and Toshi's Wall after pioneering divers that discovered many of the local sites, is one of the better walls in Southern Leyte. Turtles are frequent visitors, and there is a cave at 40 meters worth checking out if you can find it at the start of the dive—don't spend too long looking for it though, as there is plenty to see higher up the wall and it's not worth risking the bends by spending too much time at depth. The currents can be strong here, which makes for prolific and healthy coral coverage, notably huge gorgonians and black coral as well as the ubiquitous soft corals liberally festooning the reef. Batfish, sweetlips and grouper are among the reef's denizens, and barracuda often pass by.

Peter's Mound is a seamount about 200 meters offshore starting at 10 meters and dropping off to well below 40 meters. Aside from the resident surgeons, fusiliers, snapper, grouper, Napoleon wrasse and other reef fish that swarm over the vibrant, coral encrusted reef, Peter's Mound is a dive worth making if only for the fact that it is a cleaning station for large pelagics who can be found finning gently against the often strong currents (the best time to see this is when the current is running) as cleaner wrasse pick off the pesky infestations of microscopic critters from their gills, teeth, fins and scales.

— *Heneage Mitchell*

Above: Nudibranch at Peter's Mound. *Photo by Scott Tuason.*

Moalboal & Pescador

A Small but Superb Site Away from the Crowds

A few hours' drive southwest of Cebu City, across the dusty mountain roads of the interior to the west coast, is Moalboal.

One of the original dive centers of the Philippines, Moalboal owes its popularity almost entirely to scuba diving. A few steps off the beach from the main resort area of Pangasama lies a reef which is home to a wide variety of marine life. The ubiquitous fan corals and gorgonians are, of course, very much in evidence, as are sponges and crinoids, nudibranchs and several different species of shells. There are sweetlips, tangs, gobies and lionfishes all over the the dive site. A little careful exploring will usually reveal some interesting shell life too.

Tongo Point, at the south end of the beach, is covered with little cracks and caves, home to soft corals and many tropical reef fish. Anemones and clownfishes, nudibranchs and a host of other invertebrates make this a popular photographer's dive. Visibility can be changeable, depending on the weather. A great dive for novices and a popular second dive.

An underwater "island" named Lambug lies about a 45-minute *banca* boat ride away. Really an

From the beach or by boat, 10 min–1 hr

Often excellent, 10–50 meters

Can be strong in places

Outstanding—great variety and prolific

Walls and drop-offs

Good variety, prolific in places, big pelagics

Pescador, Sunken Islands

underwater mountain, Lambug is reached after descending through blue water for 27 meters before reaching the peak. There is often a strong current here too, so this really is not a dive for amateurs but for those who are up to it.

Lambug is an outstanding experience. Large pelagics cruise by all the time; we saw several king barracudas, a lone tuna, two manta rays and a whitetip shark as well as groupers, snappers and a huge shoal of *Talakitok*, or jackfish, on one 25-minute dive last year.

Pescador Island

But the jewel in the crown of Moalboal's diving is tiny Pescador Island. About 2 km offshore, Pescador has been described as "a different dive every five meters." It is quite possible to circle the island on a shallower dive. Utterly superb drop-offs, buttresses and impressive overhangs are the main features of this site, with a shallow reef running around the island. Between 22 and 25 meters is a large, funnel-shaped structure of about 15 meters, called the Cathedral. When the sunlight hits it in just the right position, the corals and sponges are dappled with beams of light, making it a beautiful sight.

Lionfishes, snappers, groupers, scorpionfishes and sweetlips are found at every depth, and on deeper dives whitetip sharks and hammerhead sharks are not uncommon, especially between the months of November and April. Less frequently, tiger and thresher sharks put in an appearance. The

Photo by Jones/Shimlock

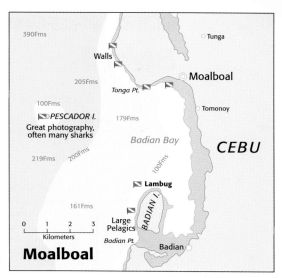

Map showing Moalboal and Pescador Island, Cebu

gorgonians are perhaps less profuse than one might imagine, but there is a lot of black coral around, as well as sea fans, sponges of all types and nudibranchs. Divers often see Spanish dancers wriggling their way sensually around the reef.

Pescador takes on a totally different perspective after dark, and it is a favorite local night dive.

Nearby, Badian Island is another spot worth visiting, though the marine life is neither as prolific or as exciting as Pescador and Lambug. However, whitetip sharks are quite common, and you may well see a banded sea snake or two, together with the inevitable anemones and sponges.

Several Moalboal dive centers arrange excursions further afield, to Bohol, Cabilao, Apo Island and other, remoter dive sites on an ad hoc basis. The communication revolution hasn't quite reached this sleepy little hamlet yet, so it's best to arrive and plan your dive outings when you get there. Whatever you may end up doing, you can rest assured that Moalboal is sure to satisfy even the most jaded diver, and has the advantage of excellent off-the-beach diving of a quality which few other dive areas in the Philippines can match.

—*Heneage Mitchell*

Opposite: The common lionfish *(Pterois volitans)*. This animal sometimes travels in packs, lurking around vertical formations such as coral outcrops or shipwrecks. *Photo by Fiona Nichols.*

Bohol

Great Diving off Cabilao, Panglao and Balicasag

Bohol, in the Western Visayas, has long been regarded as home to some of the best diving in the Philippines. Panglao Island, connected to the mainland by a bridge, is the easiest dive area to reach and has a number of excellent sites for both divers and snorkelers.

At Arco Point, near Bohol Beach Club, there is a colony of sea snakes and a tunnel starting with an entrance at 8 meters, exiting at around 18 meters. Covered with a garden of soft corals, the interior has clouds of small tropical fish, including wrasses, butterflyfishes, tangs and copper sweepers.

The northwest tip of the island has a gentle drop-off leading to a bottom which becomes deeper the further south you swim. Currents can be quite strong here, so you should dive with a guide. The gorgonians are particularly impressive although there is a good mix of hard and soft corals, as well as sponges.

There are several other spots well worth diving around the island, including the wall at Tangnan. Starting at around 6 meters, the wall falls away steeply to over 35 meters. Here, you'll find a series of small caves that are fun to

Bancas,
10 min–5 hrs,
live-aboards

10–35 meters

Can be stiff
in places

Good variety,
pristine in places

Walls, drop-offs
and coral gardens

Good variety,
good shells

Fans, gorgonians
and pelagics

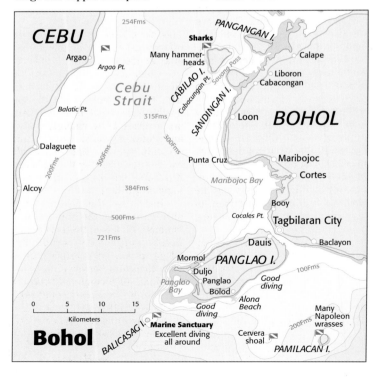

explore. Big groupers dart in and out of the holes in the corals and rocks, but look out as well for wrasses, soldierfishes, surgeons and the occasional barracuda, jacks and whitetip sharks.

Marine Sanctuary

Diving aficionados should make sure that they take the time to venture a little further afield to Balicasag Island, to the southwest of Panglao, which contains a superb marine sanctuary and has what most visitors regard as the best diving in the Visayas. Drop-offs and bottomless walls, overhangs, plentiful fans, huge table and star corals, large clumps of black coral and big fish are the main features of Balicasag. But that is not all that the sanctuary has to offer.

Shallower spots with a variety of hard and soft corals, sea whips, feather stars, crinoids, tunicates, anemones and sponges are a photographer's delight. On a good day you'll encounter schools of barracuda and jacks, batfishes, big parrotfishes and groupers. There are plenty of lionfishes about, and veritable clouds of small reef fishes.

To the east of Balicasag and southeast of Panglao lies Pamilacan Island. Pamilacan means "resting place of mantas" in the local dialect, and when diving you may be lucky enough to swim with one of these impressive creatures. A marine sanctuary has been set up on the northwestern side of the island, and it is here that you'll find superb gorgonians and hard corals along the walls, as well as an assortment of soft corals, anemones, tunicates, sponges and sea fans.

Between Pamilacan and Balicasag is the Cervera Shoal. An underwater

island just beneath the surface, dropping off to 20 meters, is home to a large colony of banded sea snakes. The corals are not particularly impressive, but it is the pelagics which are the attraction here. You can expect to see several interesting species and occasional whitetip sharks, as well as butterflyfishes, scorpionfishes, damsels and surgeons.

Cabilao

This island is located further north, off the west coast of Bohol. Cabilao is a two-and-a-half-hour boat ride from Mactan, and it is from this island that most divers start their trip. Off the lighthouse on the northwestern tip of the island there are a series of overhangs, cracks and coral gardens. Gorgonians, crinoids, sponges and soft corals can be seen adorning the walls and drop-offs, making this an exceedingly pretty dive.

But it is the hammerhead sharks for which the island is most famous. Schools of these awesome beasts congregate around the island, usually quite deep at around 40 to 45 meters, between December and June. Also commonly encountered in this excellent spot are barracudas, jacks, mackerel, tuna, triggerfishes, butterflyfishes and humphead wrasses feeding in the strong currents.

— *Heneage Mitchell*

Above: Alona Beach, Bohol. *Photo by Mike Severns.*

Below: The butterflyfish *Chaetodon lunula. Photo by Gerald Allen.*

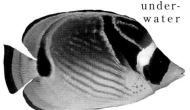

Apo Reef

A Speck in the Midst of the South China Sea

Apo Reef, in the South China Sea off the west coast of Mindoro, is actually an underwater lagoon. Between March and June, the peak season, water visibility is usually excellent, extending to 30 meters and more at most sites. But from July to January, the sea can be turbulent, making access uncomfortable to downright unpleasant. Trips to Apo are arranged through Pandan Island Resort on the west coast of Mindoro and from Puerto Galera, 125 km away. Most live-aboards feature Apo Reef on their itineraries too.

Wall diving is spectacular along many parts of the perimeter, and you don't need to go too deep to discover plenty of neat marine life.

A favorite spot on the reef itself is the wreck of a small fishing boat with a bridge which divers and snorkelers love to have their photographs taken in. Lying in shallow water, the hulk used to attract snappers and groupers, as well as hard and soft corals, sponges and a variety of other tropical marine life. The bottom has patches of table corals but visiting fishermen continue to wage war with nature very effectively, despite Apo's status as a marine sanctuary.

Dramatic Drop-offs

The northern edge of the lagoon has spectacular walls, dropping off radically from around 5 to 10 meter depths. The walls are covered with gorgonians and fans due to the currents which can get quite stiff, attracting lots of pelagics as well as

Below: The whale shark leads a solitary life, and is only rarely seen by lucky divers when it ventures inshore. Southern Leyte, Philippines.
Photo by Scott Tuason.

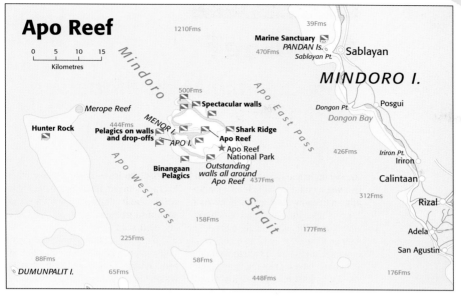

Apo Reef

0 5 10 15
Kilometres

1210Fms

39Fms

Marine Sanctuary
470Fms   PANDAN Is.
Sablayan Pt.   Sablayan

MINDORO I.

500Fms
Merope Reef   Spectacular walls   Dongon Pt.   Posgui
Hunter Rock   444Fms   MENOR I.   Dongon Bay
Pelagics on walls   Shark Ridge
and drop-offs   APO I.   Apo Reef
Apo Reef   426Fms   Iriron Pt.
National Park   Iriron
Binangaan   Outstanding
Pelagics   walls all around
Apo Reef   437Fms   Calintaan
312Fms
Rizal
158Fms   177Fms
225Fms   Adela
San Agustin
88Fms
DUMUNPALIT I.   65Fms   58Fms   176Fms
448Fms

encouraging more impressive coral formations. Watch out for the tuna, jacks, humphead wrasses, and from time to time, mantas and hammerheads. The remains of an old steamer in shallow water on the north of the reef are also quite interesting.

To the east, Shark Ridge is renowned for, of course, sharks—whitetips and blacktips most commonly—as well as mantas. The coral is not so impressive on this sloping bottom which gives way to sand and detritus at about 25 meters, but the animals are big and the diving can get wild!

To the southwest is another excellent wall, the Binangaan drop-off. Impressive gorgonians and hard and soft coral formations and schools of humphead parrotfish are seen here, as well as tuna and groupers, snappers, lots of interesting shells and some large pelagics.

Around Apo Island, to the west of the reef, there are also a number of superb sites to dive, mostly walls and drop-offs. Once again, mantas are not uncommon visitors all around the island, and the gorgonians are outstanding. Schools of tuna and other pelagics, turtles and groupers, snappers and wrasses, triggerfishes and parrotfishes seem to be everywhere. Lobsters and other crustaceans scuttle about under rocks, in crevices and fissures, while along the perimeter, blacktip, whitetip and hammerhead sharks, remoras and barracudas fin silently past. Currents are often strong, but snorkeling can be good.

Snakes Galore

Some 21 km west of Apo Reef, Hunter Rock is an underwater island and not easy to find unless you're with a good guide. Our guide, Frank Doyle of Lalaguna Beach Club, had no trouble at all, dropping us onto the shallowest point of the reef at a depth of 9 meters or so.

"Follow a sea snake down," he said, and he wasn't joking. There are hundreds of them on Hunter Rock, in crevices, under coral heads and swimming about the reef. During mating season (June through July), literally thousands of snakes appear, and the sea is sometimes unnervingly carpeted with them. The reef itself is a profusion of corals and sponges, alive with schools of tropicals—butterflyfishes, snappers, sweetlips—and larger, predatory reef fish.

— *Heneage Mitchell*

Boat from Pandan Island, 1 hr; live-aboards, 1–5 days

Usually good, 15–50 meters

Can be stiff in places

Prolific and varied

Walls and coral gardens

Prolific in places

Outstanding macro-photography

Sumilon

A Species-rich Marine Sanctuary

At the southeastern tip of Cebu lies Sumilon Island. While there are other sites around South Cebu visited by divers from Cebu and Bohol dive centers, Sumilon is a favorite, being the very first marine sanctuary created in the Philippines, though it has suffered considerable damage despite this status. Today, Sumilon enjoys better protection than before, and visiting divers are asked to contribute a small sum to help preserve it once again.

The waters are outstandingly clear around the island, especially between December and May, and there are stunning drop-offs and walls to be enjoyed with breathtaking fans and plentiful gorgonians, especially at deeper depths.

All kinds of pelagics swim around Sumilon, including leopard and manta rays, yellowfin tuna and jacks. Several shark species have been noted, not only the ubiquitous whitetips but also hammerheads and the occasional whale shark.

damselfishes, surgeons, squirrelfishes, butterflyfishes, glasseye snappers, drums and several species of parrotfishes are all there in quantity.

Pelagics are plentiful, and there is every chance of an encounter with blacktip and whitetip sharks, as well as barracuda, tuna, and game fish such as dorado and Spanish mackerel.

Apo Island

To the south of Sumilon is Apo Island (not to be confused with Apo Reef in the South China Sea, off the southwest coast of Mindoro). Apo is widely regarded as one of the best dive sites in the Visayas. In fact, many dive enthusiasts claim that it is THE best site. The marine sanctuary on the southeast side of the island is a fairytale land of hard and soft corals, with thousands of tropical reef fish blotting out the light in every direction. Gobies, tangs, wrasses, chromis or pullers,

Dive safaris from Cebu and Bohol

Usually outstanding, 15–50 meters

Can be strong

Outstanding, prolific and abundant

Walls, drop-offs

Many species, prolific and large

Fans, gorgonians and pelagics

Apo is conical in shape, and the untouched coral reef fringes the island at 15 to 20 meters. All over the reef are hills of star and brain corals, magnificent barrel sponges, a variety of stinging crinoids, pillar and staghorn corals. On the walls are magnificent gorgonians and fan corals. An outstanding dive site!

There are no dive centers on either Apo or Sumilon Island, and trips to both are arranged regularly by dive operations from Mactan, Moalboal, Bohol and several of the smaller resorts in southern Cebu. The best time to visit Apo Island is between December and May.

Siquijor Island

Between Apo and Sumilon, and a little to the east, is Siquijor Island. The inhabitants of this island are renowned (and feared) throughout the Philippines as mystics and spiritualists. Unfortunately, this has not prevented serious damage being inflicted on the reefs and shoals, and many of the great dive sites of yesteryear are history, reduced to algae-covered skeletons of coral.

There are still one or two sites worth visiting, however, including Tonga Point on the northwest coast. Here, a wall drops off quite rapidly from the relatively shallow fringing reef. Soft corals are plentiful here, and you'll find some reasonable gorgonians as you drift along the wall. Don't expect an abundance of fish life around this area, except at Apo Island, as the local fishermen are adept at harvesting everything that moves. Divers are urged to avoid dive outfits which encourage spear fishing.

— *Heneage Mitchell*

Below: Blue and gold fusilier *(Caesio teres)* form big, colorful schools, sometimes composed of several species, and frequently swarm around divers. *Photo by Takamasa Tonozuka.*

Coron Bay

Exploring a World of Wrecks off Busuanga Island

On September 24, 1944, Admiral "Bull" Halsey, seeking a safe passage through the uncharted Calamian Islands, sent out several waves of photo reconnaissance planes, When analysts compared the pictures taken, they noticed several "islands" had changed position relative to the surrounding land. Realising that they had discovered a camouflaged Japanese fleet, Halsey immediately ordered an air strike. Upon their return, US Navy pilots claimed 24 vessels sunk.

Fifty years on, 12 of these wrecks have been discovered in the protected waters of Coron Bay, lying at various depths between 15 and 40 meters.

Due to their former inaccessibility and lack of diving infrastructure, it is only recently that divers have started visiting the wrecks and outstanding coral reefs of the area. Most agree that the diving here is superb, easily as good as the wrecks of Truk Lagoon in Micronesia but much shallower.

Below: Exploring a wreck in shallow water near the entrance to Barracuda Lake, Coron Island. *Photo by Jack Jackson.*

Irako and Kogyo Maru

The southernmost wreck visited frequently by local divers here is the *Irako*. The *Irako* was a refrigeration ship, about 200 meters long displacing 9,570 tons. Now it is home to big groupers and shoals of yellowfin tuna. Lying in over 40 meters of water, the deck of this relatively intact wreck is at 28 to 33 meters.

Coron Bay

0 2 4 6
Kilometres

To the north is the 140-meter-long freighter *Kogyo Maru*. Also known as the Tangat Wreck, she is lying upright in about 30 meters of water. Divers come onto the deck at between 18 to 24 meters. The cargo holds are easily penetrable, and there are fish all over it. Look for giant pufferfish, especially around the masts, bow and stern. Soft corals and sponges, as well as some small hard corals, have attached themselves to the remains, and this is a good first wreck dive for beginners.

Mamiya Maru

West of the *Kogyo Maru* is the *Mamiya Maru,* another freighter about 160 meters in length. Lying on its starboard side in 34 meters of water, the wreck is easily penetrable in some places. The cargo holds are still full of construction materials, and anti-aircraft weapons remain on the deck. Lots of grouper have made their home on the *Mamiya Maru,* and the port side has many hard and soft corals and a variety of fish, including snappers, wrasse and lionfish.

To the north east is a gunboat about 35 meters long on the other side of Tangat Island. Lying in only 18 meters of water, this wreck is a good snorkeling site, as the bow is in only three meters.

Olympic Maru

North west of the gunboat is the *Olympic Maru,* 120 meters long and lying on its starboard side in 25 meters of water. Once again, there are plenty of grouper on this wreck, and the port side, which is only 14 to 18 meters underwater is covered in hard corals. Easy penetration of the cargo holds and engine room make this an interesting dive, but watch out for scorpionfish which are all over this area!

Tae Maru

Further away, to the northwest, is the *Tae Maru,* which is also known

Banca boat, 30 min–2 hrs, live-aboards

10–35 meters

Moderate

Good variety, prolific in places

Walls, coral gardens and wrecks

Wide variety, prolific

Wrecks galore!

as the Concepcion Wreck, a tanker about 200 meters long lying upright in 26 meters of water. You come onto the deck at between 10 and 16 meters. The bow is completely smashed, allowing for easy penetration, and the wreck is covered in hard and soft corals and sponges. Sweetlips, grouper, lionfish, surgeons, wrasse, tang and soldierfish have made this wreck their home, and barracuda occasionally swim by overhead. The currents can be treacherous sometimes, taking an unwary diver by surprise, especially when rounding the stern or bow.

The Akitisushima

Due south is the *Akitisushima,* my personal favorite, a 200-meter-long flying boat tender lying on its starboard side. The flying boat is long gone, but the huge crane used to put it into the water and retrieve it is still in one piece, twisting away from the wreck into the sandy bottom at 38 meters. More or less intact, the gaping hole in the side which caused it to sink immediately is quite apparent.

A good boatman will put a diver onto the highest point of this unusual wreck at about 20 meters, and the average depth of a dive is usually around 28 meters or so. Shoals of barracuda, tuna and yellowfin circle the wreck, and grouper, batfish, snapper and many other species of tropical reef fish have made their home here.

Apart from the wrecks, Coron also has some outstanding coral dives, and these should definitely not be missed.

Coral Diving

Off the northwest coast of Busuanga lies the island of Dimaky. Adjacent to this island are a number of excellent coral dives. On the west side of the island, a gorgeous coral garden with tame reef fish is a popular dive. A slope dropping to 17 meters is a natural home to

tunicates and sponges as well as groupers and several species of parrotfish. At the far end of the wall, there's a large swathe of staghorn coral, with an abundance of barracuda, rainbow runners and goatfish. Manta rays and turtles are occasionally seen here and more frequently at the northern end of the island.

At Dibuyan Island, the reef starts around 13 meters, sloping gently to 28 meters. Whitetip, blacktip and gray reef sharks are commonly found here, as well as surgeonfishes and batfishes. Manta rays, too, are occasionally seen. In the shallows, a fascinating profusion of small tropical reef fish can be found.

Busuanga is at the frontier of the struggle to preserve the natural resources of the Philippines. Among the creatures whose fates are inextricably linked with man's actions over the next few years is the harmless *Dugong dugon*, a relative of the manatee, or sea cow. They are only occasionally seen by divers, but their tender flesh is a favored delicacy among native fishermen, which may doom them to extinction in local waters despite the best efforts and intentions of several conservation groups operating in the area.

Barracuda Lake

Coron also has one of the most unusual dive sites in the Philippines, Barracuda Lake. To get to the lake, you have to make a climb up a limestone mountain for 15 or 20 minutes.

The water temperature in the lake varies from between 30 to 38 degrees Celsius: you can actually see the thermoclines. After simmering and boiling for a while, your host, a resident 1.5-meter king barracuda, usually appears to guide you around until it is time to leave, providing an great opportunity for photographers to get excellent close ups!

— *Heneage Mitchell*

Opposite: Coron offers some outstanding coral dives. *Photo by Ashley Boyd.*

El Nido

Fabulous Seascapes and Year-round Diving

A stunning collection of islands with high limestone cliffs predominates the idyllic seascapes of El Nido in northwestern Palawan. As one might expect, there is no shortage of fine diving to be enjoyed here. Lots of pelagics, some rare and unique species, and excellent wall and drift diving; the marine life is diverse and in places very prolific.

Diving Dilumacad

Below: High limestone cliffs and stunning islands dominate the idyllic seascapes of El Nido, Palawan. *Photo by Photo Bank.*

A popular site west of El Nido town itself, situated in the southern bowl of Bacuit Bay, is on the north side of Dilumacad Island. This is a year-round dive site, except when a strong north wind is blowing, and the location features a tunnel with a cavern in the center of it, at about 15 to 20 meters, and an entrance wide enough for two divers to swim abreast. Not far in, the tunnel widens out into the cavern with a bottom of sand, and there are clouds of small fish as well as crabs roaming the floor. The 10-meter-long way out is narrower, so only one diver can pass at a time. It exits at about 22 meters nearby lots of large rocks which frequently have big fish hanging around. Recently, while searching for the rubber cover of his depth gauge which had fallen into a crack, my buddy collided rather suddenly with a very large Spanish mackerel. Hard to tell who of the two was more surprised!

Further west around Miniloc Island, where the luxurious resort at El Nido is located, there are several worthwhile sites.

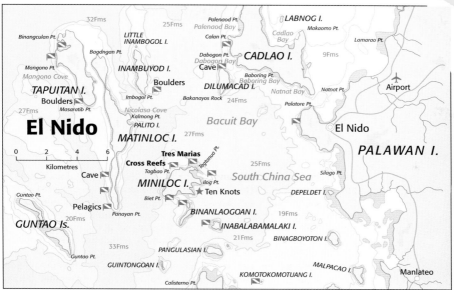

South Miniloc has a dive site between 13 and 21 meters with abundant lettuce corals, sponges and a colony of blue ribbon eels. Visited by jacks and barracuda, squids, cuttlefish and angelfishes also make their homes here. A sheltered spot, this is one of several year-round dive sites that is worth a visit.

To the north is Twin Rocks, another year-round site. It is characterized by a sandy bottom at depths varying between 13 and 21 meters, and is dotted with table corals, sea whips, corals and sponges, amongst which there are small stingrays and angelfishes.

Boulders and Big Fish

Off the northwest point of Miniloc Island lies tiny Tagbao Island. The local boatman probably knows it as Tres Marias, in reference to the three coral reefs wrinkled between the two land masses. To the southwest is a series of vast boulders, some as large as two-story houses. Because of the relatively shallow depths, the potential for snorkeling is good here, and you'll find plentiful reef fishes and colorful corals, as well as painted crayfish.

South Tip or Banayan Point on the larger Matinloc Island to the west is for lovers of pelagics. Most divers don't notice the richly coral-encrusted rocks as they are too busy avoiding mackerel, tuna and jacks finning by in the often stiff currents. It's best to head for the western side of the island, especially between March and June, as the east coast is generally a lot less attractive, though accessible all year round. Bakanayos Rock, known locally as Picanayas, has yet more boulders on the southwest side with a crew of whitetip sharks poking in and out of the holes.

To the southwest of adjacent Inbogal Point (Inambuyod) there are some impressive gorgonians and green corals on a steep wall that drops down to 35 meters. Jacks, tuna and mackerel pass by, and this site is home to a unique species of angelfish, *Pomacanthus annularis*, distinguished by its additional stripe. It is only known here and at Tres Marias.

Of the many other local dives in the area, Black Coral Forest off the west of Entalula Island deserves a mention. On a steep drop from 35 to 40 meters, it sprouts lots of acropora and black coral.

— *Heneage Mitchell*

Banca boat, 10 min–2 hrs live-aboards

10–45 meters

Usually negligible, strong in places

Outstanding in places; soft coral covering past dynamite damage

Walls, drop-offs and coral gardens

Varied, prolific; some unique species here

Walls and pelagics

Puerto Princesa

Honda Bay, Taytay and Port Barton

Puerto Princesa is the capital city of Palawan, a quaint, laidback city. Adjacent Honda Bay has some quite good sites worth a visit, serviced by several dive centers in Puerto itself and Dos Palmas resort in Honda Bay. To the north, Taytay Bay is a good option, and in the west Port Barton has some excellent sites.

Honda Bay

Around the resort island of Dos Palmas, there are several shallow sites easily accessible. Helen's Garden is diveable most of the year and is a pop-

ular night dive. A small, rounded reef with a dive platform conveniently placed by the management of Dos Palmas, this site is richly carpeted with hard and soft corals, including some impressive clumps of table and black corals. Juvenile blacktip sharks are usually spotted here, the island is a breeding ground for this species. Sergeant-majors, snapper, wrasse and trevally are among other residents you are likely to spot. This is a fish feeding station, so the fish are quite fearless. Henry's Reef fringes Arrecife Island, another shallow dive up to 10 meters with small caves and crevices to explore. Best dived

Some beach dives, mostly by boat

5–35 meters

Mostly negligible

Prolific, varied and colorful

Mostly small drop-offs, fringing reefs, seamounts

Mantas (Honda Bay), pelagics (Taytay Bay), prolific reef fish (Port Barton)

Baby blacktips, juvenile whale sharks, (Honda Bay)

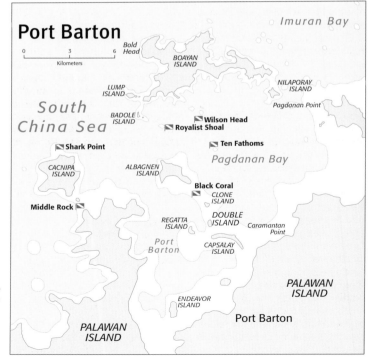

TAPUL ISLAND
BUSH ISLAND
PARUNPONON ISLAND
BUGUIAS ISLAND
FONDEADO ISLAND
STARFISH ISLAND
Verano Rocks (Twin Rocks)
Henry's Reef
East Pandan
MEARA ISLAND
SNAKE ISLAND
ARRECIFE ISLAND
Bacungan River
Honda Bay
Helen's Garden
Puerto Princesa & Honda Bay
FRASER ISLAND
PANDAN ISLAND
PALAWAN ISLAND
COWRIE ISLAND
0 2 4 6
Kilometers

during the dry season as it is buffeted by sometimes fierce winds and waves during the rainy season, this site features lionfish, cardinals, snapper, sweetlips and a good variety of nudibranchs. A good area for photographers. Honda Bay is also blessed with resident juvenile whale sharks, although local divers are unwilling to share the exact location of the site with visitors to prevent stressing the creatures. Divers from Dos Palmas Resort make regular trips to the area to record and monitor the whale sharks. Mantas can sometimes be found cruising in Honda Bay; Pandan Island is a likely place to encounter them. The reef on the east side of the island features a steep slope to 18 meters, liberally festooned with a variety of hard and soft corals and home to blennies, triggerfish and several species of parrotfish.

Taytay Bay

Further north of Honda Bay, Taytay has some excellent sites to visit. About a five-hour drive from Puerto Princesa, Taytay offers several dive centers and a variety of resorts. Some of the offshore diving is excellent, and the inshore sites are also worth a visit.

in a single dive, but you'll probably want to make more than one dive here. The furthest of the dive sites in the area, Shark Rock can experience rough seas, especially during the rainy season, so it is best to suit up in calmer water and be ready to hop off the boat on top the site to avoid seasickness and the hazards of trying to kit up in an unstable boat. Blacktip and whitetip sharks are quite common here, the corals are impressive and there is a host of tropical fish as well as painted crays and several species of crabs that call the place home. Whale sharks are also occasionally spotted here. Royalist Shoal is a seamount found at 12 meters with some of the best soft and hard corals in the area. The bottom is quite deep at 40 meters, so watch your depth. Expect to see plenty of fish life, including soldierfish, a variety of angelfish, tangs, squirrelfish, gobies, and sergeant-majors. Ten Fathoms is another seamount, this one starting at 18 meters, where you may get lucky and see hammerheads, leopard sharks and nurse sharks. Brain, star and pillar corals festoon the reef, grouper and snapper cruise the deeper sections and there are plenty of smaller tropical reef fish to see.

— *Heneage Mitchell*

Below: Jellyfish in Honda Bay. *Photo by Scott Tuason.*

Port Barton

On the west coast of Palawan, about a five-hour drive from Puerto Princesa, Port Barton is a relatively undiscovered area with some rewarding dive experiences awaiting those willing to make the trip across the rugged interior. Shark Point is a large rock you can circumnavigate

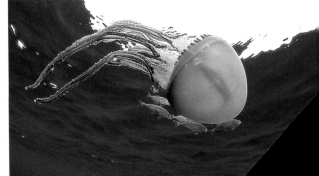

Boat or beach

 5–35 meters

 Unpredictable, can be strong along walls

 Dense, prolific

 Walls and fringing reefs

 Prolific pelagics (Gen San), good variety of reef fish (Davao)

Pelagics, gorgonians (Gen San), coral gardens (Davao)

Davao
General Santos City

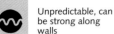

Davao City, home to the ubiquitous, smelly but delicious durian fruit, has several dive sites worth visiting, mostly adjacent to the Pearl Farm Resort. There are three dive centers in town and one at the resort.

The Ligid Caves are amongst the most popular sites around this area. A two-cave system with several entrances, the larger of the caves has some interesting black coral formations inside it, as well as a variety of sponges and tunicates. The reef itself is liberally festooned with leather corals, and lionfish, rabbitfish and parrotfish make this their home. Look for the large gorgonian fan coral with a resident razorfish and you are near a cave entrance: a good site for photographers. Pinnacle Point is another good dive for lenspersons with a huge variety of fishlife including cardinalfish, bigeye trevally, octopus and morays. Watch out for the currents here, they can be tricky. The southeast side of the reef is home to schools of surgeonfish and jacks as well as a variety of angelfish. The center of the reef has some beautiful pink soft corals and plenty of hard corals. Further down on the leeward side you'll discover clumps of black and fan corals with hundreds of little anthias darting in between them.

Pindawon Wall is just about the best wall dive in the area, with lots of overhangs, gorgonians, black and table corals. Grouper and snapper roam the deeper sections of the wall. At the shallower portions of the reef expect to find sea snakes around the large cabbage corals.

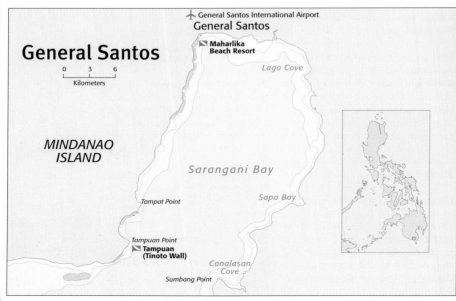

Marrissa 1, 2 & 3, named after the daughter of Pearl Farm Resort's owner, are three shallow (18 meters) reefs maintained as a marine sanctuary by the resort. Good snorkeling, lots of sea stars, staghorn and elkhorn corals and an intersting topography.

General Santos, or Gen San as it popularly known, is another recent destination that is increasing in popularity as the word spreads. The tuna fishing capital of the Philippines, Gen San's tuna fleets ply the adjacent rich seas.

The main attraction for divers is the huge Tinoto Wall, running for over 10 kilometers along the coast to the west of the city in Sarangani Bay. The wall drops off to well over 40 meters, so watch your depth here! There are over 20 sites visited by local divers on this impressive structure, all with different features. Currents can be a factor, at some points they can be fairly strong, making even a drift dive an improbable option, but an experienced dive guide can usually give a warning a few minutes before the onslaught and can get divers onto the shallow topside reef before they get washed away to sea. Huge gorgonians, sponges and a good variety of hard and soft corals festoon the wall, home to an endless variety of critters large and small.

Depending on which location you dive, you can expect to see hammerheads, blacktip and white-tip sharks, manta, eagle and other rays, tuna, rainbow runners, barracuda, Napoleon wrasse, grouper, snapper and patrols of sergeant-majors.

The topside of the wall is shallow, good for snorkeling, and extends in most places for about 50 meters from shore. Some of the more popular sites along the wall include Amadora's Diving Resort and Lau Tengco, also known as Barracuda Point.

Nearer to town is Maharlika Beach Re-sort, home to a shallow reef with plenty to see, and popular as a training site and as a night dive as well. Turtles are quite often found here, as are Moorish idols, parrotfish, wrasse, emperors, tangs, filefish and cowfish. This is also a squid breeding ground and they lay their eggs among the copious staghorn corals. Look out for the resident shoal of yellowtail barracuda here as well.

— *Heneage Mitchell*

Above: Idyllic Pearl Farm Resort on Samal Island. *Photo by Scott Tuason.*

THE PHILIPPINES

The Sulu Sea

Diving the Reefs of Tubbataha, Jessie Beazley and Basterra

The Sulu Sea is bounded on the west side by the long, thin island of Palawan, and on the east by the islands of Panay, Negros and Mindanao. Some of the best diving in the Philippines, and perhaps the world, is to be found at several remote locations within the Sulu Sea, the most famous of which is Tubbataha Reefs.

Despite its inaccessibility and its relatively short season—mid-March to mid-June—berths on any of the several live-aboard boats visiting Sulu Sea are much sought after. It's best to book as early as possible to avoid disappointment.

Tubbataha Reefs

Tubbataha Reefs National Marine Park consists of two atolls, North and South Tubbataha, separated by 4 nautical miles of water with depths reaching an incredible 650 fathoms. Most live-aboards, and the one or two large pump boats which make the trip regularly in season, start out from Puerto Princesa, capital of Palawan, and take 10 hours or so to motor to the Reefs. Puerto Princesa is actually located 98 nautical miles to the northwest of the Reefs.

The first stop is most likely to be the southern reef, which is sometimes called Lighthouse, as it encloses a small islet with a solar-powered lighthouse which identifies the area. It is worth climbing up the lighthouse, for the view of the reef and the large lagoon inside it is truly spectacular from this vantage point.

Underwater, the east side of the reef is like gently rolling hills of hard and soft corals and sponges. A wide variety of squirrelfishes, angelfishes, groupers, parrotfishes and butterflyfishes hover and swim about in an underwater fiesta of colorful abandon. You may even see a crocodilefish on the bottom between coral heads.

The reef slopes down to 18 to 24 meters in a few spots before reaching the edge of the wall stretching north for about 12 km. What remains of the *Delsan* wreck lies partly submerged near the edge of the drop-off. The vertical walls are covered with a wide variety of soft corals, tube sponges and sea fans. Moorish idols, triggerfishes, surgeons and other schooling tropicals are quite common near the drop-off, while whitetip and blacktip sharks cruise deeper along the wall. Occasionally barracuda, either alone or in a pair, will cruise by, and if you are really lucky, manta rays may pass by close enough for a good photograph.

The west wall starts more abruptly. Winding slowly towards the northwest for almost 11 km, the drop-off has large pink, purple and burgundy colored soft corals. Red and violet sea fans reach outward, and occasionally small schools of crevale jacks swim by. When the current is running, mackerel, tuna and shark also cruise close to the wall.

The north side of the reef, known for its turtles, has the same gently sloping incline leading to the actual wall, but the drop-off is not so steep in places. Hawksbill and

Live-aboard boats from Puerto Princesa

Mostly excellent, 20–50 meters

Variable

Outstanding variety, pristine and prolific

Walls and coral gardens, sand banks

Awesome variety, prolific in all sizes

Probably some of the best diving anywhere

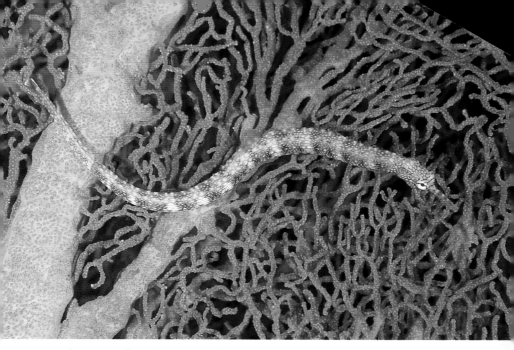

green turtles are usually to be seen, either resting or gliding leisurely near the edge of the reef. Around the area called Black Rock there are likely to be currents. Unpredictable and often swift, these can catch an unwary diver and cause problems.

Amos' Rock on North Tubbataha is in the south among the sandy cays. Here you will find a gently sloping bottom covered mostly with branching hard corals interspersed with soft corals, sponges and sea squirts. Sandy patches at around 6 to 10 meters are home to sea pens and Cerianthid anemone. This area is ideal for night dives, when a good variety of cones, cowries and olive shells can be found by sifting through the white sand. With a little bit of patience and close observation, we invariably spotted a fine assortment of species including several Triton shells.

On the west side of the islet, the reef winds from the southwest to the northeast. The walls are not so vertical but numerous varieties of sea whips, sea fans and soft corals abound among the hard corals. Coral fishes hover about, facing

mild currents, and further off the wall are schools of surgeonfishes and jacks. The wreck of a small-sized tugboat, now inhabited by plenty of small fish and an increasing number of coral colonies, sits near the wall's edge, and it offers either good snorkeling or a shallow second dive.

The north wall, near Bird Island, starts in 5 to 8 meters. Numerous fissures lead into the near vertical wall and open up into the shallows. Here, crevices and horizontal ledges cut into the drop-off where nurse sharks and, less commonly, leopard sharks may sometimes be caught resting or sleeping.

As you swim along further to the northeast, the edge drops gradually deeper. Black coral adorns the wall as well as plentiful lush soft corals and tube sponges. The sandy bottom that slowly rises to the shallows, is dotted with coral heads and wide table corals. It is not unusual to find lobsters underneath these corals. Look underneath, also, for sheltering blue-spotted stingrays and small sharks.

Keen-eyed divers have often found guitarfish (also called the

Above: Banded pipefish *(Corythoichthys intestinalis)*. Photo by Mike Severns.

shovel-nosed shark) motionless on the sandy bottom, while we have often had good sightings of manta rays in the slightly deeper waters.

The north islet is known also as Bird Island for the thousands of terns and boobies that inhabit this pocket handkerchief of land. This is an excellent spot for birdwatching and photography, but be careful of where you step as the boobies lay their eggs in the sand.

Jessie Beazley Reef

This reef lies about 18 km northwest of North Tubbataha. It is a small, circular reef that rises up almost to the surface of the sea. The surrounding blue water plunges to depths of over 500 fathoms. Marked by the shifting sand cay and the contrasting greens of the shallows, Jessie Beazley has similar features as Tubbataha Reefs, except that it is only half a kilometer in diameter. During calm, sunny days, water visibility averages an impressive 27 to 37 meters though currents can be quite strong in places.

The reef typically slopes to 7 to 12 meters before the edge of the wall itself, which drops off to over 50 meters. The shallows here are predominantly covered with Porites and Acropora corals. Near the edge, at a depth of 16 to 19 meters, are cave-like crevices with a colony of lobsters (*Panulis versicolor*). Turtles can also occasionally be seen perched among coral heads. Hanging off one side of the reef is an old anchor, encrusted with a variety of colorful corals.

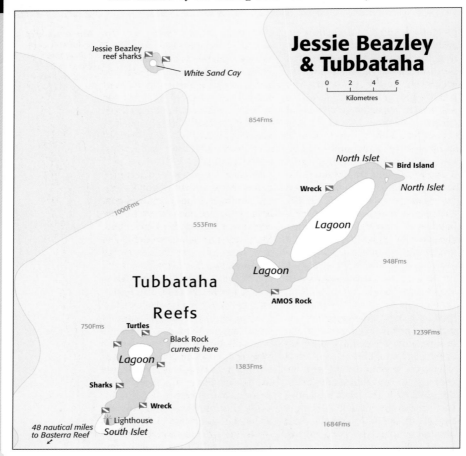

Jessie Beazley reef sharks

White Sand Cay

Jessie Beazley & Tubbataha

0 2 4 6
Kilometres

854Fms

North Islet

Bird Island

Wreck

North Islet

1000Fms

553Fms

Lagoon

948Fms

Tubbataha

Lagoon

AMOS Rock

Reefs

750Fms

Turtles

Black Rock
currents here

Lagoon

1239Fms

1383Fms

Sharks

Wreck

Lighthouse

48 nautical miles
to Basterra Reef

South Islet

1684Fms

Anthogorgia sea fans, *dendronephthya* and *antipatharian* black corals lace the wall as you descend the steep face. The wall itself is etched with small undercuts and ledges at 21 to 35 meters. Massive basket sponges, some of which measure as much as 3 meters, cling to the rock face along with a diversity of tube sponges. Small whitetip and blacktip sharks are commonly seen, and sometimes a nurse shark can be found on the sandy ledge. On the larger end of the scale, hammerhead, mako and thresher sharks occasionally cruise the clear, blue waters of the reef.

Basterra Reef

Also known as Meander Reef, this reef is rarely marked on maps and is not easily identifiable on most charts, but it lies around 48 nautical miles southwest of Tubbataha and 110 miles southeast of Puerto Princesa. It is much smaller than the Tubbataha reefs and slightly bigger than Jessie Beazley, but what it lacks in size it makes up for in real fish action.

Surrounded by waters plunging to 1,000 fathoms, Basterra Reef pushes up to the surface, a massive pinnacle capped by a sand bar, and a wreck, the *Oceanic II,* lies to the north. The majestic walls and corals of Basterra are bursting with myriad forms of marine life. In fact, the almost-round reef is considered by many to be the best diving spot in the entire Sulu Sea.

At Barracuda Slope you'll find a gentle slope of white sand, with porites and acropora corals almost breaking the surface, shelves to the edge of the wall at about 16 meters. Multitudes of small, colorful fish such as anthias, swarm like confetti around large coral heads and the table corals. These become more and more dense as you approach the edge of the wall. Perciform fish swim around in the light current and a large school of red snappers is usually seen cruising around the edge of the drop-off.

Then, at a distance, you should be able to pick up what appears to be a silvery-gray cloud in the water. At first sighting it seems stationary, suspended in mid-water, but as you move closer you realize that the cloud is a thick school of almost

Above: The engine of the wreck of a Tristar B at Basterra Reef. *Photo by Jack Jackson.*

motionless barracuda which regularly inhabit this area and after whom this site has been named.

The white, sandy slope is also an excellent place for night diving. A wide variety of shells, including terebras and *Murex*, make their home here, as does a colony of garden eels, which can be spotted peering from their holes during the day. Deeper down the wall, the common blacktip and whitetip sharks are almost always present.

From the southwest to the west side of the reef, a thick growth of massive brown corals, piled almost on top of one another, borders the impressive vertical wall which drops off from 5 to 10 meters to unfathomable depths. Squirrelfishes, bigeye jacks, assorted snappers and butterflyfishes join schools of Moorish idols and bannerfishes. Check out the crevices, too, for lobster are found here. Coral encrusted fishing lines stretch out almost horizontally from the wall, which is covered with a profusion of soft corals, sponges, black corals and gorgonians.

As one swims along, you'll see another silvery cloud cascading from the shallow reef to the depths in the distance. Closer inspection reveals it to be thousands of jacks, mingling with a large school of sweetlips and surgeonfishes.

Moving northward along the wall, in the shallower parts of the reef, there are a series of depressions that are etched into the wall. The most prominent one resembles a crater and is home to multitudes of small tropical fish, including the uncommon leaf-fish. Deeper, you'll come across boulder-like formations of massive corals at 12 to 15 meters, and this is where the current may start to move in the opposite direction, attracting plenty of fish. Look out for the surgeonfishes amidst jacks and tuna. From here, the action really begins.

Named Expressway for the current's speed at this dive site, the reef hosts an abundance of fish life which includes large manta rays, gray reef sharks and even whitetip

sharks. Not as creviced as other areas around Basterra, the edge of the wall starts at around 3 to 4 meters before plunging radically to unrecorded depths, forming an awesome cliff which angles inward to create a truly impressive overhang. This is one dive which cannot fail to excite any diver, however comprehensive his diving experience! If you can tear your gaze away, common black corals and dendrophillias are scattered sparsely along the wall.

A Wreck, Too

The scattered wreck of a large twin-hulled boat, complete with well-established coral growth, provides shelter to a variety of snappers, groupers and spade fishes, as well as smaller fishes like wrasses, chromis and thousands of sergeant-majors. What used to be one of the engines lies in 13 meters of water close to the nesting site of some triggerfish.

Near the *Oceanic II* wreck, to the north, the reef is characterized by a thick growth of a variety of hard corals. Here you may see manta rays, mating pairs of hawksbill turtles and a few solitary barracuda. Patches of coral rubble near the edge of the wall at 18 to 24 meters are favorite hangouts of sharks. Barracudas, dogtooth tuna and mackerel are commonly seen off the wall that gradually curves away to the east.

Further south, the slope steepens then drops vertically from depths of 18 to 22 meters on the east side of the reef. Every so often, divers should watch the blue water to the east for sightings of gray reef sharks, mantas, tuna, jacks and turtles. Unicornfishes and other varieties of surgeonfish are quite common in this part of Basterra. The beautiful and colorful clown triggerfish may be seen in the shallower areas, where brightly hued clams also thrive. Check out the crevices, too, for blue triggerfish and tangs.
— *Louie and Chen Mencias*

Opposite: Divers' accommodations in Bonito.
Photo by Mike Severns.

Diving in Thailand
A Kingdom Straddling Two Seas

About a decade ago, Thailand's great diving was somewhat of a secret. Back then, very few knew how great the diving is here. These days, Thailand ranks as the most popular dive destination in Southeast Asia and one of the most popular in the world. People come here for great recreational diving as well as to get certified in warm, clear waters. One of the reasons that the area has become so popular is not only the great diving, but also the fact that the country is politically stable and tolerant of foreigners.

Thailand is blessed with two bountiful seas, the Gulf of Thailand in the east and the Andaman Sea—part of the eastern Indian Ocean—in the west. The riches that these oceans contain are a delight to those of us that have had the pleasure of diving here. Furthermore, the Thai Kingdom is blessed with a remarkable history and culture, friendly natives who offer friendly service, beautiful national parks covering 13% of the country, a wide range of accommodation at every price level and some of the most delicious food in the world.

Often referred to as the "Land of a Thousand Smiles," Thailand is a joyous country to travel in. One of the first Thai phrases travelers learn is *mai pen rai,* which literally translates to "it is nothing." It also is used in the same way as "never mind" or "that's OK". However, *mai pen rai* is more than that—it is almost a philosophy that teaches one to hide problems and keep one's "public face" smiling and happy. For the visitor this attitude creates a feeling of burdens lifted.

It makes you feel satisfied, content and cheerful. While exploring the country you'll feel carefree, lighthearted and safe—you'll feel *mai pen rai.* Is it any wonder so many of us expatriates have decided to stay, or does it surprise that people visit Thailand time and time again?

Thailand's territory stretches from the eastern border with Cambodia to the western border with Myanmar (Burma), and then south to Malaysia. Because of its varied topography and delightful people, Thailand offers the visiting diver diverse undersea experiences along with an unbelievable amount of topside recreation. It's the perfect place for a diving holiday. World-class diving, heavenly tropical islands and immaculate white sand beaches await the explorer. With water visibility often exceeding 30 meters, an average ocean temperature of 27°C, and uncommonly calm sea conditions, Thailand has some of the most comfortable and safe diving environments to be found anywhere in the world.

Development of the Diving Industry

Every year more and more is published about the diverse marine life that prowls the depths of Thailand's oceans, and every year more and more divers visit the country. There are three reasons for this. First, new destinations, such as the Mergui Archipelago and the Andaman Islands in the Andaman Sea, Ko Tao in the Gulf and Ko Chang near the Cambodian border, have opened up

Overleaf: The whale shark, *Rhincodon typus,* is the largest fish known. Though this is a small specimen, it has been known to reach 15 m. *Photo by Ashley Boyd.*

Opposite: Anthias swarm a brightly colored sea fan on a wall in the Similan Islands, Thailand. *Photo by Scott Tuason.*

For Details See
Andaman Sea
Sites Map

BURMA

THAN I.
(DAVIS I.)

BRUER I.

CHRISTIE I.

AURIOL I.

ZADETKALE I.
(ST. LUKE'S I.)

ZADETKYI I.
(ST. MATTHEW'S I.)

HASTINGS I.

PULO I.

KO
CHANG

KO
PHAYAM

KO KAM YAI

KO KAM NUI

KO SURIN NUA

KO SURIN TAI

BURMA BANKS

KO TACHAI

KO BON

KO RA

KO KHAT

KO PHRA THONG

For Details See
Similan Islands Map

SIMILAN
ISLANDS

KO SIMILAN

KO MIANG

KO PAYANG

Cape Ao Kham

Thung Maphrao

ISTHMUS
OF KRA

Nong Pla

Ranong

Phato

Khuan

Ban Ratcha Krut

Na Kha

Ban Muang
Klang

Kapoe

Ban Ko Ko

KO RA

Khura Buri

Pra Tha

Bang Wan

Takua Pa

Bang Sak

Hua Mat

Lamae

Nong Met

Nong Chik

Tha Hak

Khiri

Ratthanikhom

Na Pong

Tham Waram

Thung Biri

Ban Phu

Ban Lam Ru

Plai Hang

Thap Put

Chin

Takua Thung

Tha Yu

Thai Muang

Khok Kloi

Pak Nam
Lamae

Ban Don Thup

Tha Chana

Ban Khao
Phanom Baek

Chaiya

Tha Se

SOUTHERN

THAILAND

Khao Wong

Ban Pak
Khlong Chaun

Bang Khram

Phanom

Ta Saeng Na

Phangnga

Ao Luk Nua

Khlong Hin

Thung

Lang Suan

Ban Khlong
Khanan

Cape Sui

Ban Don Bay

Surat Thani

Bang-O

Siat

Ban-Wang Ri

Khian Sa

Ban Fai Tha

Trom

Dong Tau

Ban Wiang Sa

Phunphin

Ban Na San

Phru Phri

Huai Thon

Thun

Phra Wong

Phrasaeng

Na Yai

Lan Khwai

Thung Yai

Na Lum

KO RAP

KO ANG
THONG

KO PHALUAI

KO NOK
TA PHAO

Chong Samui

KO KATEN

For Details See
Ko Samui Map

KO SAMUI

KO PHANGAN

Cape Samrong

KO TAO

Chong Tao

Sail Rock

Chong Phangan

Gulf of
Thailand

Gulf of
Thailand

Khanom

Khao Noi

Khao Yoi

Sichon

Ban Chom Phibun

Tha Mak

Tong Takhian

Ban Sa Kaew

Tha Sala

Muang

Ban Na Thap

Sale Bang Pu

Cape Talumphuk

Nai Thun

Phipun

Phromkhiri

Tan

Chawang

Lan Saka

Chong Lom

Nakhon Si Thammarat

Pak Phanang

Southern Thailand

Andaman Sea

Thalang
Phuket
KO YAO YAI
KO SI BOYA
KO LON
KO HEY
KO YUNG
KO MAI PAI
KO PU
KO PHI PHI DON
KO PHI PHI LE
KO LANTA NOI
KO LANTA YAI
Shark Point
KO RACHA YAI
KO RACHA NOI
KO KAEW
KO HA
KO NGAI
KO MUK
KO KRADAN
Hin Daeng, Hin Muang
KO ROK NAI
KO ROK NOI
KO LI BONG

For Details See
Shark Point Map

For Details See
Trang Map

Krabi
Ban Bang Phung
Khuan
Khlong Thom
Huai Sai Khao
Ban Tong I U
Sikao
Tot Chot
Khuan Pling
Ban Pa Maptrao
Kantang

Ban Nong Hat
Kapang
Ban Bang
Tham Phra
Pa Phayom
Huai Yot
Ban Na To Mun
Phraek Ha
Kachong
Trang
Na Wong
Ban Wang
Thung Khai

Na Thong
Ban Laem Tanode
Khuan Khanun
Phattalung
Ban Ko Wut
Ban Khu
Ban Khok Ya
Ban Mae Khli

Di Luang
Sathing Phra

Ban Mai Siap
Tha Pradu

Ban Pa Bon Tam
Songkhla

Ban Lo Chan Kra
Ban Pa Bak
Ban Phru Pho
Ban Tha Chamuang
Ban Suso
Palian
Ban Khlong Rap
Ban Yong Sata
Thung Wa

Hat Yai
Phru
Ban Khlong Kua
Ban Du Son
Khlong Ngae
Ban Phae
Ban Chin

Sadao
Ban To Non
Padang Besar
Kangar
Changlun
Simpang Empat
Tunjang
Jitra
Alor Setar

Langu
KO SUKON
KO PHETRA
KO BU LON LE
KO KHAO YAI
KO TARUTAO
KO ADANG
KO RAWI
KO BU TONG
KO TANGA
KO TOT

Khuan Ka Long
Pakbara Pier
Ban Wang Tong
Ban Rai
Satun

PULAU LANGKAWI (MALAYSIA)
P. TIMUN
P. TUBA
P. DAYANG BUNTING
P. SINGA BESAR

0   10   20   30
Kilometres

and been made more accessible to a wider variety of visitors. Second, Thailand's infrastructure has vastly improved, making it easier to communicate with the people who offer the diving—the dive centers. Third, the diving boats, diving resorts, diving operations and diving staff have improved their services and amenities so considerably that they now cater to the most discerning diver.

Professional level diving services are the norm in Thailand. The diving industry has exploded over the past 12 years or so, and the standard of service and professionalism in Thailand is unequalled in Southeast Asia. Most dive centers are affiliated with PADI, but SSI and NAUI instruction is available in many places. Prices vary depending on what you are doing, where you are going, and how comfortable you want to be. It is always best to contact diving centers before arriving to arrange your holiday, since at certain times of the year—especially in Phuket, where the diving is considered to be the best—dive boats are often full. If you are planning a live-aboard to the Mergui or to Similan, pre-booking is essential.

Most diving activity is supervised by a Thai or "falang" (western foreigner) divemaster or instructor. If you are a beginner, it is generally suggested that you find out as much about the dive site and the guide as possible before booking. Not all dive sites in Thailand are suitable for beginners, and not all guides are as capable as others.

Most dive centers offer both beginning and advanced or professional-level courses. High-quality underwater photography courses are available, especially on Phuket's better live-aboard dive boats. All courses are generally of the highest standard, and prices are reasonable. One advantage of learning in Thailand is that the normal class size is small, averaging between four and six students, often less.

Diving takes place in three general areas: Pattaya, near the capital of Thailand, Bangkok; around the southern islands of the Gulf of Thailand; and in the two triangles of diving in the Andaman Sea on the west coast of Thailand's isthmus. The pages that follow will describe these areas in detail and will give you an idea of what to expect.

The Andaman Sea To the northwest of the island of Phuket lie the most popular, famous and best-loved dive sites in Thailand, the Similan Islands, visited by many live-aboards. Approximately 180 km to the northwest of these islands stretches the vast Mergui Archipelago, a group of islands and banks covering 10,000 sq km of area. This archipelago is only accessible by professionally equipped live-aboard boats. About 600 km further to the northwest are the newly opened Andaman Islands. Then there is Richelieu Rock, known for its whale sharks and one of the highest densities of marine life in SE Asia.

South of Phuket lie a number of islands, most of which can be enjoyed in a day's diving excursion. Look out for trips to Ko Racha Yai and Noi, Shark Point and the delightful Phi Phi Islands. Further to the south are the province of Trang and the pinnacles known as Hin Daeng and Hin Muang, which can offer diving quality on par with Richelieu Rock.

Gulf of Thailand The friendly laid-back islands of Ko Samui and Ko Tao are located a moderate distance from Thailand's East Coast city of Surat Thani. Originally coconut plantations, these islands have developed into a paradise for people searching for a completely relaxed lifestyle. Exotic dive site names such as Ko Wao, Hin Bai and Chumpon Pinnacle all lie within easy reach of Ko Tao and Ko Samui, and some of the diving here can be spectacular. These sites present the casual diver with a pleasant diversion from such sybaritic activities as relaxing on the beach, drinking from cool coconuts fresh off the tree, or dancing to the sounds of techno music at one of the local nightclubs. Interesting diving combined with a very pleasant stay ensure an all-around great time.

East Coast Pattaya is located just a short 2-hour drive from Bangkok. A weekend escape for those living a life in the chaotic capital, Pattaya's dive sites stretch from Pattaya Bay to the newly explored areas near the border of Cambodia. Although mainly a popular place in Thailand for diving instruction, the waters around Pattaya can offer the experienced diver the opportunity to dive on ship wrecks and at the same time stay in Thailand's most comprehensive tourist resort. Further to the east, Ko Chang is being touted as Thailand's next Phuket and we shall be seeing some changes to this area's infrastructure soon.

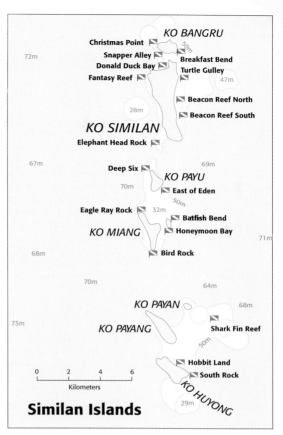

Similan Islands

Environmental Protection

Protecting the environment is a fairly new concept in Thailand and Southeast Asia, but fortunately more and more people are developing an awareness for it.

Divers have long been aware of damage to coral reefs through dynamite fishing and anchoring, but dive centers began to recognize the damage done by the divers themselves many years ago. For this reason, most centers have developed a hands-off policy. This has resulted in Thailand having some of the most environmentally progressive dive shops in the world, which has helped to keep our reefs healthy and beautiful. Divers are asked to respect the wishes of the diving community by not gathering or collecting any corals or shells, even from the beaches (removing dead shells also deprives a creature, such as a hermit crab, of a potential home). Marine items from shell shops should also be boycotted.

Environmentally, Thailand's diving fraternity has been a leader in coral reef protection in Southeast Asia. Many of Thailand's best dive sites have become protected under law. Over the past 15 years, I have seen major improvements in the quality of diving in almost all regions around the country. While other areas in Southeast Asia and the rest of the world have suffered major degradation of their reefs, Thailand's government and its dive centers have instigated sound policies in controlling damage to the coral and fish populations. These policies have included educating people on the destruction of reefs by dynamite, mooring projects in the Similans, Ko Racha, Ko Phi Phi, Ko Samui and Ko Tao, and a strict hands-off policy for divers.

As long as this positive trend continues, diving in Thailand's waters will bring pleasure, enjoyment and thrills to many people—and hopefully to their children and grandchildren as well. You will find Thailand's seas, islands and culture to be full of life, full of wonder—and full of surprises.

—John Williams

THAILAND

Similan Islands
Nine Gems Offering Some of Asia's Best Diving

Ko Similan is by far the most beautiful group of dive sites in Thailand and one of the best areas for diving in the entire world. Many divers find that the most unusual aspect about the Similans is that there are two radically different types of environments neatly packaged together into one destination.

The Similans, located about 100 km northwest of Phuket, are composed of nine granite islands covered in tropical jungle, washed by a clear, blue tropical ocean and blessed with some of the world's finest beaches. The word Similan is a corruption of the Malay *sembilan*, which means "nine," and history has it that it was a Malay fisherman who named the group "The Nine Islands." Today, the islands are identified by a Thai name and a corresponding number: for example, Ko Huyong (Island #1), located at the southern end of the chain.

In the recent past, the islands have achieved national park status, and thus are fully protected under Thai law. The National Park Authority maintains their presence on two of the islands: Ko Similan (Island #8) the largest, and Ko Miang (Island #4). The islands have also come to the special attention of the Thai Royal Family, which, we hope, protects them even further.

By drawing an imaginary line from north to south, the area divides into the two separate types of environments. The east coast with its powdery beaches features hard coral gardens which slope dramatically from the surface down to approximately 30 to 40 meters, where sand takes over as the water depth increases. On this side, the most popular activity is drift diving among healthy coral gardens and their reef inhabitants. In several sites, large coral heads or bommies rise from the bottom and are covered with soft corals, sea fans and an enormous amount of critters and unusual fish. Here the diving is easy and navigation simple, allowing each buddy pair to explore at his or her own pace.

The west coast, just a short boat ride away, can offer faster-paced, more exhilarating diving, as currents swirl around the huge granite boulders—some larger than the largest of houses. These smooth, rounded boulders create dramatic underwater formations, holes and overhangs or "swim-throughs" where divers can enjoy just swimming with the current through the openings. The drama of looking up through the clear water at these huge rocks is satisfaction and experience enough for some divers, as there are very few places like this on earth. Growing on these boulders are some of the most colorful soft corals imaginable, in many places so thick that the rock is no longer visible. In the larger passages between the boulders the fans grow to a size sometimes 3 meters across, and are often so tightly bunched together that it makes it impossible to swim through the channels. Most of the dive sites on the west coast are best seen with a dive guide, since navigation can be tricky. By diving with an experienced guide you'll no doubt increase your enjoyment of the area.

 Overnight by live-aboard boat

 Great, 18–30 meters plus

 Variable, sometimes strong

 Excellent condition, unbelievable variety

Boulders, coral walls

Small sizes but fantastic

 Unusual formations, dramatic scenery, swim-throughs, large fans and beautiful beaches

If you enjoy watching and photographing small fish, the Similans are hard to beat for the sheer numbers and varieties of tropicals. Large fish, however, are a different story, and the Similans are not well known for consistent big fish action. For this kind of diving, you must travel further north to Richelieu Rock or the Mergui Archipelago. However, luck brings an occasional whale shark, while large cow tail rays are fairly common. And, of course, the leopard shark makes his appearance on a regular basis. Whitetip and blacktip sharks are also sighted once in a while, and a few times over the years we've seen pods of false killer whales.

Like diving in all areas of Southeast Asia, you should enjoy the Similans for what they are justly famous for: wild, unspoiled beaches, magnificent coral growth, prolific fish life, crystalline waters and sensational underwater rock formations. Because of the distance from the mainland, the best way to visit the Similans is on a live-aboard boat.

We have seen a dramatic change in the quality of dive boats in Thailand over the past decade. Now, private cabins, air-conditioning and en suite bathroom facilities are the norm rather than the exception. Prices in US dollars and euros remain about the same as 10 years ago. There are now over 40 live-aboard boats operating around Thailand's West Coast to the Similan Islands and areas further north. The boats are safer than they were in the past, with modern navigational equipment and safety items in line with western standards. In general, food served aboard is excellent. Also, Phuket has become such an international place that many western food items are now available at reasonable costs. Only wine is still shamefully expensive due to high taxes. My advice: bring your own.

Trip lengths vary from 3 to 5 days; they are often longer if the boat is including the Similans as another stop on the itinerary. One-day trips are sometimes possible, but in general not recommended.

The high season in the Similans is from October until May, but diving is possible all year round. The water tends to be clearest in the summer and in the fall, but then again, the visibility is usually fairly good in the Similans, averaging about 18 to 25 meters and at times

Below: Soft coral trees (*Dendronephthya*) can grow from as small as 1 inch to more than 4 feet tall. Mergui Archipelago. *Photo by Scott Tuason.*

exceeding 40 meters! There are well over 20 charted dive sites in the Similan chain, and the following descriptions of a few of the favorites should give you an idea of what kind of diving to expect.

Christmas Point, Island #9, Ko Bangru One of the most dramatic dives in the Similans, this dive begins with a series of large arches at a depth of about 24 meters. The soft coral growth and sea fans are as large as they are anywhere, and the fish action is fast here. We often encounter small schools of blue-fin trevally feeding on schools of small fry. End your dive near the island for the best swim-throughs in the Similans, and keep your eyes open for surprisingly large jacks that hide in these passageways.

Breakfast Bend, Island #9, Ko Bangru A typical east coast dive, this is a favourite way to begin a trip. The light is beautiful early in the morning—hence its name—and the coral is in great shape. Down deeper in the sand there has been a large increase of garden eels over the past few years. In the shallows, leopard sharks are often seen resting in the sand. We've also spotted a Napoleon wrasse—a rare fish in the Similans.

Fantasy Reef, Island #8, Ko Similan One of the most popular dive spots in the Similans, these underwater rock formations cover a huge area. The friendliest fish in the Similans hang out here, including a few approachable clown triggerfishes—normally a fish difficult to get close to. Depths here range from 15 meters down to past 40 meters, and this is one of the best dives for enjoying the spectacular boulders.

Beacon Reef (south), Island #8, Ko Similan One of my favourite dives, probably because this is where I saw my first whale shark, this reef features a steep drop-off with striking diversity of hard corals from a depth of 35 meters almost all the way to the surface. This dive could easily have

the largest variety of healthy hard corals in the Similans, probably exceeding 300 species. There are plenty of nudibranchs around the coral heads, as well as rare, nervous firefishes (*Nemateleotris magnifica*), one of the most beautiful fish in the tropical sea. One of the ugliest residents of this reef are the bigeyes (*Priacanthus hamrur*) that slowly cruise the reef flats. These fishes have an amazing ability to change from a deep red color to a contrasting vivid silver. It almost appears as if they are changing their color to fit their mood.

Elephant Head, Island #8, Ko Similan Probably the most famous dive in the group, the site is named after an unusually shaped rock that juts out of the water just south of Ko Similan. The three rocks that form Elephant Head also create a natural amphitheater that feels like diving in a huge aquarium. Yellow goatfishes and snappers always hang around at the deepest level of the bowl, as well as several species of lionfishes, coral trout, and the occasional hawksbill or Ridley's turtle. The swim-throughs at deeper depths are dazzling and worth the dive experience alone.

East of Eden, Island #7, Ko Payu A typical east coast dive, this particular site has one of the most incredible underwater bommies in the Similans. Beginning at a depth of about 21 meters and rising to 12, the concentration of marine life is unequalled in the Similans. One summer, we had the opportunity to photograph, repeatedly, a cute pink frog fish who stayed regally poised in the same spot for over 2 months.

One last important comment about the Similan Islands—they are unique for another reason. Mooring projects and other environmentally protective measures have been introduced over the past few years, and, happily, the diving has actually improved. One thing is for sure, the Similan Islands will give all that you ask for—and more.

— John Williams

Opposite: Diving at Fantasy Reef, one of the most popular dive spots in the Similans. *Photo by Ashley Boyd.*

The Mergui Archipelago

A Huge Unpopulated Group of Islands and Reefs

Below: A giant potato cod (*Epinephelus tukula*) rests up in a field of coral rubble. Mergui Archipelago. *Photo by Scott Tuason.*

In the early 1990's, several dive operators out of Phuket, looking for new diving frontiers in the Andaman Sea, began exploring a series of underwater mountains 90 nautical miles northwest of the Similan Islands that came to be known as the Burma Banks. In a very short time, the banks became recognized as one of the best places for divers to observe sharks close-up and personal—

something lacking in Thailand. As it turns out, this was just the beginning. Even though these banks lie in international waters, by the middle of the decade the Myanmar (Burmese) authorities became aware and uneasy about the activity off of their coastline and asked the dive boats to seek official permission from the government to dive there. After three years of negotiations, in 1997 consent was finally given to not only visit the now famous Burma Banks, but also the islands in Myanmar's inshore waters. This opened up a whole new range of diving possibilities in the Andaman Sea, and operators soon began promoting these new destinations offering multi-day trips. Some boats visit both Thailand and Mergui on the same itinerary, while others confine the journey to only Myanmar. The main obstacle the area has to conventional diving is the distances between dive sites. A typical seven-day circuit including Thailand and Mergui can cover over 1,000 km. Obviously, day-trips are not practical for exploring the area.

Lush, Unexplored Area

Historically, the archipelago had been an important area for trade between Eastern and Western civilizations particularly in the 18th century. After World War Two with the major political changes that took place in Burma and rest of Southeast Asia, the archipelago fell into obscurity, resulting in over 50 years of very little human activity. With over 800 islands, some of them the size

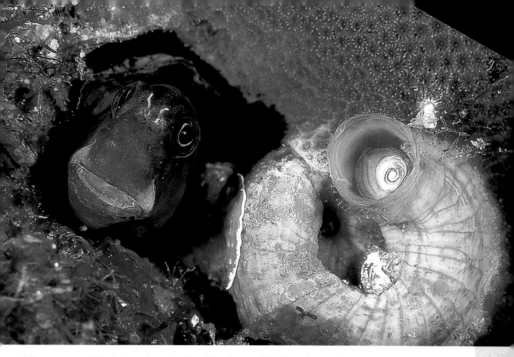

of Singapore or Phuket, and most of them completely uninhabited, the area has unlimited potential as a playground for divers, yachties, naturalists, and other pleasure seekers. Steps have already been taken to preserve the islands, and the government seems to be very interested in developing the area in a positive way.

A user fee is charged by the Myanmar authorities to enter and dive the Mergui Archipelago. All boats enter and depart via Kawthaung (Ko Song or Victoria Point are other names for it), just west of Ranong, Thailand. All boats are required to enter and exit the area from here: gone are the days when you could make a quick run from the Surin or Similan Islands.

The Burma Banks are no longer the prime reason to visit the area, as there are so many better dive sites. Although sharks and rays are seen on a regular basis both at the Burma Banks and at the islands lying further inshore, environmental problems including long-line fishing and trawling have had an effect on this type of wildlife. Much has been written about the area being a place to see sharks and

other large fish, but the main reason for visiting, honestly, is to see the incredible variety of smaller fish and reef invertebrates, many of which are not found in Thai waters. This, and the sheer immensity of the area, are reasons to go. If catching sight of large animals is the only reason for visiting the archipelago, divers will be disappointed.

Diverse Diving Environments

There are four types of diving environments in the archipelago: shallow, inshore fringing island reefs where visibility is often poor but the diversity of marine life is unsurpassed; offshore fringing reefs where the visibility is considerably better, and the coral is much healthier; pinnacles and small rocky islands which rise from the depths and attract larger marine life such as sharks and rays; and banks which rise up from depths of over 300 meters and attract different types of marine life altogether. All in all, the Mergui Archipelago contains some of the most diverse and interesting marine ecosystems in the world.

Above: This small spotted blenny plays next to a tube worm. Mergui Archipelago. *Photo by Scott Tuason.*

At least five days by live-aboard boat

Variable from 5–50 meters

Strong in many areas depending on tides

Varies from excellent to poor

Sloping mountains, walls, canyons, caves, pinnacles

Several species of sharks, ghost pipefish, seahorses, frogfish

One of the last pristine areas in the world

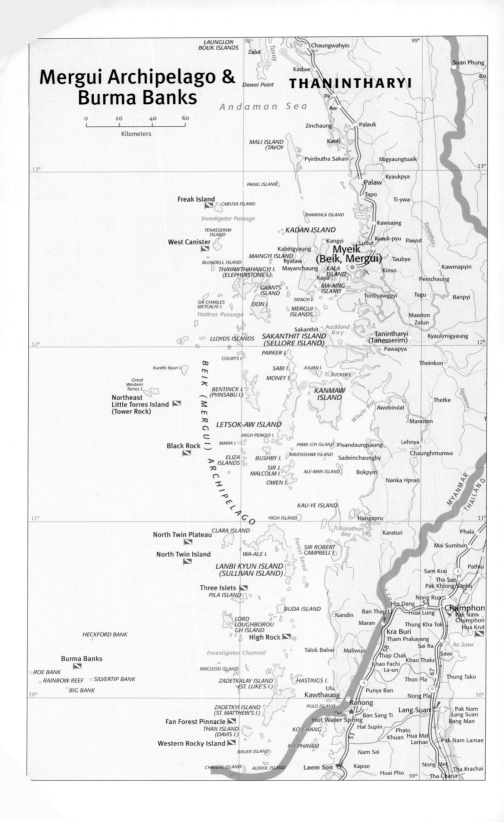

Mergui Archipelago & Burma Banks

THANINTHARYI

Andaman Sea

0   20   40   60
Kilometers

LAUNGLON
BOUK ISLANDS
Zalut
Tavoy
Chaungwahyin
Suan Phung
Bo
Kadwe
Dawei Point
Pe
Aw
MALI ISLAND
(TAVOY)
Zinchaung
Palauk
Kanti
Pyinbutha Sakan
Migyaungtuaik
Kyaukpya
PAING ISLAND
Palaw
Tapo
Ti-ywa
Freak Island
CABUSA ISLAND
THAMIHLA ISLAND
Kawsaing
Investigator Passage
TENASSERIM
ISLAND
KADAN ISLAND
West Canister
Kangyi
Lutut
Kyauk-pyu
Pawut
Kabingyaung
Myeik
MAINGYI ISLAND
(Beik, Mergui)
BLUNDELL ISLAND
Kyataw
Taubye
Kawmapyin
THAYAWTHAHANGYI I.
Mayanchaung
KALA
Kinso
(ELEPHINSTONE I.)
Kapa
ISLAND
Peinchaung
GRANTS
MA-AING
Tagu
Banpyi
ISLAND
TATAGYI I.
ISLAND
Tonbyawggyi
SIR CHARLES
METCALFE I.
DON I.
MERGUI
Mawton
ISLANDS
Zalun
Hattras Passage
Sakanthit
Auckland
LLOYDS ISLANDS
SAKANTHIT ISLAND
Bay
Tanintharyi
(SELLORE ISLAND)
(Tanesserim)
Kyaukmigyaung
PARKER I.
Pawapya
COURTS I.
Theinkon
Kunthi Kyun I.
SABI I.
JULIAN I.
MONEY I.
TUCKER I.
Great
Western
Torres I.
BENTINCK I.
KANMAW
Northeast
(PYINSABU I.)
ISLAND
Thetke
Little Torres Island
Awebindat
(Tower Rock)
LETSOK-AW ISLAND
Manoron
HIGH PEAKED I.
MARIA I.
PAWE-GYI ISLAND
Pisandaungsaung
Lehnya
Black Rock
ELIZA
BUSHBY I.
RAVENSHAW ISLAND
Sadeinchaungby
Chaunghmunwa
ISLANDS
SIR J.
MALCOLM I.
ALE-MAN ISLAND
Bokpyin
OWEN I.
Nanka Hprao
KAU-YE ISLAND
HIGH ISLAND
Hangapru
CLARA ISLAND
Karathuri
Karaturi
Phala
North Twin Plateau
Bay
Mai Sumbun
North Twin Island
WA-ALE I.
SIR ROBERT
CAMPBELL I.
Pathu
LANBI KYUN ISLAND
Sam Krai
(SULLIVAN ISLAND)
Tha Sae
Pak Khlong Saphli
Three Islets
PILA ISLAND
Nong Rua
Hin Dang
Champhon
BUDA ISLAND
Nandin
Ban Thap Li
Huai Lung
Pak Nam
Chumphon
LORD
Maran
Thung Kha Tok
Hua Krut
LOUGHBOROU
GH ISLAND
Kra Buri
High Rock
Tham Prakayang
HECKFORD BANK
Talok Babai
Maliwun
Thap Chak
Sai Ra
Sawi
Khao Fachi
Khao Thalu
Investigator Channel
La-un
Burma Banks
MACLEOD ISLAND
Thon Pla
Thung Tako
ROE BANK
Punya Ban
Nong Pla
RAINBOW REEF
SILVERTIP BANK
ZADETKALAY ISLAND
HASTINGS I.
BIG BANK
(ST. LUKE'S I.)
Ulu
Kawthaung
ZADETKYI ISLAND
PULO ISLAND
Ranong
Lang Suan
Pak Nam
(ST. MATTHEW'S I.)
Ban Sang Ti
Lang Suan
Fan Forest Pinnacle
Hot Water Spring
Bang Man
THAN ISLAND
KO CHANG
Hat Supin
Phato
(DAVIS I.)
Khuan
Hua Mat
Pak Nam Lamae
Western Rocky Island
KO PHAYAM
Lamae
BRUER ISLAND
Nam Sai
Nong Me
Tha Krachai
CHRISTIE ISLAND
AURIOL ISLAND
Laem Son
Kapoe
Tha Chana
Huai Pho

Far inshore, the islands are lush with vegetation and primary jungle, and contain some of the last jungle cats, eleplants, and other large mammals to be found in Southeast Asia. For those who are interested in more than diving, jungle walks and river trips can and should be considered as part of your trip. Birdwatchers and other observers of terrestrial life will be thrilled.

Further offshore, the islands are drier and lay in deep enough water to afford good visibility. Here the corals, sea fans, and fish life are similar to that found in Thailand, but with much more diversity of species. This makes the diving better and more exciting than in the waters to the east or to the south.

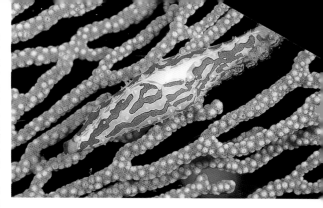

Above: Allied cowries, prized by shell collectors, are difficult to find because they are able to adapt so well to their surroundings, usually sea fans and soft corals. Mergui Archipelago. *Photo by Scott Tuason.*

island, while leopard sharks and spotted rays lie on the bottom. On and around the rocks, spiny lobster, cowrie shells, feather stars, anemones and an assortment of crabs abound. Reef fish include blue-ringed angelfish, moray eels, snappers, frogfish, and ghost pipefish.

Face to Face with Sharks

At least nine species of sharks have been reported in Burma, including bull, tiger, hammerhead, gray reef, nurse, mako, and spinner sharks. At the Burma Banks, whitetip, tawny nurse, and silvertip sharks are the ones to watch for.

Some of the more interesting dive sites in the archipelago are described below, taking a general south to north route. Keep in mind that these are just a few of the sites that you would visit on a live-aboard cruise as there are scores of dive sites here and like everywhere, some better than others.

Western Rocky Island

This limestone island features beautiful underwater terrain, including a tunnel—often full of large tawny nurse sharks—which traverses the island about 20 meters down. The island is more like a series of pinnacles rather than one big rock and the soft limestone makes for crevices offering shelter for a wide variety of sea creatures. Some of the marine life you will see here include mantas, gray reef and spinner sharks, and eagle rays in the open water next to the

The Burma Banks

Not officially part of the Mergui Archipelago as there are no islands here, the Burma Banks, located about 80 nautical miles west of Kawthaung, are a series of seamounts that rise up from over 300 meters to just below the surface. Depths average 15 to 22 meters on the flat areas on top, dropping off slowly on the edges. Some banks have a more dramatic drop-off than others, but nowhere will you find a vertical wall. Guided drift dives are the norm, usually starting on the edge of the bank in 35 meters of water where divers stare out in the blue looking for large silvertip sharks. Commonly growing to just over two meters in length, these sharks are full-bodied, fascinating animals easily identified by the white trailing edges on their pectoral fins and caudal, fins. Normally quite curious, but not aggressive, these sharks will closely approach the diver making for incredible photo opportunities.

If the sharks don't happen to be around, the dogtooth tuna, Spanish mackerel and jack fish that patrol the reef edges will delight you. You never know what you're going to see out here.

Three Islets (Shark Cave Island)

One of the most extraordinary dive sites, these three rocks that rise out of the sea from depths of 40 meters or more harbour some of the best marine life in the archipelago. Huge schools of fusilier and silversides surround you upon entering the water. The sandy base of the islands reveals unusual anemones and starfish, while the walls are covered with orange cup corals, whip corals, and green tubastrea coral. It is one of the better areas to see harlequin shrimp and harlequin ghost pipefish.

If you're looking for drama, there is a canyon that leads to a tunnel connecting the northern and southern part of the main, middle island. Here, if you're lucky, you can witness gray reef sharks swimming in and out of the canyon. The trick here is to hang out against the east side of the wall and just watch. As long as there are not too many divers in the canyon, the sharks will soon lose their shyness and swim very close to you. Up to 12 animals have been seen together.

North Twin Plateau

Located just northwest of North Twin, this large plateau starts at around six meters and carries on down to between 24 and 30 meters. It's quite a large dive site, and it's best to start in the deeper areas and find an interesting vein to explore as you move towards the surface. Lots of large sea fans make this look similar to many of the West Coast dives in the Similan Islands. Barracuda and rainbow runners cruise the outer edges of the reef, and sandbar sharks have been sighted here.

Black Rock

Probably the most spectacular site with the most potential for big stuff in the archipelago, Black Rock is a rocky island about 100 meters long, located about 50 nautical miles north of North Twin Island. Here is the closest you'll come to having a true wall dive, with depths of over 60 meters and a dramatic drop-off in most areas. Although visibility can change dramatically here due to strong currents at certain times of the month, there is plenty to see and many dives are possible on this one site. The currents can also make this an advanced dive, with up and down currents—not to mention the side-ways ones—causing all kinds of fun and games for divers. Be careful of your depths, and try and stay close to the rock itself to duck out of the currents.

Some of the fish you will see here include black-spotted pufferfish, spotted hawkfish, scorpionfish, and blue-ringed angelfish. If you are a moray eel fan, then this is your dive site. Many unusual and rarely seen morays are residents here,

Below: This small rock, typical of the sites in Mergui, is covered in a profusion of life—yellow tubastrea corals, a golden sea fan and a lone urchin, and swarmed by thousands of fusiliers.
Photo by Scott Tuason.

including extra-large common green, zebra, and fimbriated and white-eyed morays. Octopus and cuttlefish can also be found here.

Moving north, we find dive sites that are not dived that often due to the distances involved. However, they are worth noting, as they will probably be dived more often in the future as the southern sites become more crowded.

Tower Rock

Located off Northeast Little Torres Island, this island rises dramatically out of the sea and plunges over 60 meters to the bottom. Schools of mobula rays are seen here often. It's also a good place to spot sharks, but the remarkable landscape and the chance of seeing ghost pipefish is the more reliable interest.

West Canister

Located almost 80 nautical miles north of Black Rock, the island looks almost exactly like Ko Bon in Thailand, just flipped 180°. The best site is a pinnacle located almost in the middle of the small bay, and is almost connected to a ridge that runs from the westernmost point of the island. On dives we've done there, the top of the rock acts as a cleaning station for manta rays. It's a huge granite rock starting about 15 meters and continuing to over 40 meters. From there, you'll find a hard coral reef sloping down to over 60 meters. Large sea fans swathe the granite boulders, with purple, pink and orange soft corals covering most of the rock. Barracudas, fusiliers, jacks, Spanish mackerel, and rainbow runners cruise over the top of the reef. Painted crayfish hide in the overhangs.

The Mergui Archipelago has something for everyone, and although the dive sites here can often lean towards the advanced, even intermediate divers will love the place as long as the dive sites are picked carefully. As always, consult with the divemaster before diving to make sure you aren't getting more than you bargained for. Conditions change constantly due to fluctuating tides and your dive professional is the best source of current information.
— *John Williams*

Above: The tawny nurse shark (*Nebrius ferrugineus*) inhabits shallow reefs, and is therefore commonly seen at sites throughout Asia. Mergui Archipelago. *Photo by Scott Tuason.*

Ko Tachai & Richelieu Rock

Plus the Sites at Ko Bon and Ko Surin

North of the Similans lie Ko Bon, Ko Tachai, the Surin Islands and Richelieu Rock. All of these areas, with the exception of Surin, offer world-class diving that differs from the Similan Islands. You should try to make this part of your itinerary when you visit the south of Thailand.

Ko Bon This island is located about 20 km north of Similan Island #9, and features one of the few vertical walls in Thailand. The dive site is on the southwestern point and consists of a 33-m wall facing a small cove, and a step-down ridge that carries on to depths of over 45 meters. Leopard sharks are common on the ridge and on the sandy flats below the wall. Although the soft corals are not as high-profile as they are in the Similans, the colors of the corals are radically different and include shades of turquoise, yellow and blue, besides the more common pinks and purples. Ko Bon is one of the better places to see manta rays, especially towards the end of the

Below: The common reef cuttlefish (*Sepia sp.*) has the remarkable ability to change color by "flexing" iridiophores, cells in the skin that in essence bend and reflect light.
Photo by Scott Tuason.

season (April and May) when there is more plankton in the water.

Ko Tachai Twenty-five km north of Ko Bon, this isle has an offshore underwater ridge that runs perpendicular to the island. This is considered to be one of the finest dives in the Kingdom, and is famous as a place to see not only the more common species of corals, fans and schooling tropical fish, but larger animals such as rays, leopard sharks, nurse sharks and hawksbill turtles. Whale sharks make an appearance on a regular basis. Tachai also boasts a breathtakingly beautiful sandy beach on its northeastern shore.

Surin Island Although visited by several dive operators from Phuket, these islands are more appropriately famous for their beautiful coves, bays and dense jungle than they are for their diving. Spending a few idyllic days on a sail boat or other yacht here is the stuff dreams of paradise are made of, yet the serious diver will be bored easily after a few dives because of the generally poor visibility and lack of fish. This area is also accessible directly from Ban Ko Ko, on the mainland, and takes around 4 hours.

Richelieu Rock Surin's ace, however, is a small, submerged rock about 18 km east of Surin. Richelieu Rock—just exposed at the lowest of tides—rates as one of the best dive sites in the world due to the unbelievable diversity and concentration of marine life. It was also one of the best places in the world, during the

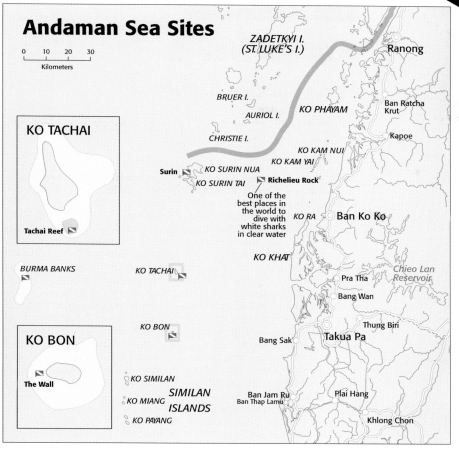

Andaman Sea Sites

0 10 20 30
Kilometers

ZADETKYI I.
(ST. LUKE'S I.)

Ranong

BRUER I.

AURIOL I.

KO PHAYAM

Ban Ratcha
Krut

CHRISTIE I.

Kapoe

KO KAM NUI
KO KAM YAI

Surin

KO SURIN NUA
KO SURIN TAI

Richelieu Rock

One of the
best places in
the world to
dive with
white sharks
in clear water

KO RA

Ban Ko Ko

KO KHAT

Chieo Lan
Reservoir

Pra Tha

Bang Wan

Thung Biri

KO TACHAI

Tachai Reef

BURMA BANKS

KO TACHAI

KO BON

Bang Sak

Takua Pa

KO BON

The Wall

KO SIMILAN
KO MIANG

SIMILAN
ISLANDS

KO PAYANG

Ban Jam Ru
Ban Thap Lamu

Plai Hang

Khlong Chon

last decade, to swim with whale sharks, the largest shark in the world. The past few years, ever since the last El Niño, the sharks have become more rare. We still see them on a regular basis, but not in the numbers we used to. Hopefully, whatever caused their decline in numbers will change and we will again see these gentle giants as before. However, the dive site is still incredible and gets better each year as less fishing is done than before.

Besides the appearance of the whale shark, Richelieu Rock offers lush soft corals, large schools of pelagic fishes, as well as countless small organisms clinging to the rock. Octopuses are abundant. Recently we had a chance to observe cuttlefish in their courtship behavior on almost every dive. The ritual can be likened to a dance as their tentacles wave wildly in all directions, and go through rapid color changes which appear to be like a quick change of costume between dance acts. Richelieu is good, too, for shell spotters. *Murex*, cowries and cones are there in abundance. Lastly, at Richelieu the guitar shark (family *Rhinobatidae*), one of the ugliest creatures alive and growing to over 2 meters in length, can be seen lying on the bottom.

These days, most of the vessels that offer four-day or longer itineraries to the Similan Islands visit these dive sites as well. In addition, most of the boats that visit the Mergui Archipelago include two or more of these dives sites in their program. Boats depart from Phuket, Ko Phi Phi, and Khao Lak, north of Phuket.

— *John Williams*

Live-aboard boat

Good, 15–30 meters

Variable, sometimes strong

Excellent

Walls, ridges, pinnacles, boulders

Fantastic

Whale sharks, guitar sharks, soft corals in a rainbow of colors, schooling pelagics

Racha Noi & Racha Yai

Fun Diving from Phuket's West Coast and Islands to the South

Though most serious divers will immediately book a longer live-aboard boat to the Similans and beyond when contemplating a Thai diving holiday, Phuket does offer some fine day trips and shorter overnight cruises to its west coast and offshore islands. One- and two-tank, half- and full-day diving excursions are available through most of the dive centers in both Patong and Kata, as well as from some hotels in the Bang Tao area near the airport, and Kamala Beach north of Patong.

Phuket's west coast offers casual diving, usually from a local longtail boat. Although not the easiest of boats to dive from, they do have the advantage of being able to pull right up to the beach and are relatively inexpensive to hire.

Some of the dive areas off the west coast include Patong Bay, Freedom Beach, Paradise Beach, Bang Tao, Kata Beach and Ko Pu. All of these spots are popular training areas and actually do offer some pleasant and easy diving, although Phuket's off-shore areas are much better. One of the best areas is right off the beach in Kata, where the coral reef parallels the bay's northern rocky point. Averaging a depth of only 5 to 6 meters, the amount of marine life surprises even the most seasoned divers. I've seen all sorts of unusual fish here including a ghost pipefish, dragon wrasses, a crocodilefish and sea robins. I've also had a lionfish swim up to a diving class and peer into each student's individual mask as if looking for an explanation. You should expect the unexpected when diving Phuket's west coast.

To the south of Phuket lie the twin islands of Ko Racha Yai (Big Racha) and Ko Racha Noi (Small Racha), which offer significantly better diving than Phuket's western beaches. Almost all diving operators offer one-day trips to both of the islands, sometimes on the same day, and there are dive shops on Ko Racha Yai affiliated with the bungalows located in both the main bays.

Ko Racha Yai

Racha Yai's best diving is off its east coast which makes it especially attractive during Phuket's off-season in the summer. Although visibility varies, it can be as good as 25 meters or more. A typical dive is

Below: Not at all camera-shy, friendly potato cod have been known to approach divers and photographers. *Photo by Scott Tuason.*

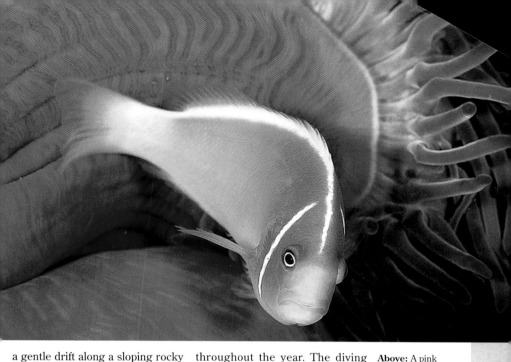

a gentle drift along a sloping rocky face sprinkled with hard coral forests of many, many varieties. Especially prominent are staghorn corals of blue and tan. Often there are large schools of false barracudas hovering over the reef, while on the reef itself are octopuses and cuttlefishes in addition to the more common tropical species. Divers of all levels of experience and snorkelers can visit Racha Yai without concern over dive hazards as the diving is easy and gentle. Water depths range from 3 to 30 meters.

Ko Racha Noi

This spot is popular for the more experienced diver, as depths are generally greater and the currents frequently stronger than at its sister island to the north. The northern tip features a large pinnacle where spotting larger marine life is possible, while the southern point is a nice drift dive with the added bonus of having a beautiful little beach to visit during your surface interval. For some reason, Racha Noi is one of the better places for divers to see manta rays throughout the year. The diving here is definitely more challenging than at Racha Yai, but the rewards can also be much greater.

Like in most places around the country, accommodation has improved significantly over the past decade and though there probably will never be accommodation on Racha Noi, Racha Yai has good accommodation in both of the pristine little bays on the northern side of the island. There are also ferries that run between Phuket and Racha Yai daily.

— *John Williams*

Racha Noi & Racha Yai
KO RACHA YAI
Basic accommodation is available on Racha Yai. No accommodation on Racha Noi
50m
Bungalow Bay
46m
36m
50m

The best diving is on the east side, making the diving here particularly attractive during the low season (southeast monsoon)
72m

55m
Northern Pinnacle
65m
36m
50m

The Wreck
KO RACHA NOI
69m
Southern Point (drift diving)
66m

Above: A pink clownfish seeks protection in the underside of the poisonous anemone. *Photo by Scott Tuason.*

Half-day and full-day trips arranged by dive centers

Average to poor, west coast. At Racha, 10–30 meters

Variable, can be strong

Good

Coral gardens, rocky points, boulders

Good

Unusual fish life, easy-to-get-to areas; good fun, fast dives at Racha. Beautiful top-side scenery

Shark Point

Shark Point, Anemone Reef and King Cruiser: Excellent Day Diving

By far the best and most popular dive sites by day-trip from Phuket or Phi Phi, these two pinnacles and the wreck dive are located approximately 25 km east of Chalong Bay in Phuket. Given marine sanctuary status in 1992, these three dive sites are the only day-trips in Thailand that offer truly world-class quality diving, albeit with limited visibility. The rock pinnacles explode with life, and the wreck attracts thousands of fish; the sheer density of marine life makes diving here a wonderful, sensual experience.

Shark Point, or Hin Musang as it is called in Thai, rises out of the water from surrounding depths of only about 18 to 20 meters. Considering the small extent of the rock above the water, the actual size of the reef underwater is a big surprise to most divers. Beginning from the relatively steep main rock

Below: The zebra shark is commonly sighted on offshore reefs throughout Thailand. *Photo by Scott Tuason.*

pinnacle, the reef flattens out to the south until it rises towards the surface again about 500 meters away. This second rock does not break the surface, and, depending on the current, is an excellent place to begin the dive.

Like many places in Thailand, Shark Point's most colorful feature is the profusion of purple and pink soft corals that cling to the rocks. The strong currents sweeping over the pinnacle provide food a-plenty for hundreds of different species of hard corals and Indo-Pacific tropical fishes.

The name of the site comes from the common leopard (zebra) shark *(Stegastoma varium)*, a docile creature that hangs out in the sand surrounding the pinnacle. These completely approachable, trusting sharks grow to lengths of a little over 2 meters, and most divers

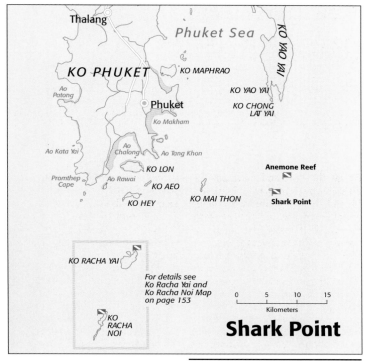

Shark Point

think that they are one of the "cutest" sharks in the ocean. Divers not accustomed to seeing sharks are genuinely surprised at how big and approachable they are. Unfortunately, many times these sharks are taken advantage of and handled unnecessarily. Handling by divers can injure the animal and expose it to infection. Touching an animal in no way benefits it and—more often than not—seriously harms it.

Anemone Reef

Hin Jom (Submerged Rock or Anemone Reef) lies just under water, about 600 meters to the north of Hin Musang. No part of the pinnacle is exposed, and under water the rock drops off more dramatically to a depth of between 20 and 27 meters until reaching a bottom of sand and oyster shells. Although not as colorful as Shark Point, the fish life here is excellent, and our friends, the leopard sharks, are often seen free-swimming at the top of the rock in 6 meters of water.

The King Cruiser Wreck

This 85-m-long car ferry was sunk in May 1997 after hitting Anemone Reef. The wreck rests at the bottom in about 30 meters of water and houses schools of jacks, queenfish and reef species like cardinalfish, snappers, lionfish and scorpionfish. Most of the hull is covered with acorn barnacles, one reason to wear gloves. Although the wreck is disintegrating, it still rises to within 12 meters of the surface, making it an easy multi-level dive

Located just south of Ao Phangnga and all of its fresh water rivers, visibility averages about 10 meters, often less. Although such conditions are not exactly the "perfect dive," the amount of marine life more than makes up for visibility. On days when the water becomes gin-clear, diving here feels like taking a breath of fresh air. The only down-sides of these sites are the visibility and the occasional strong currents, making both locations unsuitable for beginners.

— *John Williams*

Full-day trips through dive centers

Variable, 2–25 meters

Variable, often strong

Unequalled

Coral gardens, rock

Quantities and varieties excellent

Leopard sharks, large moray eels, unbelievable amounts of marine life, great soft corals and fans

Phi Phi Islands

Beaches, Bommies and Birds' Nests

Over the past several years, Ko Phi Phi (pronounced "pee pee") has grown from a peaceful little Muslim fishing village to one of the busiest international tourist destinations in the country. It now boasts at least 20 diving centers, several expensive international hotels and a variety of cheaper bungalows and guest houses. Literally thousands of people visit Ko Phi Phi daily, but after the last boat leaves, around mid-afternoon, the island regains much of its peaceful allure.

Located about 45 km east of Phuket, the Phi Phi Island group—actually part of Krabi province—is composed of the islands Ko Phi Phi Don, Ko Phi Phi Lae (translating as "Phi Phi of the Sea"), Ko Yung (Mosquito Island), and Ko Mai Pai (Bamboo Island).

Although the scuba diving is generally not considered to be at the world-class level—depending on your definition—Ko Phi Phi offers the keen diver a wide range of diving possibilities and occasionally some absolutely fantastic diving. It is a delightful place to spend a few days relaxing on its exquisite beaches, exploring its numerous coves and bays, climbing its steep vertical peaks, investigating the huge caves that hide the edible nests of swifts and—last but not least— enjoying some colorful and enticing scuba diving.

Dramatic Scenery

What sets Ko Phi Phi apart from other dive destinations in Thailand

are two features: the first are the amazing limestone cliffs that rise dramatically out of the sea and then plunge equally spectacularly straight down underwater; the second is the remarkable variety of dive sites that are concentrated in such a small area.

Nature has created the limestone rock formations and islands which form Ko Phi Phi and which have become known the world over

Opposite: Maya Bay on Phi Phi Lae, made famous by the movie *The Beach*. Photo by Ingo Jezierski.

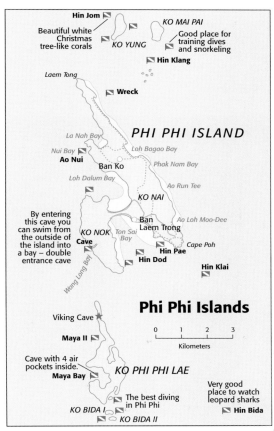

Hin Jom

Beautiful white Christmas tree-like corals

KO YUNG

KO MAI PAI

Good place for training dives and snorkeling

Hin Klang

Laem Tong

Wreck

PHI PHI ISLAND

La Nah Bay

Loh Bagao Bay

Nui Bay

Ao Nui

Ban Ko

Phak Nam Bay

Loh Dalum Bay

Ao Run Tee

KO NAI

By entering this cave you can swim from the outside of the island into a bay – double entrance cave

KO NOK Cave

Ban Laem Trong

Ton Sai Bay

Ao Loh Moo-Dee

Cape Poh

Hin Pae

Hin Dod

Hin Klai

Wang Long Bay

Phi Phi Islands

Viking Cave

0   1   2   3

Kilometers

Maya II

Cave with 4 air pockets inside.

Maya Bay

KO PHI PHI LAE

The best diving in Phi Phi

KO BIDA I

KO BIDA II

Very good place to watch leopard sharks

Hin Bida

as one of the most stunning settings in Southeast Asia. These cliffs soar over 500 meters in some areas, and beautiful green trees and bushes grow on the tops and sides of these cliffs. Swimming in a protected little cove at the base of one of these steep cliffs conjures up visions of an unearthly paradise and, no matter how popular Ko Phi Phi becomes, the stunning scenery will always create that special feeling that no one has ever been here before you.

Underwater, these towers shape a rugged, interesting environment for scuba divers, and over time the elements have created long caves, dramatic overhangs and swim-throughs in this soft rock. Some caves penetrate the rock as much as 100 meters or more, and provide the ingredients for exciting dives—if they are well planned and carried out under the supervision of a professional dive operator. Indeed, in other dive areas the scenery is often incidental to the flora and fauna, but here you'll find that the underwater landscape, itself, is impressive.

Other types of environments include vertical walls that plunge from the surface to over 25 meters. On these walls grow a profusion of soft corals, large orange-colored fans, black coral and long, stringy sea whips. Several types of unusual coral trees grow in the waters surrounding Ko Phi Phi, including a distinctive white coral bush that looks like a frocked Christmas tree—covered with ornament-like growth in the form of oysters and colorful crinoids.

In many places, the islands are fringed with hard-coral gardens, home to a wide assortment of resplendent tropical creatures. Most of the coral is healthy, although in the more popular shallow areas coral damage has occurred due to unscrupulous boat operators dropping anchor. However, in most areas coral growth and fish life is plentiful and most, but not all of the same, fish species that live in the Similans can be found around Ko Phi Phi as well.

Ko Bida Nok

One of the most popular dive sites in the group is located at the

Right: A pair of clownfish are left without a home after the host anemone folds up into a tight purple ball. Phuket, Thailand. *Photo by Robert Yin.*

Below: Two different species—the dark-spotted moray and white-eyed moray—inhabit the same hole on a site in Thailand. *Photo by Robert Yin.*

southern tip of this tiny island. The dive normally begins in a shallow bay on the eastern side of the islet. Upon descending to about 10 meters of water, you'll find vast healthy growths of staghorn and star corals and incredible numbers of anemones and anemone fish. In fact this is one of the best places in Thailand to observe the aggressive little anemonefish *Amphiprion ephippium*, which is otherwise rare in Thailand. Watch carefully as they will make a harmless attempt to bite the unwary diver. Because of their aggressiveness, these fish are easier to photograph than their more common cousins, the clown anemonefish (*Amphiprion ocellaris*), since they are constantly trying to bite your camera.

Continuing south on your dive, you'll reach a vertical wall that is exhilarating to sail over, and continue your descent head-first. You'll come to sand at about 22 meters, but there is a gorgeous little bommie off the wall, ending at almost 27 meters, that is usually covered with thousands of glassfishes, large sea fans, as well as pink and purple soft corals.

Swimming west along the wall, the terrain becomes less vertical, and schools of blue-striped snappers seek safety in numbers along the rocky bottom. You'll meet the usual pairs of butterflyfishes and plenty of small tropicals in the shallower depths. Octopuses are repeatedly found here if you look carefully in the numerous nooks and crannies, and large green moray eels are almost surely spotted.

Towards the end of the dive, you'll find a small cavern in the rock that makes a sharp right-turn just past the entrance. This cavern is a great place to spend a few minutes of your safety stop since the light filtering through holes close to the surface creates lovely patterns on the sandy bottom.

Just be sure that you leave the shallow cavern with at least 30 bar in your tank to avoid a messy out-of-air situation, and that you stay near the entrance.

Getting About

The most common type of transportation available in the Phi Phi Islands remains the versatile long-tail boat. For hire practically everywhere, these taxis will take you—for a modest fee—to secluded beaches, the birds' nest caves and any other scenic areas around the islands.

Many dive operators use these boats for diving trips, and they are quite comfortable to dive from if you listen carefully to the pre-dive briefing. If nothing else, it is a cultural experience to spend the day watching your friendly Thai captain (who usually does not speak much English, nor does he normally know how to swim) ply the waters of Ko Phi Phi, expertly handling his long-tail boat.

— *John Williams*

Day trips and overnighters from Phi Phi and Phuket

Variable, 3–30 meters

Variable, often strong, good drift diving

Colorful soft corals, healthy hard corals

Coral gardens, limestone rock, walls

Excellent quantities and varieties

Leopard sharks, dramatic landscape above and below, caves, vertical walls, diveable year-round

Trang

Hin Daeng and Hin Muang: Two Jewels of the South

Located just south of the town of Krabi, Trang is the newest diving area to open up in southern Thailand. Although not as commercially developed as some of the other sites around the country—which makes it more difficult to get to—some of Trang's diving spots are decidedly world-class. Certainly, when conditions are right, the pinnacles of Hin Daeng and Hin Muang triumph over anything in the Similan Islands.

There are four principal places for diving in this area, located south of Ko Phi Phi. These are Ko Ha Yai, Ko Rok, Hin Daeng and several islands inshore from Ko Rok and just south of Ko Lanta.

Ko Ha

This is a small group of islands almost directly west of Ko Lanta. These tiny islands, separated by channels over 50 meters deep, jut straight out of the Andaman Sea. However, unlike Ko Phi Phi, the water here is quite clear and visibility frequently exceeds 25 meters. The diving highlight here is a series of caves, or caverns, on the largest of the islands, Ko Ha Yai. The

Day trips from Ko Lanta, but only by live-aboard to the best dive sites

Inshore, 5–10 meters; offshore, 20–40 meters

Variable, often strong

Healthy and colorful

Coral gardens, pinnacles, walls

Prolific big and small fish, sharks, rays

Deep drop-offs, lush marine life, stunning islands

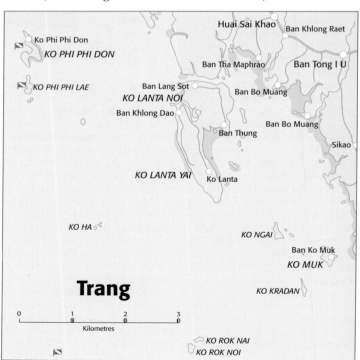

caverns are safe to enter, even without a light, as the entrances are large and there is only one way in and one way out. The best part of entering these caverns is that you can surface inside the island to view stalactites hanging down from the ceiling over 30 meters above the surface. The quality of light filtering through the water from the entrance is truly magical.

Moving inshore to the south of Ko Lanta, the water clarity begins to deteriorate, and the diving is quite shallow. There is one interesting place to explore here called the Emerald Cave, where at high tide divers can swim through a large cavern underwater to surface in a perfect little lagoon complete with its own white sand beach and splendid tropical jungle. Once inside, you are surrounded by tall cliffs, and the only way out is through the cavern. Therefore, an experienced dive guide is essential here for safe exploration.

Ko Rok

About 25 km south of Ko Ha, are two sister-islands separated by a narrow channel about 15 meters deep. These islands, Ko Rok Nok and Ko Rok Nai ("Outside and Inside") have some of the prettiest beaches in Thailand and are completely devoid of inhabitants. The islands are named for a small, furry mammal called *rok* in Thai, and this animal, along with monitor lizards, can be observed onshore— with just a little patience and a bit of luck.

The diving here is relatively shallow, with the best corals and fish life living above 18 meters. The bottom is composed of mostly hard corals, with small areas of soft corals at deeper depths. Blacktip sharks patrol the reef shallows and hawksbill turtles are sighted regularly. But the main reason for stopping in Ko Rok is that it is the perfect jumping-off point for trips out to Hin Daeng, and these twin islands make an ideal anchorage in all kinds of weather conditions.

The sole reason that diving has become popular in Trang are two pinnacles that lie approximately 25 km southwest of Ko Rok. Hin Daeng (Red Rock) and Hin Muang (Purple Rock) offer everything a

Above: A tiny lion-fish seeks shelter in the branches of a pink soft coral tree. Phuket, Thailand. *Photo by Robert Yin.*

diver could want, from dramatic walls and big fish action to lush tropical underwater gardens.

Hin Daeng

This pinnacle is easily found since it protrudes about 3 meters above the surface. Although not very impressive topside, underwater the rock is huge. The southern side descends—straight down—to over 60 meters, forming the most radical vertical drop in Thailand's seas. The wall is dotted with light growths of soft corals and a few sea fans, but is otherwise devoid of life. On the eastern side, where the slope is more gentle, two long ridges descend into the blueness and if the currents are favorable, it is possible to swim along these ridges down to 40 meters or more. Here the soft coral becomes more lush and tall, and huge schools of jacks sweep past the ridge, surrounding the diver with a shimmering wall of silver.

Ascending to the shallows we see needlefishes, or long toms, skip along the surface. Barracudas stalk their prey through the clear water. Swimming between the three large rocks that form the surface view of Hin Daeng, large schools of fusiliers dart to and fro as if they were afraid of the water surging through the channels.

Hin Muang

Located just a few hundred meters from Hin Daeng, this pinnacle lies completely submerged and its position remains somewhat of a secret. What surprised us the first time we explored the rock was the incredible amount of marine life that clung to the rock. It is as if the rock were located in another ocean and not just a short distance away from the relatively barren Hin Daeng. The name derives from the thick purple growth of soft corals that are everywhere. The rock itself is approximately 200 meters long and less

than 20 meters wide, and is shaped like an immense loaf of bread with steep, vertical sides and a rounded top. The walls are decorated with large sea fans in varying hues of red, white and orange. Clouds of glassfishes, or silver sides, school around the fans and rocky out-croppings. Carpets of anemones cover the more shallow sections of the pinnacle.

One July, the water was so transparent and the sea so smooth that I could see clearly, above me, the splash of someone throwing the dregs of their coffee overboard—with puffy white tropical clouds as a backdrop—from a depth of over 45 meters.

The whale shark is one animal that we see repeatedly around these pinnacles; we sighted these creatures on almost 70 percent of our trips last year. We've even given a name to one small 5-meter animal, since he is often present. Oscar doesn't seem to mind divers at all, and will swim right up to you— an impressive sight to behold. Oscar especially seems to like to make dramatic entrances with beginning divers around, and seems to know that this is an unnerving experience for most of them—nothing like a whale shark with a sense of humour.

On many occasions we have swum with gray reef sharks in the deep blue waters off Hin Daeng and Hin Muang. This is the only place in Thailand where I have seen more than 10 gray reef sharks together at one time. Gray reef sharks are full-bodied sharks, powerful and sleek, and they are often confused with blacktips because of their similar markings. However, unlike their cousins, these sharks are true pelagic animals, and swimming with them is a stirring, emotional experience. On one occasion, I managed to hover within 2 meters of a group of these sharks who ignored me in favor of a large school of jacks—apparently they were more mouth-watering than I was.

— John Williams

Opposite: The spotted pink lobster *(Enoplometopus debelius).* Photo by Gary Bell.

Ko Samui

Dive Courses and Idyllic Beaches

Below: Large strands of hard coral are often home to numerous small fishes and juveniles, like this undersized scorpionfish. Phuket, Thailand.
Photo by Robert Yin.

Ko Samui's allure to tourists began well over 20 years ago with the arrival of the traveler who came seeking a unique tropical paradise. Chasing idyllic places where locals were friendly and life was simple and cheap, they found Samui.

Today, surprisingly little has changed from those early days as the charm of Ko Samui—as well as the unhurried lifestyle—has remained largely intact. About the only noticeable changes today are the addition of an airport and the building of several top-class international resort hotels in a low rise, environmentally pleasing way.

Considering that most dive sites are situated at least 2 hours by boat from Ko Samui—and considering that the water clarity is not something the island is noted for—

scuba diving is surprisingly popular on the island. Remarkably, Ko Samui has developed into one of the main diver training centers in all Southeast Asia. Most instruction is completed in the shallow water directly off the coast at Chaweng Beach, Coral Cove or one of the other secluded little bays and beaches that make the island so lovely. Many diving centers will offer a couple of days on Ko Tao to finish up a diving course, but the waters around Samui are adequate for training.

For the advanced diver, Ko Samui has two main dive areas, each with an approximate 6-month opposite season. Hin Bai, or Sail Rock, located north of Samui and Phangan, is best from March until September. During the rest of the

year, the Ang Thong Marine National Park to the northwest is the choice spot. Both dive areas are interesting, and although most divers wouldn't take a dedicated dive holiday to Ko Samui, most divers will enjoy at least a few dives at both of these areas.

Hin Bai is the preferred day trip from Ko Samui since it offers the most exciting diving. The likelihood of seeing larger animals such as sharks is better here than in other areas. Similar in shape to the islands around Ko Phi Phi, Sail Rock juts out of the water and slopes beneath the surface, sometimes vertically, to just over 30 meters. You begin by exploring one of the deeper pinnacles away from the rock, which are covered in beautiful green trees of *Tubastraea micrantha*, and the bright yellow polyps of encrusting species of Dendrophylliid coral. Black coral trees with either lime green or reddish brown polyps also grow out of the crevices.

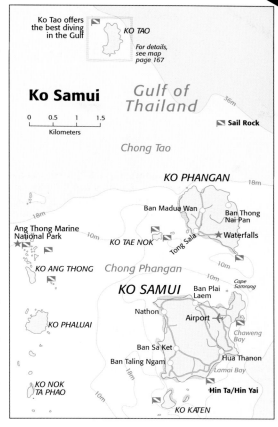

Up a Chimney

Towards the end of the dive, you'll be shown an underwater chimney located on the northwest side—the most impressive attribute of the dive. Two divers can enter at a depth of 19 meters where the cavern continues in for about 2 meters before bending towards the surface. At 12 meters you'll spot a hole that opens up laterally, guarded by a scorpionfish. Although a tight squeeze, it is possible to swim back into open water from here. Continuing up, the chimney opens at about 5 meters of water depth, and you'll exit the hole to find yourself surrounded by a magnificent carpet of anemones full of pink anemonefish.

People tell stories of shark sightings around Hin Bai. Although I haven't seen sharks myself, reliable sources say that some 15 animals, identified as bull sharks—an uncommon shark in Thai waters—have been spotted feeding from time to time at the surface. Along with the possibility of sighting a whale shark, this surely makes Hin Bai worth repeat diving.

The Ang Thong Marine National Park is a beautiful archipelago of over 40 islets, and operators offer trips to this area from December until March. While the visibility here is often poor, the snorkeling and shallow diving—as well as the striking top-side scenery—make an enjoyable outing. Ko Wao and Hin Yipoon (meaning "Japanese Rock") are the most popular areas for scuba diving and are noted for shallow caves and colorful soft corals.

Because of its laid-back charm, Samui combines many attractive factors with diving, making it a good place to sport dive or to further your dive education.
— *John Williams*

Full-day trips through dive centers; some shore diving

Variable, 2–15 meters

Variable, often strong

Fair, soft and hard

Coral gardens, rocks

Excellent variety and color

Black coral, bull sharks, occasional whale shark

Ko Tao

Lazy Lifestyle and Good Diving

The sleepy little islands of Ko Tao (Turtle Island) and Ko Nang Yuan, located approximately 65 km north of Ko Samui in the Gulf of Thailand, have exploded as a diving destination over the past few years. These days there are a number of backpacker-style bungalows, one or two upmarket resorts, and about 20 well-run dive centers offering scuba and snorkeling trips to the surrounding reefs and pinnacles.

An idyllic tropical paradise, Ko Tao seems to attract many divers looking for lengthy stays in Thailand—many backpackers travel to the island and end up spending months there. Some of the reasons for this are the relaxed pace of living, inexpensive accommodation, camaraderie between divers and dive centers, and of course interesting and relatively inexpensive scuba diving. All these combine to bring back visitors time and time again.

One of the best things about diving around these two small islands is the fact that the dive sites, unlike Phuket's and Samui's, are only minutes away. Including Ko Nang Yuan, which is only a short hop from Ko Tao, there are over 15 dives sites charted in the area. Sites range from deep water pinnacles to shallow coral gardens to rocky points complete with swim-throughs such as we found in the Similan Islands. Although water clarity can sometimes be limited, frequently the water becomes as transparent as the Andaman Sea, with visibility over 30 meters.

In Search of the Big Ones

One day a couple of years ago, I was visiting Ko Tao with a friend from the States. The day was perfect, the sea glassy and smooth, and the water crystalline, so we decided to take a dive or two. There had been much talk of whale sharks over beers the night before, since I had seen quite a

 Full-day and half-day trips through dive centers

 Variable, 3–40 meters

 Variable, often strong

 Good to average

 Coral gardens, boulders, pinnacles

 Good schools of pelagic fish, nice tropicals

Whale sharks, good soft corals. Expect the unexpected

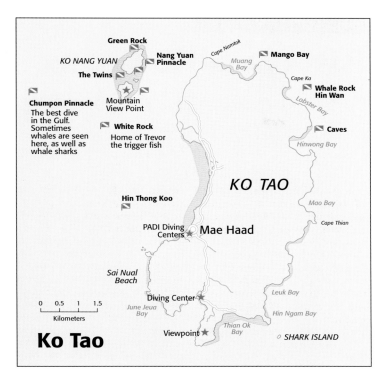

Green Rock

KO NANG YUAN
Nang Yuan
Pinnacle
Cape Namtok
Muang
Bay
Mango Bay

The Twins

Cape Ka

Chumpon Pinnacle
The best dive
in the Gulf.
Sometimes
whales are seen
here, as well as
whale sharks

Mountain
View Point

Whale Rock
Hin Wan
Lobster Bay

White Rock
Home of Trevor
the trigger fish

Caves
Hinwong Bay

KO TAO

Hin Thong Koo

Mao Bay

PADI Diving
Centers
Mae Haad

Cape Thian

Sai Nual
Beach

Leuk Bay

0   0.5   1   1.5
Kilometers

Diving Center

June Jeua
Bay

Hin Ngam Bay

Ko Tao

Viewpoint
Thian Ok
Bay
SHARK ISLAND

few on the Phuket side that year. Everyone had high hopes of today being the day that the big boys would be out to play. Well, the boys were out and then some.

As we pulled up to Chumpon Pinnacle, someone shouted "whale shark!" and sure enough, there she was next to the boat. While everyone jumped in with snorkeling gear, I hurriedly slapped on my tank so that I could follow her more easily. As the snorkelers crowded around her, she slowly moved off and only a videographer and I were able to follow. We spent the next 20 minutes swimming easily along with the shark before she swam off.

But that wasn't all. As I swam back to the boat to meet up with my buddy, a 4-meter-long sailfish (or possibly a swordfish) swam lazily below me almost the whole way back. He was a light tan colour and had a "sword" on him that extended over a meter in length.

Then, upon reaching my buddy and finally descending on the dive site proper, we descended through a spiraling school of large jacks numbering well over 1,000 individuals. We felt we were lost in some monstrous whirlpool of fish, and we were so mesmerized we completely lost sight of the rock—again.

Another long swim back to the boat with no air remaining. But it wasn't over. Some type of huge animal, surely over 12 meters, was swimming around the rock with a black back and a tiny black fin. We knew it couldn't be another whale shark with those markings, but only when we jumped in the water did we find out that two fin-back whales were frolicking with our group. Divers swam with these whales for over 1 hour. This was definitely a dive of a lifetime—even though we never found the dive site.

It is a longish trip to Ko Tao, but as it offers the best diving in the Gulf of Thailand, combined with the pleasantries of a sybaritic shore life, it is well worth a visit. You may not see whale sharks or swordfish on every dive, but you'll certainly be more than charmed by the local inhabitants of the reefs.

— *John Williams*

Opposite: The sleepy little island of Ko Tao is fast becoming a popular dive destination. *Photo by Ashley Boyd.*

Pattaya & Ko Chang

Fun Resort with Some Interesting Diving Options

Pattaya, Thailand's first resort built for foreign tourists, became infamous as an "R&R" destination for American soldiers during the Vietnam War. The first dive shop opened for business during this time and as a result, many servicemen and their visiting families became some of the first foreigners to scuba dive recreationally in Thailand. Today, huge high-rise hotels follow the curve of the bay and Pattaya, while still popular with international visitors, has become more attractive as a weekend getaway for residents of Bangkok.

Although Pattaya is far more densely populated than other tourist areas in Thailand, it remains popular as this city beside the sea is bustling and energetic. Even

though Pattaya has received considerable negative press, it has a certain character that people return for. Pattaya is definitely an active resort and diving enthusiasts will find plenty of different dive sites and courses to keep them busy.

Since Thailand's recreational diving industry was born in Pattaya, dive centers there have set valuable examples to other more recently opened diving businesses in other parts of Southeast Asia. Their main activities are teaching introductory courses and open-water certification courses to new divers. In addition, they specialize in advanced training programs for divers, offering scheduling that is especially suited to residents working in Bangkok—both foreign and Thai.

Below: Highrise hotels line the curve of Pattaya's bay. *Photo by Ingo Jezierski.*

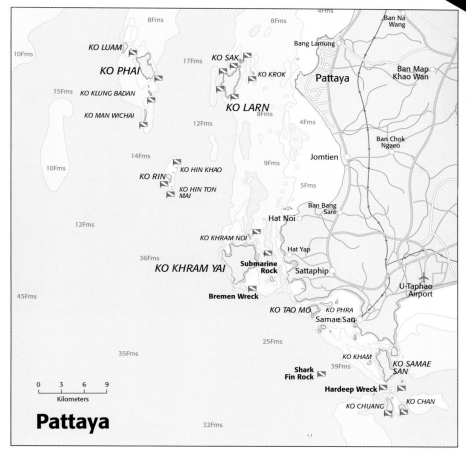

Pattaya

8Fms
8Fms
4Fms
Ban Na Wang
10Fms
KO LUAM
Bang Lamung
17Fms
KO SAK
Ban Map Khao Wan
KO PHAI
KO KROK
Pattaya
15Fms
KO KLUNG BADAN
KO LARN
8Fms
KO MAN WICHAI
12Fms
4Fms
Ban Chok Ngaeo
14Fms
Jomtien
10Fms
9Fms
KO RIN
KO HIN KHAO
KO HIN TON MAI
5Fms
12Fms
Ban Bang Sare
Hat Noi
KO KHRAM NOI
Hat Yap
36Fms
Submarine Rock
KO KHRAM YAI
Sattahip
U-Taphao Airport
45Fms
Bremen Wreck
KO TAO MO
KO PHRA
Samae San
25Fms
35Fms
KO KHAM
KO SAMAE SAN
Shark Fin Rock
39Fms
0 3 6 9
Hardeep Wreck
Kilometers
KO CHUANG
KO CHAN
Pattaya
32Fms

All dive centers in Pattaya conduct one-day diving trips, and some are now starting to delve into the live-aboard scene, offering longer trips to Ko Chang near the Thai-Cambodian border.

One problem that has frustrated dive operators is the lack of clear environmental policy. Combined with a solid population growth over the past 10 years, this has caused many dive sites to deteriorate. To side-step this, operators have been forced to go further afield.

Visitors to the area will soon discover that some of the best wreck diving in Thailand is found here. Although there are several wrecks around, the three best sites in the area are the *Hardeep,* the *Bremen* and the Vertical Wreck.

The *Hardeep* is considered to be one of the best wreck dives and

stores offer one-day and two-day trips to the site. Located between Ko Samaesan and Ko Chuang, the *Hardeep* is a 42-m-long freighter that sank in 1942 and now rests on her side in 21 to 27 meters of water. As with all wrecks, one of the main reasons people dive on it is because of certain eerie emotions they experience when the ship first becomes visible through the gloom. This aside, the best reason for diving on sunken ships is that they are a magnet for incredible amounts of marine life.

Today, the wreck is still and tranquil—except for the masses of tropical fish who have made this disaster their home. It is also home to colonies of fan corals and large barrel sponges. Although visibility is not dependably clear here—averaging about the same as in the rest

Full-day trips through dive centers; live-aboards

Variable, 2–25 meters

Variable, often strong, especially on wrecks

Good in some places

Coral gardens, rock, boulders

Not bad, some unusual animals

Wreck diving

of the Gulf—the prolific marine life and the possibility of a safe penetration into the wreck makes the dive one of the most inviting in the whole area.

The second popular wreck is the *Bremen,* located near the village of Sattahip, south of both Pattaya and Jomtien. Although the profile of this 100-m steel ship is weakening each year due to gradual deterioration, the wreck attracts large schools of yellowtail snappers and barracudas during slack tide. An excellent deep dive for an advanced course, the wreck rests at a depth of about 25 meters and visibility ranges from around 7 to 10 meters.

The Vertical Wreck is, no doubt, the best wreck dive in Thailand. This freighter, when it was sunk, was still full of gas and the stainless steel tanks, located on the bow, still hold gas to this day making the bow buoyant. Thus, when the ship sank, the stern sunk to 60 meters and the bow remained just below the surface. This is why it's called the Vertical Wreck.

The problem with the wreck is the distance to it from port. Most trips leave from Sattahip for an overnight journey out to the wreck.

The problem lies in the fact that there is no protection once you arrive, so if the weather is rough, you must jump in and do your dive, if you can, and then suffer through a long journey back! However, if the weather is fine, then you're lucky and will have yourself a great day or two of diving.

Besides being unusual in that the wreck is vertical, the other unusual thing about the wreck is the extreme water clarity, especially for the Gulf. Visibility can reach over 60 meters on a good day. The ship, like most wrecks, attracts huge schools of baitfish, not to mention crustaceans and reef fish. The ship cannot really be penetrated, though the super structure is intact and very interesting.

Due to the depth of the wreck, Pattaya dive shops have started offering Tech Diving, including Trimix and deep air courses. This makes Pattaya one of the only places in Thailand that can offer such courses and have the diving to back them up.

For those divers interested in more than ship wrecks, coral diving in Pattaya can be satisfying as well. Often dive centers will offer a coral dive during their trip to the *Hardeep,* as Ko Chuang and Ko Samaesan have healthy coral down to as deep as 30 meters. Although larger animals such as sharks and rays are occasionally seen, the big attractions here are the abundance of corals, both soft and hard, and beautiful colorful anemones.

The island of Ko Rin probably offers Pattaya's best diving. The underwater profile is more interesting here compared with other places, and water clarity can be excellent, sometimes exceeding 25 meters. Rocky canyons form swim-throughs which are not only wonderful for divers but create currents to wash around the rocks, causing great environmental conditions for the vast array of marine life that lives here. Although the day can be long due to the distances involved in getting to different sites in the area, those looking for clearer water will find the longer traveling times more than worthwhile.

South to Ko Chang

Recently there has been much discussion of the diving possibilities at Ko Chang. Also, the government has just started a campaign to turn Ko Chang into a second Phuket. Greedy hands are rubbing together, and there is talk of making the island a more expensive resort, effectively getting rid of backpackers and other "undesirables". Whether this happens or not— since the eyes of the government are on Ko Chang, there are bound to be changes.

Some people claim that the diving in Ko Chang is at least as good as in the Similan Islands. However, the area suffers from very inconsistent visibility and the dive sites lie very far apart. So, instead of making a comparison between the Similans and Ko Chang, a more reasonable comparison would be with Ko Tao. With its low-rise buildings, large forested areas, and lack of bars and the other undesirable features of Phuket, Ko Chang could

well turn into another hugely popular place for diver certification courses and for good diving excursions afterwards.

The area itself is rich in history and culture as it is located almost right on the border with Cambodia. With the political turmoil in Cambodia, very little tourist development has occurred here. The hilly, jungle-covered islands are striking in their beauty, and many of the beaches rival those of our southern islands. The potential for tourist development is good.

What excites the diving operators who express their opinions about diving around Ko Chang are the underwater pinnacles located offshore of Ko Chang and Ko Raet, underwater topography that hosts and attracts a wealth of flora and fauna. The best diving in both the Andaman Sea and the Gulf of Thailand are the pinnacles because of the rich conditions found there. No only will bigger animals such as sharks and rays be more common, but the coral and fish life on these pinnacles are far denser. When the Ko Chang area gets the boats capable of making long journeys, or start live-aboard operations, then the area will most likely turn into a very popular diving destination.

The best diving spots in both the Andaman Sea and the Gulf of Thailand are on pinnacles because of the rich conditions there, which create healthy environments for marine life. Once Pattaya's dive operators begin conducting regular live-aboard trips to the area, we will all be hearing much more about this destination.

As with the island of Ko Samui, to the south, Pattaya is probably not the place for a dedicated diving holiday. But for those divers looking for an active sporting life—or a busy nightlife—as well as diving, Pattaya could be the answer. For the student of scuba, Pattaya offers many opportunities on all levels. For a week or a weekend, Pattaya has the potential to keep even the most active diver happy.

— John Williams

PERIPLUS TRAVELMAPS
The first choice of experienced travellers in Asia!

ASIA'S #1 SELLING MAPS

AUSTRALIA, NEW ZEALAND MAPS

Australia	ISBN 962-593-641-6
Brisbane	ISBN 962-593-049-3
Cairns	ISBN 962-593-048-5
Darwin	ISBN 962-593-089-2
Melbourne	ISBN 962-593-050-7
Perth	ISBN 962-593-088-4
Sydney	ISBN 962-593-640-8
New Zealand	ISBN 962-593-092-2
Auckland	ISBN 962-593-130-9

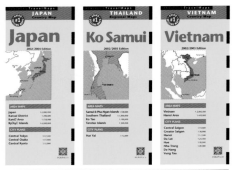

CAMBODIA, LAOS, MYANMAR, THAILAND, VIETNAM MAPS

Cambodia	ISBN 962-593-794-3
Laos	ISBN 962-593-069-8
Myanmar (Burma)	ISBN 962-593-070-1
Thailand	ISBN 0-7946-0014-X
Bangkok	ISBN 0-7946-0015-8
Chiang Mai	ISBN 0-7946-0016-6
Ko Samui	ISBN 962-593-993-8
Phuket	ISBN 962-593-575-4
Vietnam	ISBN 0-7946-0070-0

CHINA MAPS

China	ISBN 962-8734-02-4
Beijing	ISBN 962-8734-03-2
Hong Kong	ISBN 962-593-571-1
Shanghai	ISBN 962-8734-04-0
Taiwan	ISBN 962-593-090-6
Taipei	ISBN 962-593-132-5

INDIA, NEPAL, SRI LANKA MAPS

India	ISBN 962-593-047-7
Nepal	ISBN 962-593-062-0
Kathmandu	ISBN 962-593-063-9
Sri Lanka	ISBN 962-593-112-0

INDONESIA MAPS

Indonesia	ISBN 962-593-042-6
Bali	ISBN 0-945971-49-4
Bandung	ISBN 0-945971-43-5
Batam	ISBN 0-7946-0024-7
Bintan	ISBN 0-7946-0068-9
Jakarta	ISBN 962-593-980-6
Java	ISBN 0-7946-0025-5
Java & Bali	ISBN 0-7946-0007-7
Lombok	ISBN 962-593-639-4
Sulawesi	ISBN 962-593-734-X
Sumatra	ISBN 962-593-735-8
Surabaya	ISBN 0-945971-48-6
Yogyakarta	ISBN 0-945971-42-7

JAPAN MAPS

Japan	ISBN 0-7946-0069-7
Kyoto	ISBN 962-593-143-0
Osaka	ISBN 962-593-110-4
Tokyo	ISBN 962-593-109-0

MALAYSIA, SINGAPORE MAPS

Malaysia	ISBN 0-7946-0026-3
Johor & Melaka	ISBN 0-7946-0027-1
Kuala Lumpur	ISBN 0-7946-0020-4
Penang & Langkawi	ISBN 0-7946-0029-8
Sabah	ISBN 0-7946-0030-1
Sarawak	ISBN 962-593-780-3
West Malaysia	ISBN 962-593-778-1
Singapore	ISBN 962-593-994-6

PHILIPPINES MAPS

Philippines	ISBN 962-593-113-9
Manila	ISBN 962-593-124-4

Periplus Travel Maps are available at bookshops around the world.
Any inquiries/orders, please write to:
Periplus Publishing Group
130 Joo Seng Road #06-01/03 Singapore 368357
tel: (65) 6280 1330 fax: (65) 6280 6290 email: inquiries@periplus.com.sg

Other titles from
Periplus Editions

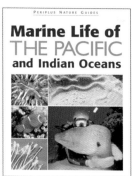

**Marine Life of the
Pacific and Indian Oceans**
ISBN 962 593 948 2
US$16.95

This handy reference guide showcases 350 of the most colorful and commonly encountered species in the region. Features photos from many of the world's best underwater photographers.

Tropical Reef Fishes
ISBN 962 593 152 X
US$9.95

Tropical Marine Life
ISBN 962 593 157 0
US$9.95

Written by leading authority Dr Gerald Allen, these two handy field guides are essential for snorkelers and divers alike.

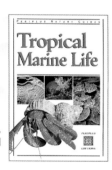

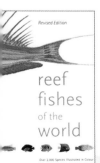

Reef Fishes of the World
ISBN 962 593 960 1
US$19.95

This comprehensive book identifies the world's reef fishes, with notes on habitats and key identification points.

If you cannot find these books where you live,
please write to us for the name of a distributor closest to you:

Periplus Publishing Group
130 Joo Seng Road #06-01/03 Singapore 368357 tel: (65) 6280 1330 fax: (65) 6280 6290
email: inquiries@periplus.com.sg

Contents

The following sections provide background information about traveling in the various countries, including transportation options, visa regulations, health and emergency services, and information about accommodations and food. A special emphasis has been placed on dive operators and diving services.

INDONESIA

MALAYSIA

Regarding enforcement, NSWA's active participation in the development of an entrance fee system for Bunaken National Park has now insured sustainable financing for an effective patrol system to curb illegal and destructive practices such as blast and cyanide fishing techniques. The Association also instituted a voluntary but strict ban on all anchoring within Bunaken National Park and has brought in internal regulations to prevent degradation of dive sites by tourism activities.

Dive operators (NSWA members)

Blue Banter, Jl Piere Tendean, Manado 95111, Tel: +(62-431) 851-126, 851-174, Fax: +(62-431) 862-135 , b_banter@manado.wasantara.net.id, Contact person: Bruce Moore, www.bluebanter-manado.com

Bunaken Divers, Pantai Pangalisang, Bunaken Island, Tel: +(62-431) 859-379, info@bunakendivers.com, Contact person: Thomas Korompis, www.bunakendivers.com

Bunaken Chacha Dive Lodge, Tanjung Parigi, Bunaken Island, PO Box 1316, Manado, 95010, Tel: +(62-812) 430-1672, cha2@indosat.net.id, Contact person: Raphael and Reiko Downey, www.bunakenchacha.com

Celebes Divers, Jl Raya Trans Sulawesi, Kalassey, Tel: +(62-431) 826-582, +(62-811) 437-416, Fax: +(62-431) 826-581, celebes@kudalaut.com, Contact person: Paola Bearzi, Massimo Boyer, www.kudalaut.com

Eco-Divers, Tasik Ria Resort, Jl Raya Trans Sulawesi, Tasik Ria, Manado 95351, Tel: +(62-431) 824-445, Fax: +(62-431) 823-444, info@eco-divers.com, Contact person: Jim and Cary Yanny, Kim Hessel, www.eco-divers.com

Froggies Divers, Pantai Liang, Bunaken Island, PO Box 1520 Manado 95015, Tel: +(62-812) 430-1356/1464, manado@divefroggies.com, Contact person: Christiane Muller and Tommie Massie, www.divefroggies.com

Lumba Lumba Diving, PO Box 1721, Manado 95017, Tel: +(62-431) 826-151, Fax: +(62-431) 826-512, lumbalumba@manado.wasantara.net.id, Contact person: Juud and Roel Jong-Dikkers

Murex Dive Resort & Live-Aboard, Jl Raya Trans Sulawesi, Kalassey, Manado, Tel: +(431-62) 868-513, 826091 Fax: (62-431) 826-092, 846287, info@murexdive.com, Contact person: Angelique Batuna, Danny Charlton, www.murexdive.com

Sulawesi Dive Quest, Liang Beach, Bunaken, PO Box 1030, Manado, Tel: +(62-431) 814-235, 813-771, info@sulawesi-dive.co.id, Contact person: Frans, www.sulawesi-dive-quest.com

Thalassa Dive Center, Desa Tongkaina, Kecematan Bunaken, Manado 95016, Tel: + (62-431) 850-230, Fax: +(62-431) 850-231, info@thalassa.net, Contact person: Simone Gerritsen, Mara Segrada, www.thalassa.net

Two Fish Divers, Pantai Pangalisang, Pulau Bunaken, Tel: +(62-811) 432-805, twofish@indosat.net.id, Contact person: Nigel Thomas, Tina Melson, www.twofishdivers.com

Dive operators (non-NSWA)

Barracuda Dive Resort, Molas, Manado, Tel: +(62-431) 854-288, 854-279, 862-033, baracuda@manado.wasantara.net.id, Contact person: Michael Smith, Bpk Richmond, www.dive-barracuda.com

Kungkungan Bay Resort, Jl Tandu Rusa, Bitung, PO Box 16, Bitung 95500, Tel: +(62-438) 30-300, Fax: +(62-438) 31-400, kbresort@manado.wasantara.net.id, Contact person: Mark Ecenbarger, www.kungkungan.com. KBR is a five-star resort in every sense of the word. A labor of love for the Ecenbarger family, this small retreat offers the best of all worlds—excellent diving staffed by perhaps the best critter spotters in the world; sumptuous spreads at breakfast, lunch and dinner; and a well-trained staff that caters to every need. It is pricey, and often booked full, but a vacation at KBR is not one soon to be forgotten.

Minihasa Prima Resort, Jl Raya Trans Sulawesi, Tasik Ria, Manado 95351, Tel: +(62-431) 826-407, 826-551, Fax: +(62-431) 826-406, mpresort@mdo.mega.net.id, Contact person: Oliver Chan

Nusantara Dive Center (NDC), Molas Beach, PO Box 1015, Tel: +(62-431) 863-998, 863-992, Fax: +(62-431) 860-368, ndc@manado.wasantara.net.id, Contact person: Katiman Herlambang, www.ndc-manado.com

TO THE NORTH

Currently there are no resorts in the north and only live-aboards can reach the great diving there. A few operators do visit the Sangihe Talaud Islands by charter but only one operates trips there regularly. Murex, which also has a resort in Manado, departs on the *Serenade* or the *Symphony* every Saturday.

Murex Dive Resort & Live-Aboard, Jl Raya Trans Sulawesi, Kalassey, Manado, Tel: +(431-62) 868-513, 826091 Fax: (62-431) 826-092, 846287, info@murexdive.com, Contact person: Angelique Batuna, Danny Charlton, www.murexdive.com

CENTRAL AND SOUTH SULAWESI

To reach the Togians and Banggai Islands, it is best to go by live-aboard—Murex operates on a charter basis. There are a few resorts that operate in the Togians, but communication is irregular at best.

Marlin Dive Centre (South Sulawesi), Tel: +(62-411) 858-762, Fax: +(62-411) 831-003, jansoon@indosat.net.id, www.arinidiving.com

KLM Felidae, info@divetastic.com, www.divetastic.com

Murex Dive Resort & Live-Aboard, Jl Raya Trans Sulawesi, Kalassey, Manado, Tel: +(431-62) 868-513, 826091 Fax: (62-431) 826-092, 846287, info@murexdive.com, Contact person: Angelique Batuna, Danny Charlton, www.murexdive.com

Wakatobi Resort, Tel: +(62-361) 284-227, +(62-81) 2380-9491, Fax: +(62-361) 284-226, office@wakatobi.com, www.wakatobi.com. The resort operates its own charter flight, which leaves from Bali to arrive at the privately built and operated airstrip. The flights, which last three hours, leave for the resort at 8 am and return at 3 pm.

Walea Dive Resort (Togian Islands), Tel: +(62-873) 761-966-490, Fax: +(62-873) 761-966-491, www.walea.com

Java

Jakarta, with its estimated 12 million people, is the center of Indonesia's government and commerce, as well as being the hub for diving west Java and Pulau Seribu. There are several dive operators in the city to choose from. While these diving centers primarily provide scuba diving instruction, they also organize regularly scheduled weekend trips.

Bubbles Divers, Tel: +(62-21) 7581-16221, 7581-6233, Fax: +(62-21) 7581-6221, info@bubblesdivers.com, www.bubblesdivers.com

Divemasters Indonesia, Tel: +(62-21) 570-3600 ext. 9037, Fax: +(62-21) 719-8974, 420-4842, divers@aquasport.co.id

Dive Indonesia, Tel: + (62-21) 570-6878, Fax: +(62-21) 719-4168

Kristal Klear Dive, Tel: +(62-21) 7581-8025, kkdtour@indosat.net.id, www.kristalkleardive.com

Ocean Divers, Tel: +(62-21) 525-1991, Fax: +(62-21) 520-3227

Kura Kura Resort, Tel: +(291) 595-931, 595-932, kurakura@idola.net.id, www.kurakuraresort.com. The resort operates a charter flight from Jakarta or Surabaya, which drops guests at a nearby island only minutes away. Alternatively, travelers can fly into Surabaya or Jakarta and catch a connecting flight to Semarang, where all that waits is a three-hour speedboat ride to the island.

Bali

To make someone jealous, tell him you're going to Bali. The word itself will conjure up an intoxicating vision of a tropical paradise.

The waters off Bali are very rich; and while the diving is not as immediately impressive as that in Eastern Indonesia, it is very good, and gets more interesting the more you dive. Bali's combination of beautiful surroundings, convenient diving, tourist services and interesting culture is hard to beat.

Getting there

The best way to arrive in Bali is at the Ngurah Rai International Airport which, despite its often being referred to as "Denpasar" is actually on the isthmus connecting the Bukit Badung peninsula to Bali, much nearer to Kuta Beach than to Bali's capital city. Daily Garuda flights from

Jakarta, Yogyakarta, and many other Indonesian cities connect to Ngurah Rai, and a growing number of international flights — including those from Australia, Hong Kong, Japan, the Netherlands and Singapore—land there as well. Flights from the Soekarno-Hatta International Airport in Jakarta are frequent, and if you land in Jakarta before 5 pm you can usually get a connection to Bali, although in peak season these 90-min flights are almost always full.

International airlines

Many international airlines have offices in the Grand Bali Beach Hotel in Sanur, Tel: +(62-361) 288-511. Hours are Monday to Friday, 8:30 am to 4:30 pm, and Sat 8:30 am to 1 pm. Their direct lines, all +(361) area code, are:

Air France 288-511
Ansett Australia 289-636
Cathay Pacific 286-001
Continental Micronesia Tel: 287-774
Japan Airlines (and **Japan Asia Airways**) 287-577
Lufthansa 287-069
Malaysia Airlines 285-071
Northwest Airlines 287-841
Qantas 288-331
Singapore Airlines 288-511
Thai Airways International 288-141

Several other airlines have offices in the Wisti Sabha Building at the Ngurah Rai Airport:

Air New Zealand 756-170 and 751-011, ext. 1116
China Airlines 754-856 and 757-298
EVA Air 298-935
KLM-Royal Dutch Airlines 756-127
Korean Air 289-402
Royal Brunei 757-292

Getting around

Airport taxis One-way fares from Ngurah Rai Airport to the tourist centers are fixed. You pay a cashier inside and receive a coupon, which you surrender to your driver. (There will be touts and freelancers offering their services but these are never a better deal.) Fares range from $2 to nearby Kuta Beach to $10 to Ubud, far inland.

Minibuses All hotels have minibuses for hire with a driver or an English-speaking driver/guide. Rates run $3 to $5/hr, with a 2-hr minimum. Day rates run $30 to $40, more for an air-conditioned vehicle.

Bemos Public minibuses in Bali are called "*bemos*," a compression of *becak* (bicycle-like pedicabs) and mobile. This is the way the Balinese travel and is the cheapest way to get around the island. Fares are very inexpensive and you could probably get all the way across the island for less than $2, but you will need to know some Indonesian or be very good at charades to make sense of the routes and drop-off points.

For a diving visitor to Bali, *bemos* are most useful for short day trips around the area or to hop locally around town. Get one of your diving guides or someone at the hotel to explain the ins and outs of the local routes.

Vehicle rental It is best to leave the driving in Bali to someone who knows how to negotiate the roads and traffic. The roads are narrow, twisting, and full of hazards: unmarked construction sites, chickens, dogs, children, Vespas as wide as cars due to huge baskets of produce, and tough, unflinching truck drivers, to name just a few. You can rent a small (150cc) motorcycle for $7/day if you have an international motorcycle driver's license, but you better know how to ride.

Renting a car—particularly since you will be carrying diving gear—is a more practical solution. These run $15/day for little Suzuki jeeps; more for larger, more comfortable Toyota Kijangs. Rent through an agency (even Avis has outlets) or from numerous local rental companies. Ask at your hotel or comb the streets where there's an agent on nearly every block. Be sure your rental includes insurance for loss and damage.

Photography

The biggest range of photographic equipment and supplies can be found in Denpasar at Tati Photo, Jl Sumatra 72, Tel: +(62-361) 226-912, and Prima Photo, Jl Gajah Mada 14, Tel: +(62-361) 222-505.

The best E6 processing in Bali is at Bali Fotografi in Kuta. They offer color and black and white print developing and processing, film sales, and camera cleaning and repair. Bali Fotografi Jl Raya Kuta 57X, P.O. Box 2088, Kuta 80361. Tel: +(62-361) 751-329, Fax: +(62-361) 755-827.

INDONESIA

Dive operators

Bali has at least 80 dive operators, some excellent, some okay, and some frightening. Those listed below have a good reputation. Still, there is considerable variation even among these operators, and if possible you should always meet with them first.

Most operators on the island keep their main offices in the South, in the tourist triangle—Kuta, Nusa Dua, and Sanur. Some of these maintain branches, with tanks and compressors, in the Northwest or Lovina or at Candi Dasa on the East Coast, and there are local operators clustered around the good sites, such as Tulamben. The bigger outfits maintain desks at the major hotels, or at least keep brochures at the desk.

Bali is not very big, and you could dive any site on a day trip starting from a hotel or *losmen* anywhere in the South. We don't recommend this, however, as you probably will spend half of your vacation cooped up in the back of a van or minibus, as your driver fights his way through an unending stream of local traffic.

If this is your first trip to Bali for diving, you should plan to stay at Tulamben for at least a couple of days. This is the most popular purely diving area, and from here you can run across to Menjangan on a day trip without too much trouble (it is a pleasant drive along the relatively empty north coast road; there is nothing pleasant about the drive from the south) or, going the other way, run down to Padangbai to dive the East Coast or Nusa Penida.

If you are a serious diver, and you have the time, a "dive safari" is highly recommended—this involves staying a few days at Pemuteran or Banyuwedang (on the north coast), diving Menjangan; then a few days at Tulamben, diving that area; then a few days at Candi Dasa or Padangbai, diving the east coast; and finally a few days in the south, diving Nusa Penida (or stay on and dive Penida from Candi Dasa or Padangbai). This will give you a taste of the island's different diving areas, and also its different towns and environments, with the minimum amount of driving.

Any of the bigger dive operators will book you a package that includes any combination of the sites. These days, you can even do most of this ahead of time through the web and e-mail.

Courses

Like everywhere else in the world, and for the same business and marketing reasons, most of the operators in Bali are or have become PADI franchises, some of them having earned stars and golden palms and other merit badges. The bigger operators offer basic and advanced certification and other resort courses, averaging $300 to $400 for open water certification.

Bali is not a bad place at all to learn to dive, and Tulamben is probably the best area for this. If you decide to do this, we recommend that you make your decision on who to take a course from based on the knowledge, attitude, and experience of the person who will be teaching you, period.

Prices

The cost of diving in Bali is pretty standard among operators, and is almost always priced in dollars. A basic day's package, including two full tanks, weights, transportation, and a guide, runs $40 to $60 for a shore dive (e.g. Pemuteran, Tulamben), $65 to $90 for a dive that requires a boat ride (e.g. Menjangan, Tepekong), and $80 to $120 for a dive that requires a long boat ride (e.g. the far side of Nusa Penida, Gili Selang).

THE NORTHWEST (INCLUDING SECRET BAY AND MENJANGAN)

This is the furthest area from the airport and the resorts of the South. Although most of Bali's operators offer Menjangan packages, unless you want to spend half of your day on the road, you are better off staying at one of the resorts in the area. The cluster of resorts in Pemuteran offer the most variety, but the upmarket Mimpi Resort is a good option. There is a single operator at Gilimanuk, which specializes in that site. There is diving at the little resort beach of Lovina, on the North Coast about 25 km west of Singaraja, but it is not exceptional. However, if you are on a very tight budget, diving Menjangan out of Lovina might still be the best option.

Archipelago Dive Sarana, Tel: +(62-362) 92-623, Fax: +(62-362) 93-264, tamanri@indosat.net.id, baliwww.com/arkipelago

Mimpi Resort and Dive Center Menjangan, Tel: +(62-82) 836-2729, Fax: +(62-82)

836-2728, menjangan@mimpi.com, www.
mimpi.com; Main office, Tel: +(62-361) 701-
070, Fax: +(62-361) 701-074, sales@mimpi.
com.

Pondok Sari Desa Pemuteran, Tel/Fax:
+(62-362) 92-337

Reef Seen Aquatics Dive Center, Tel/Fax:
+(62-362) 92-339, reefseen@denpasar.was-
antara.net.id

Secret Bay Dive Center and Resort, Tel:
+(62-365) 61-037, Fax: +(62-365) 61-320, dive-
dive@indo.net.id. The resort, set up by Dive
and Dive's (see below under Sanur), is a
refurbished *losmen* just in back of the ferry
terminal. It is well designed for divers,
particularly underwater photographers, with
camera cleaning tables, washbasins, and
charging facilities. It faces the quiet bay.

Spice Dive, Tel: +(62-362) 41-305, 41-509, Fax:
+(62-362) 41-171, spicedive@singaraja.was-
antara.net.id, www.damai.com/spicedive

Taman Sari Bali Cottages, Tel/Fax: +(62-
362) 93-264, Tel/Fax: +(62-361) 286-879,
tamanri@indosat.net.id, www.com/tamansari

Taman Selwi Wahana, Tel/Fax: +(62-362)
93-449, taslina@dps.mega.net.id

YOS Marine Adventures, Tel: +(62-361) 775-
438, 775-440, 752-005; Fax: +(62-361) 752-985,
yosbali@indosat.net.id, www.yosdive.com

TULAMBEN AND AMED

Most divers travel to Tulamben on a package tour from Kuta, Sanur, Nusa Dua, or
Candi Dasa, but independent-minded divers
can make their way by rented car or, if not
carrying gear, motorcycle. It's about 4 hrs
from Kuta or Nusa Dua, 30 minutes less from
Sanur. The traffic through Candi Dasa will
likely be heavy, but the last hour of the trip
—from Candi Dasa onward—is very scenic.
　　Operators in Tulamben offer tanks,
weights, and equipment rental, along with
guides for independent divers who arrive on
their own, and we highly recommend staying in Tulamben if you want to dive here
or in Jemeluk.

Dive Paradise Tulamben, Tel: +(62-363) 22-
913, 41-052, Fax: +(62-363) 41-981. The Paradise, associated with the resort of the same
name, is the orginal Tulamben operator, and
still a good one. It may no longer be the only
operation in town, but for many divers who
have been coming over the years, the
Paradise remains a sentimental favorite. The
prices are also a bargain.

Ena Dive Center and Water Sports runs
the small Saya Resort, Tel: +(62-361) 288-829,
281751, Fax: +(62-361) 287-945, enadive@den-
pasar.wasantara.net.id, enadive.wasantara.
net.id, www.enadive.wasantara.net.id

**Mimpi Resort and Dive Center Tulam-
ben**, Tel: +(62-363) 21-642, Fax: +(62-363) 21-
642, tulamben@mimpi.com, www.mimpi.com.
This is definitely the high end of the Tulam-
ben accommodations, and like the other
Mimpi resorts, very tasteful and comfortable.
It has a pool, though it is always freezing cold.
The restaurant, on a deck facing the water,
has the best food in the area, but this isn't
saying much. Compared to the others, the
Mimpi has a more refined, suit-and-tie feel.
Stay here if you can afford it.

Tauch Terminal Bali, Tel: +(62-361) 730-200,
Fax: +(62-361) 730-201, tauchtermi@den-
pasar.wasantara.net.id, www.tauch-termi-
nal.com. Clean, basic air-conditioned rooms
are offered. Has a training pool and classroom.

　　There are a few *losmen* near Amed and
further south along the coastal road. Some
of these offer snorkeling, and have offered
diving, but cannot be recommended at this
time. To dive Amed, you are still best off coming in with your operator by car with tanks
and equipment from Tulamben, and hiring
a *jukung* from Jemeluk Bay to take you out.

Candi Dasa and Padangbai

It is not too inconvenient to dive the East Coast
sites from the South, nor in fact is it difficult
to dive them from Tulamben (the drive is
more pleasant). But if you are serious about
this area, it is best to stay in either Candi Dasa
or Padangbai. These sites are very dependent
on conditions, and it's nice to be able to look
out at the actual water you are going to be
diving in the mornings and evenings, to get
a feel for what you are up against.
　　Candi Dasa itself is quiet and less crowded
when compared to Kuta and Sanur to the

south, but it is a veritable New York City compared to Tulamben. It has at least 50 hotels, *losmen* and homestays, and plenty of restaurants. Because the fringing reef here was "mined" for construction material, Candi Dasa's beautiful beach is now history. Ugly groins have been built to stop the erosion, but it seems unclear if they are helping.

Geko Dive, Tel: +(62-363) 41-516, Fax: +(62-363) 41-790, gekodive@indosat.net.id, www.gekodive.com. No one in this operation has lost his wonder for the underwater world, or for Bali. They have started a plastics program to help clean up the area, and when the rupiah crashed, established a medical fund to cover health care costs for the Padangbai community. Their boats are fast and slick, their captain is skilled, and their prices are good.

Spice Dive, Tel: +(62-363) 41-725, Fax: +(62-363) 41-171, spicedive@singaraja.wasantara.net.id, www.damai.com/spicedive/

Padangbai is a quiet and somewhat odd little town. The local Balinese community seems very tight, and still curious about the ways of foreigners, as if this isn't a tourist town at all. Yet this is the terminus of the Bali-Lombok ferry, and a constant stream of backpacking tourists passes through.

Nusa Penida
(see The South)

There are no operators on Nusa Penida itself, and the best way to dive it is from Padangbai or the South: Sanur or Tanjung Benoa. The time across the Badung Strait depends on the boat and the location, but can be as short as 35 minutes with a strong vessel (e.g. twin 85hp outboards or better).

The South

Most of Bali's tourist services, and dive operators are no exception, are clustered in the South, in Kuta, Sanur, and Tanjung Benoa/Nusa Dua. Again, we would use a South-based operator only for diving the South or Nusa Penida, or perhaps for a single day on the East Coast. Because of travel time, for diving the Northwest or for serious diving in Tulamben or the East Coast, it is better to stay in those areas.

KUTA

A town has grown up around the beach here that has become the tourist center of Bali. Today, Kuta, which now extends north up to Legian, bustles with activity, its streets and tiny gangs (alleyways) lined with shops, restaurants, discos, and *losmen*. Although it has long been fashionable to malign Kuta, the place has an irrepressible, youthful charm.

Archipelago Diving, at the Sol Elite Paradiso Hotel, Tel: +(62-361) 761-414 ext. 7153, Fax: +(62-361) 756-944, tamanri@indosat.net.id, baliwww.com/arkipelago

AquaMarine Diving, Tel: +(62-361) 730-107, Fax: +(62-361) 735-368, info@AquaMarineDiving.com, www.aquamarinediving.com

Pro Dive Bali, Tel: +(62-361) 753-951, Fax: +(62-361) 753-952, prodivebali@bali-paradise.com, www.prodivebali.com. This is the Bali franchise of Pro Dive, the world's largest dive operation. Well run, with an experienced team. They offer diving at all of the basic sites. Departures are regularly scheduled.

SANUR

Sanur was Bali's first resort town and is, in a sense, the gray eminence of the tourist triangle. Compared to Kuta, it is quiet and dignified (or just dull, depending on your point of view and, inescapably, your age) and compares to Nusa Dua as old wealth does to new. The town is very quiet at night and the beach here, protected by the reef flat, is very calm. People who intend to spend a long time on Bali often stay in Sanur.

Dive & Dive's, Tel: +(62-361) 288-652, Fax: +(62-361) 288-892, divedive@indo.net.id. This well-regarded outfit specializes in photographers and Japanese clients. They can arrange multi-day dive tour packages and trips around Bali, and have set up a center at Gilimanuk for macrophotography specialists (see above). They offer one of the fullest ranges of sites.

Ena Dive Center and Water Sports, Tel: +(62-361) 288-829, 281-751, Fax: +(62-361) 287-945, enadive@denpasar.wasantara.net.id, enadive.wasantara.net.id, www.indo.com/diving/ena. One of Bali's pioneer operators, specializing in Japanese, European, and Southeast Asian clients.

TANJUNG BENOA

Nusa Dua offers luxury, and isolation from touts, peddlers, stray dogs, cold-water showers and other indignities. It's also quite antiseptic, preferred by the international jet set. The lodgings here are not cheap. Dive operators keep desks at most big hotels.

Bali Hai Diving Adventures, Tel: +(62-361) 720-331, Fax: +(62-361) 724-814, diverse@indosat.net.id, www.scubali.com. This outfit is a specialist for Lembongan Island and Nusa Penida, and they offer several packages.

World Diving Lembongan, Tel: +(62-81) 2390-0686, Fax: +(62-361) 288-500, info@world-diving.com. www.world-diving.com

Wally Siagian, Tel: +(62-361) 775-998, walldive@denpasar.wasantara.net.id. Wally is an independent dive guide on Bali, earning a modest living by crafting custom tours for individuals or small groups, particularly photographers, scientists, or other divers with a special interest in marine life. He is certainly the most knowledgeable diver on the island, and working with him would be a good choice if you are looking for some special animals or want to dive an unusual location. He has his own compressor and gear, and can get vehicles and boats as needed. His rates are reasonable.

YOS Marine Adventures, Tel: +(62-361) 775-438, 775-440, 752-005, Fax: +(62-361) 752-985, yosbali@indosat.net.id, www.yosdive.com. This professional, family-run business has established a good reputation for itself. YOS diving runs fast boats from the main Tanjung Benoa center to Nusa Penida, and takes divers by land to any of the other sites.

East of Bali

The season for the best diving conditions varies for many of the sites east of Bali. Like the sites in north Komodo, the best months to dive Moyo, Sangeang, Satonda and Maumere are from March through December. Sumba, in the south, is best from December through April.

Most cruises begin, and end in Bali. For the lone resort on Moyo, charter planes take guests to Sumbawa, where they are picked up by a custom-built yacht for transport to the island.

Adelaar Cruises, info@adelaar-cruises.com, www.adelaar-cruises.com

Aman Wana Resort, Tel: +(62-371) 22-233, Fax: +(62-371) 22-288, amanwana@amanresorts.com, www.amanresorts.com. Once the preferred choice of Princess Diana, this opulent tent-resort spoils guests with outstanding location, service, diving and dining.

Baruna (Adventurer and Explorer), Tel: +(62-361) 753-820, baruna@indosat.net.id, baruna@denpasar.wasantara.net.id, www.komodo-divencruise.com

Blue Marlin Dive Center, Tel: +(62-370) 634-387, info@dreamdivers.com, www.diveindo.com

Dive Asia Pacific (MV Pelagian), Tel: +(66-76) 238-762, 238-763, Fax: +(66-76) 238-947, diveasia@diveres.com, www.dive-asia-pacific.com

Dive Komodo (MV Evening Star), Tel: +(62-361) 728-878, greg@evolving.com.au, www.divekomodo.com

Grand Komodo Tours (Tarata, Temu Kira), Tel: +(62-361) 287-166, Fax: +(62-361) 287-165, info@komodoalordive.com, www.komodoalordive.com

Kararu Dive Voyages, Tel: +(62-361) 282-931, info@kararu.com, www.kararu.com

Komodo Dancer, Tel: +(62-361) 730-191, Fax: +(62-361) 733-942, info@indonesiacruises.com, www.indonesiacruises.com

Pindito, Tel/Fax +(62-361) 282-494, pindito@indo.net.id

Reefseekers Dive Center, Tel: +(62-370) 641-008, Fax: +(62-370) 641-005, dive@reefseekers.net, www.reefseekers.net

Komodo

As with the other sites east of Bali, the best way to visit these diverse islands is in the comfort and (in some cases) luxury of live-aboard boats, of which there are many. Live-aboards in Komodo fall into two categories—traditional wooden sailing *phinisi* converted into western standard boats complete with A/C and attached baths; or steel-hulled motor yachts.

The QE II of the fleet is the incomparable *Pelagian*, which sets the standard in luxury, comfort and service in the dive industry worldwide. Both Baruna boats are steel-hulled vessels that have been renovated in Surabaya to a comfortable, if ordinary standard. Kararu Dive Voyages have the most luxurious boat in the traditional fleet, followed by the *Pindito* and *Adelaar*, with Grand Komodo at the bottom, offset by being the cheapest by far.

Some trips will begin or end in Labuanbajo, Flores or Bima, Sumbawa, but the erratic nature of "regularly scheduled" domestic flights to these cities makes this a highly risky proposition. As always, check with the operator when planning your trip.

The KMTA (Komodo Marine Tourism Association) is a group of dive operators, including live-aboards, resorts and dive shops, which dive within the park boundaries. Using methods similar to those in Bonaire National Park, the KMTA is striving to attain a mandate to limit the number of operators in the park area, to control diver impact on popular dive sites and to help patrol the park area through the KomodoWatch program. Ten mooring buoys have been installed in the park for large live-aboards, and in 2002 the KMTA and the Komodo Foundation will install a hyperbaric chamber in Labuanbajo.

The Nature Conservancy is winning a crucial battle to protect Komodo's incredibly rich and beautiful coral reefs. But the park, like the reefs, is also under siege. As the surrounding areas become fished out, fishermen from the region and from as far away as Sulawesi are targeting Komodo's sanctuary. To fight back, TNC has helped the government beef up its park-protection force. It has funded the addition of two floating ranger stations, manned by rangers and soldiers who patrol round-the-clock against blast and cyanide fishermen and coral miners.

As part of the "3Es" program—Education, Empowerment, and Enforcement—the Komodo Foundation and TNC are promoting community-awareness programs, to persuade villagers both inside and outside the park to stop blast and cyanide fishing and to stay off the reefs. Educational programs targeting reef biology, endangered animals, waste management and dangers of bombing reefs have entered villages and are slowly changing ideas and attitudes.

TNC and other environmental groups need to concurrently offer the largely subsistence fishermen alternative ways to support themselves and their families. TNC has also installed a number of fish-aggregation devices—large, floating bamboo platforms that are anchored in 1,500 to 2,000 meters of water over 20 kilometers offshore. Algae and other microorganisms that grow on the undersides of the platforms attract fish. More than 400 former reef fishermen use hooks and lines to catch Spanish mackerel, skipjack and yellowfin tuna.

The Komodo Foundation is also working to protect the environment with their recycling program for Labuanbajo and Komodo National Park. As well as monthly clean-ups and special events such as Earth Day, the Komodo Foundation runs a regular garbage pick-up service for the town of Labuanbajo.

Dive operators

Adelaar Cruises, info@adelaar-cruises.com, www.adelaar-cruises.com

Baruna (Adventurer and Explorer), Tel: +(62-361) 753-820, baruna@indosat.net.id, baruna@denpasar.wasantara.net.id, www.komodo-divencruise.com

Dive Asia Pacific (MV Pelagian), Tel: +(66-76) 238-762, 238-763, Fax: +(66-76) 238-947, diveasia@diveres.com, www.dive-asia-pacific.com

Dive Komodo (MV Evening Star), Tel: +(62-361) 728-878, greg@evolving.com.au, www.divekomodo.com

Grand Komodo Tours (Tarata, Temu Kira), Tel: +(62-361) 287-166, Fax: +(62-361) 287-165, info@komodoalordive.com, www.komodoalordive.com

Kararu Dive Voyages, Tel: +(62-361) 282-931, info@kararu.com, www.kararu.com

Komodo Dancer, Tel: +(62-361) 730-191, Fax: +(62-361) 733-942, info@indonesiacruises.com, www.indonesiacruises.com

Pindito, Tel/Fax: +(62-361) 282-494, pindito @indo.net.id, www.pindito.com

Puri Komodo, info@purikomodo.com, www.purikomodo.com. The one resort in Komodo worth visiting, Puri Komodo is relaxing retreat spread over 25 hectares in an immensely pleasing tropical setting.

Reefseekers. The premier dive operator in Labuanbajo. British-owned and managed. dive@reefseekers.net, www.reefseekers.net

Alor

To dive Alor, guests must first fly to Kupang, the capital of West Timor. Since the direct flight from Darwin was halted, getting to Alor has become considerably more difficult. There are flights from Bali, but these typically have stopovers in towns like Maumere, Bima or Labuanbajo along the way. The travel time may be long and arduous, but it is well worth the effort.

For Alor's only land-based operator, Dive Alor, guests must overnight in one of a number of hotels before catching a morning flight to Kalabahi, Alor's provincial capital. Once there, you will lodge in basic, but clean and comfortable *losmen*-style rooms, and depart early each morning on the company's spacious houseboat for a one to two hour steam to sites outside the long harbor. If diving by live-aboard, divers will be picked up and taken to the boat, for an overnight steam north.

Dive Alor, Jl El Tari 19, Kupang, NTT 85111, Tel: +(62-380) 821-154, Fax: +(62-361) 824-833, divealor@telkom.net, www.divealor.com

Grand Komodo Tours (Tarata and Temu Kira), Tel: +(62-361) 287-166, Fax: +(62-361) 287-165, info@komodoalordive.com, www.komodoalordive.com

Kararu Dive Voyages, Tel: +(62-361) 282-931, info@kararu.com, www.kararu.com

The Northeast

Like many of the sites scattered throughout the vast Indonesian archipelago, those in the northeast typically can only be reached by live-aboard.

BANDA SEA

Due to the recent political and religious turmoil in Ambon, land-based operators there and in the Banda Sea have ceased operations; unless you travel on one of the few live-aboards that visit this region, diving here will remain closed.

Banda has two dive seasons—one in April, the other in October. The months before and after are usually quite good. Visibility in the off-season is restricted to 15 to 25 meters, but during the peak months can reach upwards of 40 to 50 meters.

Dive Asia Pacific (MV Pelagian), Tel: +(66-76) 238-762, 238-763, Fax: +(66-76) 238-947, diveasia@diveres.com, www.dive-asia-pacific.com. The *Pelagian* will visit Banda on and off over the course during any given year, depending on the political climate and interest generated by divers. Cruise director Larry Smith knows these islands better than anyone in Indonesia, and it is his expertise that promises the best experience possible.

IRIAN JAYA

Irian Diving, Tel: +(62-951) 327-371, Fax: +(62-951) 325-274, info@IrianDiving.com, www.iriandiving.com. Owner Max Ammer is the most knowledgeable operator in the area, with several years of exploration in the waters around Irian Jaya. Irian Diving operates two dives camps, with speedboat access to a number of world-class sites nearby.

Kararu Dive Voyages, Tel: +(62-361) 282-931, info@kararu.com, www.kararu.com

Pindito, Tel/Fax: +(62-361) 282-494, pindito@indo.net.id, www.pindito.com

Live-aboards

The criteria for choosing a live-aboard dive boat include:

Price: Average daily rates for cabins with A/C and attached bath are $250 to $300, for A/C and shared toilets, $200, and for fan-cooled cabins $125 to $150.
Food: Most ships cater predominately Asian menus. The more expensive packages include western cuisine, with imported meats and condiments. In some packages soft drinks and alcohol are included; in others these are billed separately.
Tenders: Tenders may be fiberglass, aluminum or inflatable, but all are powered by outboard motors. For the environmentally-minded, four-stroke engines are the least polluting outboard by far. Entry from the mother boat to the tender is usually by gangway. Getting in the tender after diving is most important—is there a ladder, or must you pull yourself up?

Air: Does the boat use airbanks or compressors? Airbanks allow tanks to be filled quickly and quietly, otherwise the compressors are working non-stop. Are the compressors regularly maintained? Is nitrox available?

Dive Guides: Are the dive guides Western or Indonesian? Are all the guides internationally certified? Do the guides cater to photographers? Do the guides give thorough briefings before each dive?

Camera Facilities: Are there camera tables? Are there dedicated rinse tanks for camera equipment? Are there battery chargers? Is there E6 processing? Is there an on-board TV for playback of video?

Comfort Zone: Is there hot water? Are there on-deck showers? Are towels provided? Is there a water-maker on board? Is there adequate refrigeration? Does the crew speak English? Does the ship cater for special diets?

Safety Zone: Does the ship have life rafts and life preservers? Does the ship have radar, sonar and GPS? Does the ship have a SSB radio and satellite phone? Are safety sausages, dive computers and diver alert horns available? Do tenders have walkie-talkies? Are there fire extinguishers readily accessible? Is there a ship's emergency briefing?

Communication: Does the ship have a satellite phone? Is there an email capability? Is there an on-board computer with maps and descriptions of dive sites? How can people contact you in case of an emergency? Can the ship access real-time weather reports?

Conservation: How does the ship handle its garbage? Do the guides routinely handle marine animals? Does the ship use moorings when available? Is the crew environmentally aware? Does the operator support local conservation groups?

Dive operators

Baruna (Adventurer and Explorer), Tel: +(62-361) 753-820, Fax: +(62-361) 753-809 baruna@indosat.net.id, baruna@denpasar.wasantara.net.id, www.baruna.com, www.komodo-divencruise.com

Dive Asia Pacific (MV Pelagian), Tel: +(66-76) 238-762, 238-763, Fax: +(66-76) 238-947, diveasia@diveres.com, www.dive-asia-pacific.com

Grand Komodo Tours (Tarata and Temu Kira), Tel: +(62-361) 287-166, Fax: +(62-361) 287-165, info@komodoalordive.com, www.komodoalordive.com

Kararu Dive Voyages, Tel: +(62-361) 282-931, info@kararu.com, www.kararu.com

Komodo Dancer, Tel: +(62-361) 730-191, Fax: +(62-361) 733-942, info@indonesiacruises.com, www.indonesiacruises.com

Murex Live-Aboard (Symphony and Serenade), Jl Raya Trans Sulawesi, Kalassey, Manado, Tel: +(431-62) 868-513, 826091 Fax: (62-431) 826-092, 846287, info@murex-dive.com, Contact person: Angelique Batuna, Danny Charlton, www.murexdive.com

Pindito, Tel/Fax +(62-361) 282-494, pindito@indo.net.id, www.pindito.com

Malaysia Country code: 60

Malaysia has radically developed its tourist infrastructure in the past few years, so that now travelers have a wide choice of accommodation and travel options almost everywhere in the country. The capital, Kuala Lumpur, boasts shops as sophisticated as those in Hong Kong or Singapore, yet, happily, at grass roots level, *kampung* or village life remains much the same as ever. The Malaysians are a hospitable people, whether Malay, Chinese, Indian or mixed race in origin. The diving can be very good, particularly off the the island of Sipadan. Note: Malaysia can be dialed directly from Singapore.

Air travel

Kuala Lumpur International Airport is 50 km from Kuala Lumpur and is the air travel hub of the country. Apart from the national carrier, Malaysian Airlines, some 35 airlines serve the city from all continents. Other destinations in Malaysia which have international airports include Langkawi, Penang and Kota Kinabalu. A shuttle service exists between Kuala Lumpur and neighboring Singapore while frequent daily flights link the Peninsular Malaysia with the East Malaysian states of Kuching and Kota Kinabalu.

Land travel

Travel within Malaysia is equally convenient. Shared taxi services exist between many large towns and the country has a good railway system. Air-conditioned express buses also operate regularly on inter-city and inter-state routes.

Sea travel

Ferry services link the country's many islands with the mainland. Along the East Coast ferries operate on a regular basis to the most popular islands of Tioman, Perhentian and Redang, while ferries between Kuala Perlis or Kuala Kedah and Langkawi run hourly. There is also a high-speed catamaran five times weekly between Penang and Langkawi.

Visas

All travelers must be in possession of a passport valid for at least six months. Citizens of most Commonwealth and EU countries are granted a visa-free entry for 14 days. Extensions can be made for a period up to three months at immigration offices, providing an onward ticket and sufficient funds are shown.

Health

This rarely presents a problem in Malaysia. A tropical country, it does have mosquitoes but malaria is rare. The most common complaints are usually too much sun and upset stomachs. Both can be remedied by taking preventive measure or paying a visit to a pharmacy or *klinik*—found all over the country. In emergencies, there are government-run and private specialists in all the major towns with doctors who speak English. Generally, the water throughout the country is safe, though opting for boiled water is a wise precaution.

Money exchange

Banks and money-changers will convert travelers' checks and foreign currency to the Malaysian dollar, or ringgit, as it is known, in all the major cities. Opening hours are generally 10 am to 3 pm but may vary from state to state. Credit cards are widely accepted. Carry plenty of small change and notes—invaluable for taxis and buses.

PRACTICALITIES

MALAYSIA

The ringgit was one of the first of the Asian currencies to fall in the late 1990s, and at the time we went to press it was trading at US$1=M$3.8. Travelers should check for regular updates.

Weather

Divers in Malaysia will enjoy tropical weather year-round. During the northeast monsoon (November to late March) the East Coast is mostly wet and the West Coast, dry. With the Westerlies, between April and October, it is the East Coast that is dry, and the west that is rainy. The same is largely true of Sabah. Temperatures at sea level rarely fall below 22°C and infrequently rise above 32°C.

Accommodations and food

There is no shortage of luxury hotels in Malaysia's capital and resort destinations. However, there is also a wealth of less expensive accommodation and simple guesthouses throughout the country. You can pay anything from M$20 (US$5) for a double room in a guesthouse to over M$400 (US$100) a double room in a 5-star resort. See the individual areas for more details.

Malaysian cuisine is spicy and delicious, combining pungent spices with local vegetables, fish and fowl. Throughout the country, hawker stalls serve fast food, Malaysian-style, for a few ringgit. Indian food and Chinese cuisine are also widely available, while international dishes can be found in restaurants in the more popular resorts.

What to bring

Divers should bring only the essentials. Weight restrictions apply on some of the flights served by small domestic airplanes. All resorts and dive operations will rent the basic equipment, but a suit is a recommended extra. Lycra or 3 mm will generally be fine. Bring sufficient batteries, sun cream and spares for your dive gear if you are diving off the islands.

Dive emergencies

The best advice for divers is always to dive conservatively. If an emergency arises, there are naval decompression chambers at Tanjong Gelang on the East Coast (near Kuantan) and Lumut on the West Coast of Peninsular Malaysia.

Kuala Lumpur City code: 03

Dive Operators

There are a number of dive operators based in Kuala Lumpur. The following are recommended:

Borneo Divers and Sea Sports (KL) 127M Jalan SS21/37 Damansara Utama, 47400 Petaling Jaya, Selangor. Tel: 60-3/717-3066; Fax: 60-3/718-4303. E-mail: information@borneo-divers.info, reservations@borneodivers.info, www.borneodivers.info/
Known for its excellent PADI 5-star IDC facility and diving operation in Sabah, this company runs tours to Sipadan and the islands in Tunku Abdul Rahman Marine Park. See the section on Sipadan, below, for full details. In Kuala Lumpur, it operates a 5-star dive center and a comprehensive underwater photo center, and is a fully licensed travel reservation agency for bookings to its Sabah-based diving and beyond, as well as a well-equipped dive shop.

Planet Scuba This PADI 5-star IDC is located in Bangsar, KL: www.planetscuba.com.my/

Scuba Malaysia: www.scubamalaysia.com/ Email: scubamalaysia@hotmail.com

Sipadan

Sipadan Island is located in Sabah, East Malaysia, off the coast of northeast Borneo. Access is either via Singapore, Johor Bahru or Kuala Lumpur to Kota Kinabalu, the capital of Sabah, then by a domestic service of MAS to Tawau or Semporna on the southeast coast. From there you can travel by speedboat to Sipadan.

There are three companies operating dive resorts on the island. The only way of reaching Sipadan is through their organizations.

When to visit

July through September are busiest and theoretically the best months to dive off Sipadan, with the northeast monsoon. Late November through January are the worst, with decreased visibility, colder air and waters, but a better possibility of seeing mantas, whale sharks and hammerheads.

Diving

Sipadan is not for neophyte divers. While only basic certification is required, experience will ensure a far better time. No certification courses are offered on Sipadan, but Borneo Divers offer some advanced courses.

What to bring

UW flashlight, insect repellent, and a wet suit of at least 3 mm thickness.

Dive operators and resorts

Because of impending new restrictions on diver numbers to Sipadan, prices and packages were not available at the time of printing. In the past, packages at Sipadan ranged from US$125 to US$175 a day. We advise you to contact the operators directly.

Borneo Divers and Sea Sports (Sabah) 9th Floor, Menara Jubili, 53 Jalan Gaya, Kota Kinabalu, 88000 Sabah. Tel: 60-88/222-2226, Fax: 60-88/221550 and 265055. E-mail: information@borneodivers.info, reservations@borneodivers.info, www.borneodivers.info Borneo Divers runs the Sipadan Island Dive Lodge on the island. Prices include airport transfers, air fares from Kota Kinabalu to Tawau (where it has a branch office), transfers from Tawau to Sipadan, meals, twin-share accommodation and diving. Equipment is for rent on the island by prior arrangement. Specialty cavern courses are available.

Pulau Sipadan Resort (PSR) 484 Block P, Bandar, Sabindo; P.O. Box 61120, Tawau 91021, Sabah. Tel: 60-89/765-200; Fax: 60-89/763-575. Email: prst@po.jaring.my, www.sipadan-resort.com PSR offers food and accommodation packages ex-Tawau or including airport transfers, round-trip from Kota Kinabalu. Non-divers: 20% off. Up to three boat dives per day; unlimited beach diving and night dives in front of the resort, which is closest to the drop-off. PSR also offers dive packages to Mabul, Kapalai and Lankayan.

Sipadan Dive Centre (SDC) 1 11-03 Wisma Merdeka, Jalan Tun Razak, Kota Kinabalu, 88000 Sabah. Tel: 60-88/240-584, Fax: 60-88/440-415. Email: sales@sipadandivers.com, www.sipadandivers.com

Kota Kinabalu and Layang-Layang

City code for Kota Kinabalu: 088

Kota Kinabalu can be reached by regular daily flights from West Malaysia, Singapore and other regional destinations. Local buses run from the city center to the beach at Tanjung Aru and to other suburban locations. Taxis are available at ranks in the center and are metered.

Accommodations and food

Hotel rooms vary from the expensive to the simple. Two luxury hotels offer fine accommodation, one in the heart of town and the other at Tanjung Aru. There are plenty of restaurants to suit all tastes and budgets. Kota Kinabalu excels in its seafood and has a wealth of temperate-climate vegetables from the highlands. You can pay anything from M$5 for a simple meal in an open-air market, to a US$100 for a lavish dinner in a fancy hotel.

Dive operators

Borneo Divers A 1002, 10th Floor, Wisma Merdeka. P.O.Box 14527, 88851 Kota Kinabalu, Sabah. Tel: 6088.223.490, Fax: 60-88/221550 and 265055, www.borneodivers.com Operates trips to Tunku Abdul Rahman National Park (as well as Sipadan)

Coral Island Cruises 1002 10th Floor, Wisma Merdeka, Jalan Tun Razak, P.O. Box 14527, Kota Kinabalu 88851, Sabah. Tel: 60-88/223-490, Fax: 6088.223.404. Email: info@coral-island-cruises.com, www.coral-island-cruises.com Runs day trips to Tunku Abdul Rahman National Park and arranges trips to Layang-Layang Island Resort.

Layang-Layang Island Resort Box No12, Block A Unit A-0-3, Megan Avenue, No 12 Jalan Yap Kwan Seng ,50450 Kuala Lumpur, Tel: + 603-21622877 Fax" + 603-21622980, Email: layang@pop.jaring.my, www.layang-layang.com The only commercial operation on this remote oceanic atoll, Layang-Layang Island Resort has 70 guestrooms and is open for nine months every year, from February to October. Packages include full board, twin-sharing accommodation and three boat dives.

Pulau Payar

City code for Langkawi: 04

Pulau Payar is accessible from the island of Langkawi, a popular tourist destination and a duty-free island off the west coast of Peninsular Malaysia.

Getting there

Ferries run from the mainland for M$10 one-way between Kuala Perlis and Langkawi. A daily ferry operates from Penang to Langkawi for M$35 one-way. The island is linked by frequent MAS flights from the capital of Kuala Lumpur, by daily flights from Singapore and seasonal flights from Penang.

The *Langkawi Coral*, a high speed catamaran, leaves from the Kuah jetty on Langkawi each morning at 10.30 am, returning at 3.30 pm. The trip takes 50 minutes and the vessel docks at a recently built reef platform.

Accommodations and food

Langkawi's hotels and beach resorts offer a wide range of accommodation, from 5-star deluxe class to moderately low-priced hotels and chalets at budget prices. Expect to pay M$200 to M$2,000 for a room in a deluxe class hotel and as little as M$15 for a budget chalet.

Seafood is a specialty in Langkawi and there are plenty of small restaurants in Kuah. Breakfast or lunch may cost as little as M$5 to $10 per person, and dinner is around M$15.

Dive operators

Langkawi Coral Lot 1-21, Jetty Point Complex, Langkawi, Kedah. Tel: 60-4/966 7318; Fax: 60-4/966 7308. www.langkawicoral.com/ Email: sales@langkawicoral.com

Sriwani Tours & Travel The owner of the *Langkawi Coral* offers a daily trip to Pulau Payar, for M$220 per adult, including transfers, buffet lunch, boat rides and snorkeling equipment. Diving costs are extra. Email: www.3routes.com/asia/mala/mala/4934.html

Terengganu

This state's coastline offers a score of delightful offshore islands and the best snorkeling and diving in Peninsular Malaysia.

Getting there

Access to the offshore islands is by boat from Kuala Terengganu, Kuala Besut, Tanjong Merang, Dungun and Marang.

All these coastal villages and towns are linked by bus or taxi from the state capital, Kuala Terengganu, and with Kuantan, south, in the state of Pahang.

If visiting a resort, the hotel boat will pick you up at the relevant port. If you want to dive or snorkel on an individual basis, you have to negotiate a fare with one of the boats that ply the route. You can get to Perhentian from Kuala Besut. It takes approximately 90 minutes and costs around M$20 per passenger. You can also get to Lang Tenggah from here. Redang is accessible from Kuala Terengganu and Tanjong Merang.

From Dungun, you can hire a boat to Tenggol. It takes some 60 minutes. Costs depend on how many share a boat. Kapas is accessible from Marang in 30 minutes. Costs vary similarly.

Dive operators and resorts

All the companies and dive operators listed under Kuala Lumpur offer inclusive-cost dive trips to these islands. Most of the better hotels along the coast also have operational headquarters and booking offices in Kuala Lumpur.

Perhentian Island Resort Perhentian Besar. Book in Kuala Lumpur: 22nd Floor, Menara Promet, Jalan Sultan Ismail, 50250 Kuala Lumpur. Tel: 60-3/243-4984; Fax: 60-3/244-8530, 1, 2, Email: pir@po.jaring.my, www1.jaring.my/perhentian/
This small hotel is accessible from Kuala Besut and offers a variety of accommodation from dormitory beds to air-conditioned chalets.

Berjaya Redang Beach Resort Pulau Redang, P.O.Box 126, Main Post Office, 20928 Kuala Terengganu, Terengganu; Tel: +609 697-3988; Fax: +609 697-3899; toll-free: 1 800 88 8818. Email: reserdept@b-redang.com.my, www.berjayaresorts.com.my/redang-beach/info.html.
This 150-room international standard resort hotel is situated on the southern shores of Redang and offers good facilities for snorkeling and diving. Access is 35 minutes by private ferry from Kuala Terengganu.

Primula Park Royal Resort On the beach at Kuala Terengganu. Primula Parkroyal Kuala Terengganu, Jalan Persinggahan, 20400 Kuala Terengganu, Terengganu Darul Iman, Email: maxcarry@tm.net.my, www.primulaparkroyal.com/ Offers daily diving trips to Kapas Island.

Tioman and Aur

Tioman offers visitors plenty in the way of recreation and excellent beaches. There is an international-standard hotel with an 18-hole golf course, and scores of other smaller, bungalow-style guesthouses and hotels. Costs from M$5 for a room upwards. Pulau Aur, the easternmost island of the Malay Peninsula, is not anywhere as well known as her famous relative, Tioman, but the diving is just as good.

Getting there

Forty-three nautical miles from Mersing on the eastern coast of Peninsular Malaysia, the daily ferry takes 90 minutes. There is also a hydrofoil service from time to time. From Singapore (122 nautical miles away) the journey by high speed catamaran takes 4.5 hours.

Tioman also has daily flight connections with Kuala Lumpur via Berjaya Air, which takes 70 minutes. Information through Malaysian Airlines. Pelangi Air also has daily flights from Singapore, which is 40 minutes. Information through Singapore Airlines.

The journey to Aur from Mersing takes around 4.5 hours, while from Singapore the journey can take between 8 and 10 hours, depending on the chartered vessel.

Accommodations

Berjaya Tioman Beach Resort P.O.Box 4 Mersing, 86807 Johor, Malaysia. Tel: +609 419-1000; Fax: +609 419 1718; Email: reserv@b-tioman.com.my, www.berjayaresorts.com.my/tioman-beach/info.html This hotel offers international-standard rooms and suites. It is also operates a PADI dive center with regular departures to all the best dive sites.

Dive operators

Dive Asia operates two dive centers on Tioman, a 5-star PADI IDC facility at Kampong Salang, and another center at Kampong Tekek.

91, Jalan Endau, 86800, Mersing, Johor. Tel: 07-799 1769, 799 4098; Fax: 07-799 4099; Direct line: 6-09-419 5017, Email: enquiry@diveasia.com.my, www.diveasia.com.my Dive Asia offers two dives, lunch and equipment from M$160 per day, Open Water Courses (M$795), Advanced Open Water Courses (M$550) and specialty courses. The friendly dive shop rents tanks and gear, and sells a good range of diving equipment and spares.

Tioman Island Resort (see above, Berjaya Tioman Beach Resort) operates a PADI dive center on the beach by the hotel. Tel: 60-9/419 1000 and ask for the dive center extension. Daily dives cost M$105 including equipment, Open Water Courses (M$800) and Advanced Open Water Courses. The center's dive store sells diving equipment.

Atlantis Bay Resort, Aur c/o Scubacorner in Singapore, www.scubacorner.com.sg; Big Bubble Centre in Singapore, www.bigbubble.com.sg, bbcdiver@starhub.net.sg

Live-aboards

Live-aboard possibilities can be checked out through the marinas at Tanjung Aru (Kota Kinabalu) and Port Klang (Kuala Lumpur).

The Reclaim II

From April to October, the *Reclaim II* visits the Riau archipelago every weekend, and is also available for charter. Owned and operated by Singapore-based Marsden Bros Dive Center, this 56-foot motor yacht has spacious teak decks, three air-conditioned cabins sleeping eight passengers, two bathrooms, a galley and dining area. The live-aboard trips are distinguished by their professional and fun crew, excellent cuisine and adventure diving in secluded waters. **Marsden Bros Dive Centre** 25 Faber Park, Singapore 129113. Tel: (+65) 6778-8287, Fax: (+65) 6773-2265, Email: marsbros@pacific.net.sg, www.marsbros.com

Big Bubble Centre in Singapore organizes live-aboard trips to Malaysia. This PADI 5-Star Dive Centre is at 68 Neil Road, Singapore 088836, Tel: (+65) 62226862, Email: bbcdiver@starhub.net.sg, www.bigbubble.com

The Philippines Country code: 63

The Philippines is an island nation—7,107 of them at best count. Travel and trade between the islands has been a predominant feature of life here for centuries. Tourism is a major dollar earner and there is no shortage of domestic destinations. The traveler these days also has a wide range of transportation options, from jet planes and air-conditioned coasters to simple inter-island ferries, fast super cats and colorful, crowded jeepneys. A welter of development throughout the islands is continuing to produce world-class hotels and resorts, both luxury and budget in concept, in some of the most unique and intriguing corners of the country. Eco-tourism is gaining ground too, and divers arrive in droves to discover what must be one of the best organised industries in Asia, given the tyranny of distance and poor communications which still plague some parts of the country.

In Manila and many provincial capitals, such as Cebu and Davao, giant shopping malls are becoming part of the everyday scene. The Philippines, despite its often stormy political and economic fluctuations, continues to grow at a pace which amazes even some Filipinos themselves, but the outgoing, friendly character of the people is more or less intact anywhere you may happen to roam.

Air travel

The county's leading gateway, Ninoy Aquino International Airport (NAIA) in Pasay City, Manila, has been subject to much criticism in the local press for its lack of infrastructure. In fact, if travelers follow a few simple rules, they will survive NAIA easily. After exiting the customs shed, one can avail of the Avis coupon taxi system, which, although costing more than a regular taxi, is a fixed price paid in full before departure. If you are being met by a hotel or travel agent's representative, look for the person carrying a sign identifying themselves after exiting customs.

You can also opt for a DOT approved metered taxi to the left of the entrance to the parking area and waiting shed across from the main exit from the arrivals hall where greeters are supposed to meet arrivals. As a rough guide, expect to pay around US$2 to $3 to Makati or Manila, $3 to $5 or more to Quezon City and beyond, depending on traffic. The guard on duty is supposed to give you a slip of paper with your destination and the taxi's plate number on it in case you have any complaints. Although technically monitored by the DOT, in our experience, there may sometimes be an attempt to "negotiate" what is supposed to be a metered taxi fare.

Mactan International Airport on Mactan island, Cebu, is the up and coming gateway, and is served by airlines flying direct from Japan, Singapore, Malaysia and elsewhere. It is a $4 to $5 taxi ride away from the center of Cebu City, $2 or less or less to any resort on Mactan Island. Taxis in Cebu and Manila are ALWAYS supposed to use their meters: ignore any protestations to the contrary.

Both airports have tourist information centers, currency exchange facilities and duty free shops, as well as car rental agencies and hotel hospitality desks. Inbound passengers have a duty free allowance of $1,000, which can be used up within 48 hours of arrival at any of the huge Duty Free outlets in Manila (close to the airport), Subic, Angeles, Cebu, San Fernando Pampanga and elsewhere.

There is a departure tax of 500 pesos for all international flights. International flights require you to check in two hours before departure as exit queues can be long. Do reconfirm your onward flight within 72 hours of departure and allow for the often heavy traffic, especially in Metro Manila.

Domestic airlines

Several domestic airlines serve the provinces. Prices are very reasonable, and the coverage is quite extensive. Divers (and golfers) can join Philippine Airlines' "Flying Sportsman's Club" to make use of the increased baggage allowances. It costs 50 pesos to join. Apply at the nearest PAL office for more information. Domestic flights require check-in one hour before departure. Unclaimed seats are given away to standby passengers 35 minutes before take-off.

Domestic airports around the country are mostly quite efficient, though take-off and landings can sometimes be a bit hairy. Note that the departure tax is 50 pesos for domestic flights originating in Manila: regional airport charges vary. PAL has its own ultramodern Domestic Terminal in Manila, other airlines use different terminals, so check which terminal your flight is leaving is from.

Domestic airline destinations

Although domestic routes are subject to change, the following list of domestic airlines and the destinations they fly is accurate as of going to press.

Philippine Airlines Reservations (63-2) 855-8888 Destinations: Manila, Cebu, Davao, Cagayan de Oro, Zamboanga, Bacolod, Iloilo, Butuan, Kalibo (Boracay), Puerto Princesa, General Santos, Tagbilaran, Tacloban, Legaspi City, Laoag, Tuguegarao.

Air Philippines Reservations: (63-2) 855-9000 Destinations: Manila, Cebu, Bacolod, Cagayan de Oro, Cotabato, Davao, General Santos, Iloilo, Kalibo (Boracay), Legaspi City, Puerto Princesa, San Jose (Occidental Mindoro), Zamboanga, Dumaguete.

Cebu Pacific Reservations: (63-2) 636 4938-45. Destinations: Manila, Cebu, Iloilo, Cagayan de Oro, Davao, Bacolod, Tacloban, Kalibo (Boracay), Roxas, Dumaguete.

Asian Spirit (info@asianspirit.com) Reservations: (63-2) 851 8888; 514 4310 to 12. Destinations: Manila, Caticlan (Boracay), Masbate, San Jose (Occidental Mindoro), Tagbilaran, Virac, Baguio, Calbayog, Catarman, Marinduque, Naga, Busuanga (Coron) Tablas (Romblon). Inter-island: Cebu-Cagayan, Cebu-Caticlan, Cebu-Tagbilaran, Cebu-Surigao.

Air Ads (www.flyaai.com) Reservations: (63-2) 833 3264. Destination: Caticlan (Boracay).

Pacific Air (paco@mnl.sequel.net) Reservations: (63-2) 832 2731; 833 2391. Destinations: Caticlan (Boracay), Coron, Baguio.

Land travel

Filipinos love to travel, and there is always a way to get somewhere. A wide variety of buses, from luxury air-conditioned liners to diesel spewing behemoths serve anywhere that can be reached by road. Jeepneys and motorised tricycles go where the buses can't, which can make for exciting, if uncomfortable, excursions. Carry all your valuables with you, preferably in a belt bag, as bag slashings are not uncommon on some routes, especially on regular buses plying the Batangas to Manila route.

Sea travel

Many visitors who have the time might prefer the option of sailing between the islands. While luxury yachts can be chartered by the affluent few, several shipping lines, such as **WG&A**, **Negros Navigation** and **Sulpicio Lines** have excellent services connecting Manila and Cebu with dozens of ports around the country. Accommodation ranges from deck space to first-class suites, and there are quite passable restaurants and discos aboard some of the vessels.

Inter-Island travel around the Visayas is often on fast **Super Cat Ferrys**.

At some point, it will almost certainly be necessary for you to board a *banca* boat, the ubiquitous motorised outrigger canoe. Sit where the boatman tells you and be prepared to get splashed now and again. The driest part of the boat on a smaller *banca* is usually under the bow, so stow anything that has to be kept dry there.

Visas

Most Foreign Nationals with valid passports and an onward ticket are given 21 days or so upon entry, depending on the visitor's country of origin. For longer trips, visa extensions up to one year can be arranged in the country at regional Bureau of Immigration offices or through a local travel agent, but if you plan to stay longer, you should apply for a 59-day Temporary Visitor's Visa at any

Philippine Embassy or Consulate. Formalities and fees are minimal, usually taking a few hours to process.

Health

The Philippines has some excellent medical facilities, and others which are not so excellent. Dentistry is cheap and often of extremely high standard, and there are several good medical centers in Manila.

Most sicknesses occur through over-indulging in the many delicacies of the islands. Over-exposure to the sun is another common cause of discomfort, especially for fair-skinned divers soaking up a few rays between dives. Proper precautions should be taken to avoid sunburn, as the local remedy of applying vinegar or other, more pungent, liquids on affected parts is best avoided.

Tap water is often heavily chlorinated in cities, and mostly not to be consumed before prolonged boiling outside of them, especially by those with delicate stomachs. Bottled mineral water is widely available, but watch out for the ice in the soft drinks.

Weather

There are two seasons in the Philippines: the dry season (from March to May) and the rainy season (from June to February). Tropical depressions, storms and typhoons affect parts of the country from June to October, especially in the so-called "Typhoon Belt" from Southern Luzon to the Visayas. Between storms, the weather is often quite balmy for long periods. December through February are the coolest months. Average temperature is 22° C, humidity is 77%.

Money exchange

Visitors can bring in any amount of currency, but you should declare any amount over US$3,000 or equivalent in cash to avoid any complications when exiting. The export of more than 1,000 pesos is disallowed, but note that it is necessary to produce official Central Bank Receipts issued by authorised currency exchange dealers to change your excess pesos back to another currency before leaving.

Banking is notoriously awkward in the Philippines. In an emergency, it is usually safer to use the Standard Chartered or the Hongkong Bank to have funds telegraphically

transferred (TT'd) from outside the country. Most international credit cards are honored after verification. Many urban centers now have ATMs that will give a cash advance in local currency with a credit card. It is advisable to check first before booking into a resort or paying for services as some merchants cannot verify cards quickly. Traveler's checks, although safer, are harder to encash and are exchanged at a lower rate than cash. Keep the original receipts you were given when you purchased the check.

At the time of writing, US$1 = P50+/-, but the currency is prone to volatility.

Photography

There are few places which restrict the taking of photos, and there are always plenty of interesting subjects to shoot. Serious photographers will want to bring their own slide film, especially those using Kodachrome. However, Kodachrome cannot be developed in the Philippines. E6 processing is available, but only in Manila and on some live-aboards by prior request. Fuji Superia is available in Manila at about $7 a roll.

Although they claim to be film safe, some X-ray machines at airports in the Philippines are not. Insist on having precious films inspected by eye and keep them in lead-lined bags if at all possible. Small lithium and even alkaline batteries are not readily available outside of major population centers, and spares for cameras and strobes, especially O-rings, seals, gaskets, etc., are almost non-existent, so be sure to pack plenty of spares.

Communications

With the advent of cellular communications and deregulated telecommunications, many resort areas in the Philippines that until recently relied on expensive, slow, extremely frustrating and often inaccurate reservation systems now transact business on the internet. This has allowed many dive resorts to make a quantum leap forward in their communications in many previously "remote" areas. Internet access can be found in most cities and in a growing number of resorts such as Puerto Galera, Boracay, the Visayas, and Mindanao.

There is extensive cellular coverage throughout the archipelago. International GSM roamers can utilize local Globe, Piltel, Smart and other cellular communications services in many areas.

All telephone numbers listed in this section are listed with the local area code. If you are dialing from a land-line with the same area code, drop the part in brackets. To dial any telephone, cellular or otherwise, from outside the country, drop the zero and add the international access code and country code (63). Thus, a Manila number 123 4567 becomes (02) 123 4567 when dialed from outside Manila and (63-2) 123 4567 when dialed from outside the country.

Please note: to the absolute annoyance and frustration of subscribers, telephone numbers tend to change periodically as the country's booming telecommunication providers upgrade their systems.

Technical diving

Technical diving is widely available throughout the Philippines, IANTD, PADI and ANDI being the most popular certification agencies. Most areas frequented by divers have several interesting sites for "techies." such as caves and wrecks, as well as deep drop-offs and walls. Needless to say, getting the proper instruction for any intended dive is vital, and there is no shortage of highly qualified technical instructors available at most destinations.

The world's deepest mixed gas dive record (308 meters) was set in Puerto Galera in 2001 by John Bennett, a locally based techhical diving instructor, in the deep waters off the coast. This was John's third record-breaking dive around Puerto Galera, and the level of support he got from other local techies is a testament to the popularity and professionalism of technical divers in the Philippines.

Manila City code: 02
Intl. telephone access code: 63-2

Manila Bay is not recommended as a dive spot. However, Manila is a good place to start planning your diving vacation as it is home to several retail stores worth a visit as well. The **Philippine Commission on Sports SCUBA Diving (PCSSD)** (ercajigal@tourism.gov.ph) is also headquartered in Manila, at the Department of Tourism (DOT) building at Agrifina Circle, Tel: (02) 524 7141 loc 382 & 388; 524 3735. The PCSSD is the regulatory body of the local SCUBA industry. Registered dive operators are bound by a code of ethics and safety. The PCSSD operates two recompression

chambers, one in Manila, (02) 426 2701 local 8991 and one in Cebu (032) 233 9942. Whenever possible, check to see if the dive center you plan to dive with is registered as it can say a lot about the operator's integrity.

There is another chamber in Subic, Tel: (047) 252 7052; 252 7566, operated by the Subic Bay Freeport Authorities.

The Philippine Diver (diver@diver.com.ph; www.diver.com.ph) is a glossy, full-color magazine filled with information, articles and complete PCSSD listings, is available through subscription ($35 for one year for four issues) and at many dive centers and resorts throughout the country. Tel: (02) 7211969, Fax: (02) 7211991 for more details.

Most live-aboard vessels and many resorts around the islands have offices in Manila, and there are several dive tour specialists around town as well.

Whitetip Divers (sales@whitetip.com; http://www.whitetip.com) Joncor ll Building, 1362 A. Mabini St, Ermita, Manila. Tel: 521 0433, 526 2629, 526 8191, Fax: 522 1165 Sells diving gear including Scubapro, Uwatec, Dacor, Zeagle, and Sherwood brands, Bauer compressors, Luxfer and Catalina tanks, and is an excellent source of information wherever you wish to dive. Whitetip also has branches in Cebu located at Unit 2 Borromeo Arcade Bldg., F. Formoso St., Cebu City (whitetip@cebu.weblinq.net, Tel:(032) 254 2623); in Bantayan, Dumaguete City (whitetip@mozcom.com, Tel:(035) 255 2381); and in Davao located at DPA Bldg., Sta. Ana Wharf, Davao City (whitetipdavao@whitetip.inbox.as).

Dive Buddies (divebuddies@divephil.com; http://www.divephil.com) has two stores in Metro Manila, at Robelle Mansions, 877, J.P. Rizal St., Makati City, Tel: (02) 899 7388, Fax: (02) 899 7393, and at L&S Building, 1414 Roxas Boulevard, Manila, Tel: (02) 521 9168-69, Fax: (02) 521 9170, is another full service retail store and package specialist worth visiting. Available brands include Beuchat, OMS, Aeris and Ikelite. Dive courses (PADI, NAUI, SSI and CMAS) are taught using an in-house swimming pool. Technical diving training and equipment is available, and there is an in-house tank hydro-testing and inspection facility. Dive Buddies also has a cosy, budget dive resort, Dinky Little Dive Camp, in Anilao.

Aquaventure Philippines (aqua@aquaventure.com; http://www.aquaventure.com), is the longest and best established dive retail, training and travel operation in the country. Major brands of equipment available include Aqualung, Spiro, Sea Quest, Suunto, and Technisub. Technical diving courses and equipment are also offered. Aquaventure House is a custom-built, three-story building featuring a dive training pool with view windows. Located at 7801 Saint Paul St., San Antonio Village, Makati City, Tel: (02) 899 2831, Fax: (02) 899 2551.

Other stores in Manila are at Unit 6, 8137 Plaza, Amber Drive, Ortigas Center, Pasig City, Tel: (02) 637 4317. Other Aquaventure branches are found in Cebu, Tel: (032) 234 2639, Fax: (032) 234 2603, at 2nd Flr. Myra's Pension House, 12 Escario St. Lahug, Cebu City; and at the Amanpulo Resort in Pamalican Island, Palawan, Tel: (02) 759 4040. Aquaventure also has a resort in Anilao, Batangas, Aquaventure Reef Club, Tel: (02) 899 2831, Cel: (0912) 254 7140.

Scuba World Inc (swidive@i-manila.com.ph; http:www.scubaworld.com.ph), a PADI 5-Star facility, is headquartered at 1181 Vito Cruz Extension, corner Kakarong St, Tel: (02) 895 3551; 890 7805; 890 7807, Fax: (02) 890 8982. Offering complete retail services, featuring Mares, Tusa, and Suunto. Scuba World is affiliated with PADI, NAUI, CMAS, BSAC and PDIC. Customized scuba training classrooms and a swimming pool rounds out the facility. Complete Technical Diving services are also available. Other branches are found in San Juan at 714 Jose Abad Santos St. (Tel: (02) 726 0115; 724 8880) and at 90 A. Aguirre Avenue, BF Homes, Paranaque (Tel: (02) 807 8134; Fax: 809 4268).

Other Scuba World outlets can be found in Boracay (Tel: (036) 288 3310) and Cebu Tel: (032) 254 9554, (032) 340 5938, Fax: (032) 254 9591).

Scuba World operates several liveaboard vessels including the MV *Island Explorer*, MV *Oceanic Explorer* and MV *Big Blue* and smaller vessels such as the *Dolphin Explorer* and the *Sea Gypsy*. Reservations for Tubbataha and other remote dive sites are taken at any Scuba World outlet.

Asia Divers (manila@asiadivers.com; http://www.asiadivers.com), a Puerto Galera-based PADI 5-Star IDC facility dive resort, recently opened their own dive center in Manila at 1741 Dian St., Abimir Place, Palanan, Makati City (Tel: (02) 834 2974, Fax: 551 8063). Other branches are in Small La Laguna, Puerto Galera, Mindoro Oriental (Tel: 849 7430) and in Cebu at Unit 22 Mercedes Commercial Center, A.C. Cortez Avenue, Ibabao, Mandaue City (Tel: (032) 344 6819, Fax: 344 6820). Retail equipment available includes Cressi-Sub, Bodyglove and Aropec. Complete PADI training to Master Instructor is available, as is technical diving equipment and training.

Other dive centers around Manila you should check in with include:

Eureka, Level 3, Power Plant Mall, Rockwell Center, Makati City 1299, Tel: (02) 756 0170, Fax: (02) 756 0149, euraka@eurekadive.com, dealers of parkway and Cetacea products, a PADI Dive Center.

Nautilus Dive & Sport Center, Midland Mansion Unit 1, 839 Pasay Rd., Makati City, Tel: (02) 812 2848; 817 7293, cell 0917 792 8074, nautilusdive@surfshop.net.ph

Dive Shoppe (diveshop@skyinet.net) at 71-B Constancia Building, Timog Avenue, Quezon City, Tel: (02) 921 2020; 928 2376; Fax: 413 6737 cell (0917) 533 1266, agents for Seac Sub, a PADI dive center with good Anilao connections.

Cocktail Divers (cdiver@vasia.com; http://www.wetexpedition.com) U/g 33, Citiland 8, 98 Gil Puyat Avenue, Makati City, Tel: (02) 892 1443 operates three dive centers and a resort in Puerto Galera (cell (0917) 813 5392). Under German management, they have dive equipment for sale and rental, PADI instruction, dive travel services and parasailing and water-skiing equipment and instruction.

La Union   City code: 072
Intl. telephone access code: 63-72

Getting there

La Union is accessible by road from Manila. If you prefer not to rent a car, with or without a driver, there are several bus companies running regular air-conditioned buses daily to La Union from Manila (Partas, Rabbit, Farinas, Maria De Leon, Times Transit), about a 6-hour trip costing around $5.

Ocean Deep Dive Centre (scuba@slfu.com, www.oceandeep.ws), is located at Poro Point in San Fernando, La Union 2501 tele-Fax: (072) 8884440. Ocean Deep is home to Tim Aukshun, PADI Regional Course Director. Naturally, expert training to all levels is available here. Equipment sales, rentals, hotel and travel reservations can also be made at Ocean Deep.

Expect to pay around $30 for a dive with equipment, guide and boat. Jellyfish particles are quite common in the warmer upper layers of water at some times of the year, so full coverage, such as a lycra suit, is recommended. 14 Mile Reef and further north can be arranged. Diving is mainly done off 2-man *banca* boats, which can sometimes get a little hairy. They cost around $5 per head per dive. To the north of San Fernando a few miles is a good surfing beach with cheap cottages ($15 a night) at San Juan.

There are several smaller resorts next to each other along the coast here, all with reasonable rooms and good restaurants. Some of these are Southern Palms Resort, (Tel: (072) 888 5384; Bali Hai Resort; Cabana Resort, (Tel: (072) 242 5585; and China Sea Resort, (Tel: (072) 242 0822, all located on Bauang Beach, La Union. Room rates vary between $20 and $40 a night for a double room; look for seasonal discounts.

Subic Bay City code: 047
Intl. telephone access code: 63-47

Getting there

International flights from Taipei have now opened up the way for further development of the tourist industry in the Free Port Zone of Subic Bay.

A 3-hour drive from Manila, Subic is visited by hordes of "Duty Free Day Trippers" from Manila, eager to spend their duty free allowance at the stores inside the Free Port Zone, formerly a US Navy Base. Victory Liners (Tel: (02) 3611506) is the easiest way to get there if traveling by bus. They run several air-conditioned trips daily to and from Olongapo. Tickets are under $S 3.50.

A wide variety of accommodation is available locally, from 5-star hotels to small nipa huts and bungalows at prices to suit all pockets. The beaches bordering the bay are becoming increasingly popular as weekend get-aways for Manila-based families, and there is a variety of nightlife and dining

options available. By the Sea, Barrio Barretto, Subic Bay, Olongapo, (Tel: (047) 222 4560, Fax: (047) 222 2718 is a popular hotel with rooms from $10 and up. White Rock Hotel, Matain, Subic Bay, Olongapo, (Tel: (047) 232 4446), has just reopened. Rooms are pricier here, starting at around $90. There are several other places to park yourself ranging from a few dollars a night upwards.

Subic Bay Aquasports (sbas@svisp.com) Bldg. 249 Waterfront Road, Subic Bay Freeport Zone, SBMA, Olongapo City. (Tel: (047) 252 7343; 252 3005, telefax (02) 813 5677. A Duty Free SCUBA retail outlet and organiser of fine wreck diving aboard a variety of vessels, Aquasports also offers PADI instruction, air and equipment rentals. A 2-tank dive with a boat will cost around $65, including a guide.

Nasugbu

Getting there

Southwest of Manila, after a 2-hour drive which takes you over the mountain at Tagaytay with its breathtaking views of Taal Volcano poking out of Taal Lake finds one in Nasugbu in western Batangas. There are several decent places to stay along the coast here, at nearby Matabungkay Beach for example, but limited diving infrastructure.

BLTB Bus Co has a regular service to Nasugbu, but a hire car is a better bet.

Aside from bringing all your equipment from Manila and winging it, which is a viable option for those who know the area's dive sites well enough, visiting SCUBA divers really have three choices.

The Fortune Island Resort (Tel: (02) 818 3458) offers accommodations around $70 a night with SCUBA equipment for rental (bring your own). Situated at perhaps the best dive spots in the area.

Maya Maya Reef Club, (inquiry@maya-maya.com; http://www.mayamaya.com), cell (0918) 909 7170, Fax: (0918) 932 0483, has a marina full of exotic yachts and speedboats that set the scene here, and the place is popular with Expats and locals alike seeking to escape the grime of Manila. Single occupancy rooms start at around $75, including breakfast. Book first, and ask about seasonal and other discount packages.

Coral Beach Club (Tel: (0917) 901 4635; coralbch@skyinet.net; http://www.coral-beach.ph) is a place to get away from it all where you can relax and enjoy the fine life outside of the city. Located right on the beach, one can delight in overlooking the beautiful white sand and some of the most dramatic sunsets in the world. Rooms are priced at $40 and above. They have a PADI 5-star facility by Dive Ventures (Tel: (0917) 762 6473) that offers diving lessons and equipment rentals with guide and boats.

There are several beach resorts along the coast from Nasugbu to Matabungkay and further South with varying degrees of value and amenities available. These are worth checking out.

There are many small resorts, bungalows and cottages for rent along the coast hereabouts from Balayan to Nasugbu for those traveling with their transport.

Anilao

Getting there

Most dive operators in Anilao can provide their guests with some form of transfer if they need it. Adventure lovers without their own car can take a bus to Batangas and then a 30-minute or so jeepney ride over some quite bumpy roads to Anilao. Once there, one can negotiate a *banca* boat at the town pier or take a chance on getting another jeepney along the road that winds along the brows of the lush, tropical hills overlooking the sparkling Balayan Bay.

Anilao is all about diving. Since 1967, when Thelma Zuniga of the 70-room Aqua Tropical Resort first built two little nipa huts on the rugged coastline to accommodate visiting divers, Anilao has blossomed and grown. There is no 'strip' here; in fact, it is very awkward to even visit another resort if you don't have a car. However, the diving is excellent, and most of the better established resorts serve great buffets at mealtimes, some time for beach hopping, in reality more like rock hopping, is limited for most visitors. Listed are only a few of the many resorts along the rugged Balayan coastline offering SCUBA diving packages.

Anilao Seasports Anilao, Mabini, Tel: 8011850. Single rooms from $40 up. Full diving package with meals, 2 dives and accommodation from $120 per day.

Aqua Tropical Resort, Barangay Ligaya, Anilao, Batangas. Tel: 523 1989, 523 1842 or 522 2536. Aqua Tropical Resort has 70 rooms set in beautifully landscaped grounds with a large swimming pool. PADI, NAUI and ADSI instruction is offered, and there are trips to all the surrounding dive sites going out at all hours of the day.

Japanese and Taiwanese dive operators have been sending groups of divers over regularly to Aqua Tropical for decades now, and the resort's high standards reflect this. Packages start at around $100 per person, all inclusive.

Aquaventure Reef Club. Barangay Bagalangit, Mabini. Cell: (0912) 254 7140; (0917) 847 4417, Fax: (02) 895 7932. The Anilao outlet of industry leader Aquaventure Philippines Inc., the reef resort is a cosy getaway with, as do all the resorts around here, a heavy bias towards diving. Rooms start at $46 a night with a 10% discount Monday to Friday. Aquaventure Club members get a good discount here!

Dinky Little Dive Camp (divebuddies@divephil.com.ph; http://www.divephil.com) is operated by Dive Buddies Philippines. Check out the Dive Buddy Directory on their web site. Tel: (02) 899 7388, Fax: (02) 899 7393 for reservations.

Dive & Trek Resort Bauan, Batangas, telefax: (02) 851 8746; (0918) 552 0299; 833 8021. This is a diver-friendly resort that offers reasonable prices. PADI courses can also be arranged for guests.

Bonito Island Resort, Barangay Pisa Tingloy, Tel: (02) 812 2292, 94, 97; 818 0114; 818 0015; is an exclusive island resort catering to discriminating divers. Secluded and surrounded by superb diving, Bonito is a good choice for both serious divers and honeymooning couples. Call for rates as well as other information.

Balay San Teodoro, Mabini, Batangas; balay@edsamail.com.ph; (02) 943 2808; (0919) 205 7116. Located near Anilao's prime dive spots, Balay is an artistically inspired resort with cosy accommodations and complete dive amenities. Balay caters dive packages for both non-divers and divers, inclusive of food and/or dives, with rates from $30 and $60 respectively.

Puerto Galera

Getting there

Regular air-conditioned BLTB and JAM Transit buses leave from Lawton Bus terminal in Manila to Batangas Pier, where several ferries leave for Puerto Galera daily. The last trip is usually around 1.30 pm on the small car ferry; allow at least three hours for the bus trip. Private *bancas* also make the crossing from Batangas, Mayanaga and Anilao piers, charging from $35 upwards for the one-hour trip. Most resorts and dive centers in Puerto Galera can arrange painless transfers at any time of the day or night with short notice (depending on the water conditions in the Verde Island Passage).

The **Sikat Bus and Ferry** service, which leaves at 9 am promptly every morning from the **Citystate Tower Hotel**, Tel: (02) 521 3344, Fax: (02) 526 2758, costs around $15 each way and is still the best way to go for budget-minded travelers.

Passengers usually take a *banca* boat from the quaint Puerto Galera pier to the beach of their choice. Rates are supposed to be posted at the pier; if in doubt, ask someone who looks like they live there. Expect to pay about $10 for a boat to Sabang, less to Small and Big La Laguna Beaches respectively.

An irregular jeepney service plies between Puerto and Sabang Beach to the East and White Beach to the West, depending on the condition of the road.

Coco Beach Resort (resort@cocobeach. com tel: (02) 521 5260) has a free bus and ferry service for its guests, which picks up at several major hotels around Manila at 6 am. The Park Hotel and La Laguna Beach Club, can arrange for a seaplane to drop you off right on the beach.

There is no shortage of budget rooms on the many beaches within 5 km of the picturesque port of Puerto Galera. From busy Sabang Beach in the East to the quiet White Beach to the West, nipa huts and cottages, with or without catering facilities, can be rented from $5 a day and up. Small, self-contained dive resorts, such as Capt'n Greggs on Sabang, a BSAC center, and PADI Five-Star IDC dive resorts such as Atlantis Hotel (www.atlantishotel.com on Sabang, El Galleon (www.elgalleon.com) on Small La Laguna and La Laguna Beach Club (www.lalaguna.com.ph), on Big La Laguna go for

between $15 and $30 and up a night and are very good value. As with all the local shops, multilingual PADI instructors and divemasters are readily available to teach any number of courses and specialties.

The local diving community has regulated prices so all dive centers are supposed to charge the same for all diving services. Open Water courses start at around $275 to $310, Advanced from $200 to $220. A boat and dive guide is $25 per dive. Many of the dive centers carry a range of equipment for sale. Ask at any dive for up to the minute information on dive safaris to the Sibuyan Sea, Apo Reef, Coron and other remote sites originating in Puerto Galera. Technical diving is very popular in Puerto, many dive centers offer courses with ANDI, PADI, IANTD and others. Nitrox and IANTD Technical Diving courses and complete technical diving equipment, including rebreathers, are widely available.

SABANG BEACH

Among the many choices available, **Capt'n Greggs** (info@captngreggs.com.ph), Tel: (097) 349 6691, is a BSAC International School. **Atlantis Dive Resort** (info@atlantishotel.com http://www.atlantishotel.com), Tel: (097) 349 7503 is a PADI 5-Star IDC center. **Big Apple Dive Resort** (Big-Apple@qinet.net), Tel: (0912) 308 1120, (043) 724 8545, is a PADI resort and **Octopus Divers** at Villa Sabang, Tel: (0917) 562 0160, has its own training pool. These four dive centers have rooms and cottages for rent from between $10 and $25 and up a night. Most of the local nightlife is squeezed onto Sabang Beach.

Other dive centers on this beach include: **South Sea Divers** (Tel: (043) 724 8547; (0917) 747 5355) and **Cocktail Divers** (cdiver@vasia.com; http://www.wetexpedition.com), telefax (02) 892 1443. Cocktail Divers also operates a full service dive center, parasailing and water-skiing lessons, and a Dive Travel center in Manila

SMALL LA LAGUNA BEACH

El Galleon and **Asia Divers**, a PADI 5-Star IDC facility owned by PADI Course Director Allan Nash (manila@asiadivers.com, http://www.elgalleon.com), Tel: (0917) 814 5107, (0912) 308 3190, telefax: (097) 378 2094, **Sunsplash** and **Scubaplus**, a PADI facility (martin@scubaplus.com; http://

www.scubaplus.com), cell (0912) 388 4831, and **Carlo's Inn**, cell (0912) 301 0717; and **Cocktail Divers** (see listing for Sabang) are all quality resorts with dive franchises on the premises. As with most other beaches, there are lots of cheap ($7 and up) cottages around: try Nick and Sonia's first.

Other Dive centers on Small Lalaguna Beach include another **Asia Divers** outlet (admin@asiadivers.com, http://www. asiadivers.com), Tel: (097) 378 2094, Fax: (097) 386 5252), set back a little way behind the **Full Moon Restaurant**. Small La Laguna is also where you will find the smaller but highly professional **Action Divers** (info@actiondivers.com; http://www.actiondivers. com), Tel: (097) 375 1968, Fax: (097) 377 6704.

BIG LA LAGUNA BEACH

La Laguna Beach Club, or **LBC** (lalaguna@llbc.com.ph, http://www.lalaguna. com.ph), cell (0973) 855545, (0912) 363 6061, cell/fax (0973) 878 409, is the premiere spot on this cosy beach. Fan rooms are $30, aircon $40, but check with the management for package rates, seasonal and other discounts. Good food and a private pool are among the attractions here. PADI Course Director and IANTD Instructor Frank Doyle runs the PADI 5-Star Resort facility.

El Oro resort has budget rooms and a **Cocktail Divers** outlet too; there are plenty of other reasonable accommodation options to choose from.

WHITE BEACH

Not as developed as the other areas, White Beach has retained its laidback character over the years. Cottages here are usually a bit cheaper than at other beaches. There are currently two small dive centers operating along White Beach as this is written.

Other resorts with private beaches worth mentioning are Coco Beach Resort, Tel: (02) 521 5260, (0918) 595 4191, a luxurious and secluded resort getaway in a very tropical setting with Philippine Divers Corporation (pauchtom@batangas.i-next.net), cell (0912) 318 7994; (0917) 890 0200, franchise serving visiting divers. Double rooms are priced from around $63 and up, with seasonal and other discounts applicable. Tennis courts, a convention center and a lovely swimming pool complement the excellent food and service here. Encenada Beach Resort, Tel: (0912) 301 2289, has cottages and

rooms with fan and aircon. Expect to pay up to $40 a night for a comfortable cottage, less for a room. Encenada has its own dive center as well.

Boracay City code: 036
Intl. telephone access code: 63-36

Getting there

Philippines Airlines flies daily from Manila to Kalibo, a 90-minute air-conditioned bus ride from Caticlan, where a short ferry ride can usually drop you off close to your resort. If the weather doesn't permit, then you may have to cross the island, either by motorcycle taxi or on foot. For other airlines servicing Kalibo and Caticlan, Boracay's airports, refer to the Domestic Airlines section. Asian Spirit has regular flights to the strip at Caticlan. For romantics with time on their hands, it is also possible, though not recommended, to take one of several ferries from Manila or Cebu to a nearby port, such as Romblon, and to negotiate the sometimes rough sea passage onward from there. In season, WG&A Superferries runs a service to Boracay.

Along the famous white beach of Boracay there are a number of accommodation options to suit all budgets. Many resorts maintain offices in Manila too, making booking a snap. There are usually plenty of options available to travelers preferring not to reserve in advance, though in peak season, January to May, especially around Easter, it is advisable to book ahead if possible.

At least 16 dive centers are doing a thriving business, and more are on the way. Windsurfing is very popular on Boracay as well. A wide range of restaurants and bars and several great night spots complete the picture.

Many of the resorts listed here sell packages including round trip airfares and transfers; it is worth calling first to compare prices and amenities.

With comfortable rooms and suites, some air-conditioned, mostly starting above $60 a night, many of the up-scale resorts are still good value for money. Check for significant seasonal and walk-in discounts.

For the less wealthy but comfortminded, **Morimar Boracay Resort** Tel: (036) 288 3120; **Pink Patio**, Tel: (02) 845 2222 local 25; sales@pinkpatio.com; Tel: (036) 288 3888 and **Cocomangas** (02) 521 9443; are good choices, priced from $20 and up.

Budget travelers might want to try **Greenyards**, **Morning Star** or **Highland Springs**, all priced under $20 a night in peak season.

Dive centers on Boracay are very competitively priced and can be booked directly or through agents in Manila. All have multilingual PADI instruction. Dives are priced around $20 with complete rentals, many shops have day trips including boat and lunch for $50; a PADI Open Water course is around $270, Advanced $180. Due to the extreme depths sometimes attempted by the foolish few, several stores have dive computers for rent.

Divegurus

(georgewegmann@hotmail.com), Tel: (036) 288 5486, cell (0918) 919 3830, are some of the longest serving members of the local diving community, and they also have a Tabibuga, a 70ft steel boat runs daytrips and safaris to more of the best diving near and around Boracay. Victory Divers Tel: (036) 288 3209 are also Boracay veterans who specialise in discounted Habagat specials (Habagat is the wind that blows for long periods from June to November, the off-season).

Scuba World

(swidive@i-manila.com.ph; http://www.scubaworld.com.ph), Tel: (036) 288 3310, operates a full service dive center along the beach. Lapu Lapu Diving Safari (info@lapulapu.com), Tel: (036) 288 3302, Fax: (036) 288 3015, have been operating in Boracay for over a decade now. Other dive centers include Red Coral Tel: (036) 288 3486 and Calypso Tel: (036) 288 3206, Fax: (036) 288 3478; calypso@i-next.net.

Marinduque

Getting there

Not much goes on around this sleepy little Island, except for the annual Moriones Festival, which is frequently depicted in glossy DOT posters. The actual event is really quite tame, but the diving around Marinduque is well worth the effort.

There are a number of small resorts dotted around the island. Take a jeepney or bus along the Western coastal road and pick one that seems to suit you. There are no full-service dive centers, but there are a few operators with scuba gear for rent who are willing to arrange full-day dive trips if they are around. Check at any resort or hotel for more information, but be prepared for disappointment as the operators are unreliable and frequently not around. Most divers visit Marinduque's offshore islands to the west and south by live-aboard dive safaris originating from Puerto Galera and Boracay.

Mactan/Cebu City code: 032
Intl. telephone access code: 63-32

Getting there

Minutes from where Cebu's first tourist, Magellan, met his untimely end while interfering in a squabble between local chieftains, Mactan's busy airport spills out planeloads of international travelers, many of them package tourists from Japan, to enjoy the resorts of Mactan and historic Cebu's cosmopolitan beat. Cebu is a hub city, a major shipping center and the jump-off point for the rest of the Visayas.

Mactan Island is separated from Cebu City on the main island of Cebu by the Mactan Straits: a single bridge spans the gap, connecting the two.

Diving and water sports have been at the forefront of the development of tourism, a top dollar earner for the region. Cebu has several retail outlets serving the booming SCUBA market, among them **Aquaventure Cebu** aqua@aquaventure.com (Tel: (032) 234 2639, Fax: (032) 234 2603, at 2nd Flr. Myra's Pension House, 12 Escario St. Lahug, Cebu City, **Scuba World**, (swidive@i-manila.com.ph; http://www.scubaworld.com.ph), 800 Ma. Cristina cor. M. Yap Sts., Capitol, Cebu City, **Whitetip Divers** (whitetip@cebu.weblinq.net; http://www.whitetip.com), Unit 2 Borromeo Arcade Bldg., F. Formoso St., Cebu City, Tel: (032) 254 2623, **Asia Divers**info@asiadivers.com, Unit 22 Mercedes Commercial Center, A.C. Cortez Avenue, Ibabao, Mandaue City (Tel: (032) 344 6819 Fax: 344 6820), and Liquid Assets, Cebu Grand Hotel Complex, Tel: (032) 254 6359, Fax: (032) 231 4980.

Most resorts around Mactan have diving services on the premises; if not, you are never too far away from a dive center: there are over 100 dive operator permits issued every year by the local Lapu Lapu City Government! Most dive shops arrange one to five day dive safaris to nearby Cabilao Island as well as to other exotic Visayan dive spots.

At the top end of the range, **Scotty's Dive Center** at Shangria-La's Mactan Island Resort, Tel: (032) 231 0288, local 8846, Fax: (032) 231 5075, has rooms starting at $100 a night. A huge pool and outstanding landscaping complement the luxurious appointments. Scotty's Dive Center, past the pool towards the beach, has more down-to-earth prices and years of experience diving around Mactan and the Visayas. Equipment rents out for $20 a day, Dive Safaris are from between $89 and 165 a day, from economy to luxury. PADI courses are available.

Further south, on the east coast, there are many resorts servicing divers: most have decent off-the-beach diving. Rentals and instruction tend to be a little higher priced than usual. PADI Open Water Courses sell for around $350 at many dive centers.

High-end resorts on Mactan include the Maribago Beach Club, Tel: (032) 232 5411) and Tambuli Beach Club, Tel: (02) 522 2302 to 03. Rooms are around $80 to $100 and more a night in these places, with facilities to match.

For the serious diver, it is hard to beat Club Kon Tiki Resort, telefax (032) 340 9935. Genuinely run by divers for divers, Kon Tiki's international instructors teach PADI, NAUI, CMAS and SSI SCUBA courses in a very professional classroom with all the AVA's and up-to-the-minute teaching aids. It has one of the best dives ('House Reef') in Mactan right off the beach. Rates for rentals, training and dive trips are typically lower than most other operations on the Island, more in line with Puerto Galera and Boracay. Rooms are cosy, with a choice of air-conditioned or fan, and start at around $23 a night. Seasonal and other discounts can be negotiated.

Hadsan Beach Resort is another less expensive option worth checking out with two dive centers operating out of it: Sazanami Marine Sports, Tel: (032) 254 0568, cell (0912 501 2702, Fax: (032) 254 0745, caters mostly to the Japanese and are not so adept at English, a situation common in many resort-based dive centers, and Scubaworld ((032) 340 5938) also operates a concession at Hadsan Beach.

Whilst not really close to Cebu City, mention should be made of Argao Beach Club, Casay Dalagueta, Cebu, Tel: (032) 213532, (63-2) 812 1984, a few hours south of the city on the east coast. Rooms go for $60 and up here, but there is some excellent diving quite close by that is otherwise hard to reach.

MOALBOAL

On the western side of the Island, Moalboal was one of the original SCUBA diving centers in the Philippines. Most of the SCUBA operations and accommodations here are relatively humble, with prices to match. Although there were eight dive shops operating the last time we visited, only one, Seven Seas Aquanauts (the parent company of Savedra Divers), is registered with the PCSSD. It seems several of the dive operators are either too poor to register, or perhaps are unnecessarily suspicious of the government-sponsored program to promote and enhance SCUBA diving in the islands.

To get to Moalboal, one can either rent a car or takes a three-hour bus trip on the rough and rugged road over mountainous central Cebu. Buses leave every half hour from the Librando bus station in Cebu. Upon arrival at Moalboal, grab a tricycle and head off to Panagsama Beach. Accommodations here range from $5 to $70 a night. The food is also very affordable hereabouts, with several surprisingly good options.

Visaya Divers Corp, Panagsama Beach, Moalboal, Cebu, offers diving from $12 a dive if you have your own gear, $17 without, and teaches PADI Open Water Courses for $220, Advanced for $150, standard for the area.

Savedra PADI 5-Star IDC Center, www.savedra.com, Moalboal, Cebu, Tel: (032) 474 0014, Fax: (032) 474 0011, is a professionally run diving outfit with complete Nitrox and Technical Diving facilities. Rooms for rent cost $25 for fan, $30 and up for air-conditioned. Seaquest Dive Center, www.seaquestdivecenter.com, Moalboal, Cebu, Tel: (032) 349 9629, is another well-established dive operator with a branch and a resort at Alona Beach, Bohol; Sumisid Lodge, has fan rooms for around $10, air-conditioned for about $25 a night. Depending on the season and the bookings available, it is often possible for you to negotiate a better deal on accommodations as well as diving services.

A walk along Panagsama Beach will introduce you to most of the dive operators doing business. Ask for rates and facilities before committing: remember, not all dive operators are created equal.

NORTHERN CEBU

Not as well developed as the south, there are only a few places catering to SCUBA divers in the north.

As dive operators tend to come and go in remoter locations, it is best to ask for local advice with regards to dive operations doing business before planning a journey up north unless planning to stay at Alegre Beach Resort (msrophpi@csi.com.ph), at Calumboyan, Sogod, North of Cebu City, Tel: (02) 634 7505; (032) 254 9800; gm@algrebeach resort.com, is an excellent private resort. Packages here go for around $270 net per person for two nights/three days twin sharing deluxe accommodation with four dives.

Malapascua Island is one of the most raved about dive sites now because of the spectacular thresher sharks that inhabit its waters. From Cebu, one can take a bus at Northern Bus Terminal priced at $3 for a four-hour ride or a taxi at half the time for around $20 to Maya. From Maya are passenger *banca* trips priced from $2 to $10 that take you to Malapascua Island in 30 minutes. Resorts worth checking out are Malapascua Exotic Island Dive and Beach Resort, www.malapascua.net, Tel: (032) 437 0983 to 84; (0918) 774 0484), Sea Explorers, www.seaexplorersscuba.com, Tel: (032 234 0248); Blue Water and Cocobana. Dives cost around $25. For more information, check with any of the dive operators listed in the Mactan/Cebu section.

Southern Leyte

A true frontier for divers and travelers, Southern Leyte has stunning natural attractions above and below the water. Waterfalls and walls, caves and whale sharks attract a growing number of visitors, and new sites are being opened up all the time. This is one of the only places left in the Philippines where many dive sites are reached by tricycle!

Getting there

Getting to Southern Leyte can be half the fun, a daily Super Cat fast ferry leaves Port 4 of Cebu City for Maasin every morning at 8:30, takes about 2.5 hours to get there.

There are several dive operators in the area, but don't expect state-of-the-art dive centers, just plenty of outrageously good diving. Try any of the following for more info:

Peter's Dive Resort, www.whaleofadive. com, Lungsodaan, Padre Burgos, Cell: 0919 585 389; scuberph@yahoo.com;

Davliz Scuba Center, Cantutang, Padre Burgos, run by David Jackson or

Blue Depth Dive Resort, Cantutang, Padre Burgos, managed by Joyce Teves.

Bohol City code: 038
Intl. telephone access code 63-38.

Up and coming Bohol has an increasingly diverse choice of accommodation and dive services. Most of these originate on Panglao Island, across the causeway south of the provincial capital Tagbilaran City.

Getting there

Bohol can be reached by regular domestic flights to Tagbilaran City from Manila or Cebu, or by comfortable, fast ferry boat services from Manila, Cebu and from throughout the Visayas—Mindanao region. Once there, most divers head for Alona Beach on Panglao Island, where the scuba diving business is flourishing.

Local prices are fairly standard. Dive safaris start at $55 to $80 a day. Boats rent out for about $6 a day per person. A PADI Open Water Course is around $250, Advanced $170, Equipment costs about $10 a day.

Cebu Sea Explorers (cebu@seaexplorersscuba.com; http://www.seaexplorersscuba.com) c/o Alona Tropical Beach Resort, Panglao Island, cell (0918) 770 4709; (038) 411 2244; (038) 411 4517, also has branches on Cabilao Island and at El Dorado Beach Resort (cebu@seaexplorersscuba.com) in Dumaguete, Negros Oriental. Owner Chris Heim, a Swiss national, is a PADI Course Director who holds several IDC's in the Visayas every year and franchises eight dive centers throughout the Visayas and in Puerto Galera.

Bohol Divers Lodge, Alona Beach, Panglao Island, Bohol, Tel: (038) 502 9050, cell (0917) 320 1940, is operated by long-time resident Frenchman Jacques Trotin, www.seaquestdivecenter.com.

Balicasag Island Dive Resort, Balicasag, Panglao (Tels: (038) 411 2192; (038) 502

6001; for reservations call (02) 524 2502; (02) 524 2495), has single rooms starting at $37, doubles at $43. PADI Open Water Courses are $300 here, complete equipment rentals for around $28 a day, air for $10 a fill.

Alona Divers, Alona Beach, Tawala, Panglao, telefax: (038) 502 9043, is a cosy dive resort managed by German Peter Buermann and his charming wife Maritess.

Atlantis Dive Center, www.atlantisdive-center.com Alona Beach, Panglao, Tel: (038) 502 9058; is one of the longest running operations on the island owned by Kurt Biebelmann.

Other dive centers worth checking out on Panglao include: **Genesis Divers**, cell (0918) 770 8434, Fax: (038) 502 9056; **Sharky's Divers**, and **Swiss Bamboo House**.

Other dive centers around Bohol include **Polaris Dive Center** on Cabilao Island, cell (0918) 773 7681, Fax: (038) 253 0265 and **Sierra Madre Divers**, located at Bohol Tropics in Tagbilaran City, cells (0912) 720 1047; 707 0669, cell/fax: (0912) 720 0078.

Coron

There are a few landlines in Coron: they are all difficult to reach. **Swagman Travel** (bookings@swaggy.com) has an office in Coron and transacts bookings and other business through a radio connection to their head office in Manila (Tel: (02) 523 8541, Fax: (02) 522 3663). Several of the dive operators in Coron have e-mail and/or Manila representative offices that take bookings and arrange transfers.

Getting there

Refer to Domestic Airlines section for information on airlines flying to Coron from Manila. For the adventurous, Inter-island ferries ply the route to and from Coron and Batangas (Viva Shipping Lines) and Manila (Asuncion Shipping Lines, North Harbour).

Philippine Divers Corporation, cell (0912) 318 7994; cell (0917) 890 0200, operates the diving facility, 'Dugong Dive Center', at Club Paradise, Dimakya Island, Busuanga, off the northeast coast of the Island of Busuanga. This is a first-class resort with rooms starting at around $110 a night and up.

Reservations should be made first so that the resort can meet the plane in Coron and escort visitors on the land and sea trip to the hotel. Although too far from the 'Ghost Fleet' of Coron Bay to place divers on the famous wrecks, there is plenty of excellent coral diving within easy reach of the resort.

Around Coron itself, several small lodge-type of hotels have sprung up to cater to the increasingly large number of divers visiting the area. Several outlying islands have resort developments of varying sophistication.

Kalamayan Inn (kalmayan@mozcom.com; http://www2.mozcom.com/~kalmayan), Coron, Busuanga Island, Northern Palawan, Tel: (02) 633-4701, Fax: (02) 633-4855 has eight air-conditioned rooms and a bar and restaurant called 'The Tourist Trap'. It is a few minutes walk from most of the dive centers in Coron.

Sangat Island Reserve, www.sangat.com.ph, info@sangat.com.ph, on Sangat Island is situated right in the middle of the best wreck diving in the Philippines with its own 'House Wreck' a few meters off the white sand beach. Eight cottages, a restaurant and a PADI oriented dive center round out the facilities. Satellite phone: 00873 762 612 318 from 8am to 5pm.

Discovery Divers, www.vasia.com/ddivers; ddivers@vasia.com;), Barangay 5, Coron, Busuanga, have many years experience diving the wrecks and corals of Coron Bay. They also teach PADI courses, Open Water at $269, Advanced at $199. A dive with your own equipment costs $16, or $18.50 if full rental gear is required. A speedboat is available for hire at $180 a day.

Dive Right (diving@mozcom.com; http://www2.mozcom.com/~diving) arranges tours and accommodation as well as PADI courses. They also retail Zeagle and other equipment.

ABC Divers (Tel: (036) 288 3302, Fax: (036) 288 3015 for reservations and information) conducts dive safaris and is a PADI facility.

Coron Tours and Travel (corontur@pworld.net.ph) are agents for Asian Spirit and can be very helpful in getting seats on planes that claim to be booked out and at reserving a room at the resort of your choice. Tel: (02) 838 4964-65.

El Nido

Getting there

Corporate Air, Tel: (63-2) 804 0408, directly to El Nido from Manila, cost is about $120 one way. Alternatively, you can fly to Puerto Princesa, one way, and suffer for up to 12 hours in a jeepney from Puerto Princesa to Taytay and then across the island to El Nido over often muddy roads which frequently require a shovel and a good pair of shoulders to negotiate. Or you can fly to Coron and hire a *banca* boat to El Nido, a trip of several hours to a full day, depending on the waves. The price should not exceed $100, and is usually open to negotiation. A weekly boat trip to and from Boracay sometimes runs in season.

Once in El Nido, the best hotel in town is the Bayview Hotel, where a single room is just over $3 a night. When we were there, electricity was on from 5.30 pm until 11 pm. There are no private bathrooms, but the toilets flush and bathing is by 'bucket bath'. There are also plenty of cottages for rent at around $7 and up a night.

There are three dive shops in the town proper: the oldest is Bacuit Diver Services, run by German Willy Amman and his wife Nora. It is 100 meters east of the Pier and charges $20 for one dive, $30 for two. Boat charges of $30 are divided between divers. A PADI Open Water Course costs $200, Advanced $250.

The town itself is not big—you can walk from end to end in a couple of minutes.

Miniloc Island Resort and Lagen Island, both situated in El Nido bay with outstanding natural views and first class facilities, are operated by 10 Knots Development Corporation, 2/f, Builder's Center Building, 170 Salcedo St., Legaspi Village, Makati City, Tel: (02) 894 5644, Fax: (02) 810 3620. You should reserve first as both resorts are not especially welcoming to transient visitors. They have rooms from $130 and up. These prices include all diving and other activities. PADI and NAUI instruction is available, an Open Water Course costs $350. Pangalusian Island Resort, another 10 Knots property in El Nido Bay, suffered a devastating fire in mid-1998 but is now operational.

MINDANAO: CAMIGUIN, GENERAL SANTOS AND DAVAO

Although parts of Mindanao are considered unsafe due to ongoing hostilities between Muslim rebels and outlaws (such as the Abu Sayyaf in Jolo and Basilan), there are plenty of areas where tourists are welcome and can expect high standards of safety and security. Fortunately, the diving in these areas is excellent and the local facilities are good and reasonably priced.

General Santos City

Intl. telephone access code: 63-83

Getting there

Regular flights by PAL serve the city, there are ample choices for accommodation and entertainment. The 'Tuna Capital' of the Philippines (because of the large numbers of tuna trawlers at port here), Gen San, as it is more popularly known, has one of the best walls to be found anywhere in the country.

There is only one dive center in town, operated by Englishman Chris Dearne.

Tuna City Scuba Center, Cambridge Farm Hotel, Purok Malakas, Philippines 9500. Telefax (083) 554 5681, cell 0917 330 1237. divegensan@gs-link.net

Davao

Intl. telephone access code: 63-82

Getting there

Davao is served by regular domestic flights daily. A thriving city, home to the smelly durian fruit and orchid farms, Davao enjoys a balmy tropical climate year round. Some good dive sites and several choices for discriminating divers to choose from.

Pearl Farm Resort, http://www.century-hotels.com/hotels/dpf_factsheet.htm, Kaputian, Samal Island Davao, Tel: (82) 221 9970 to 78, Fax: (82) 221 9979 a luxurious resort with some fine dive sites immediately adjacent, rooms start at around US$90 per night. pearlfarm@skyinet.net

Amphibian, Stall IA, VAL Learning Village, Ruby St., Marfoni Heights Subd., Davao, Tel: (82) 227 2049

City Shack Corporation/Whitetip Divers Davao, www.whitetip.com, PPA Bldg. Santa Ana Wharf, Davao City, Tel: (82) 227 6175. ctshack@dv.weblinq.com

Camiguin

Intl. telephone access code: 63-88
(unless otherwise stated)

Getting there

Fast ferry services from Cebu City or Balingoan (88 km by regular bus services from Cagayan de Oro City, which in turn is served regularly by several domestic airlines and by fast ferry services from Cebu City).

Camiguin Island, just south of Bohol, is a delightful tropical paradise with plenty to see and do topside as well as some outstanding diving under the waves. There is a good choice of resorts on the island, and a couple of dive centers too.

Genesis Divers, www.genesisdivers.com, Caves Resort, Agoho, Camiguin Island, telefax (88) 387 9063, genesisc@cebu.weblinq.com, have been around for a while, and is a sister company to Genesis Divers on Bohol.

Mantangale Alibuag Dive Center, Lapasan Highway, Cagayan de Oro, Tel:(8822) 722 591 Fax: (88) 856 2324, mantadive@col.com.ph. Not actually on Camiguin Island, but the dive center here regularly visits Camiguin and other outlying sites such as Constancia Reef.

Live-aboards

Live-aboard diving in the Philippines is an experience which, once tasted, is usually repeated. From $65 to $180 and more a day, a full range of vessels and destinations await divers with a yearning to discover some of the best diving in Southeast Asia.

The Sulu Sea dive sites, such as Tubbataha, Jessie Beazley and Basterra, are accessible for three or four months of the year (March to June), and only by live-aboard. Book early to ensure a slot. Other locations frequently visited by live-aboards include El Nido, Coron, Bohol and the Visayas, Apo Reef and the Sibuyan Sea. Some outfits also dive the Spratley Islands.

At the bottom end, large *bancas*, or pump boats, and sailing yachts carry six to eight people in relative comfort. Some have air-conditioning, but most don't, though sleeping on the deck under a blanket of stars is quite okay for most of us. Camps are often made on deserted islands (make sure you tidy up properly before leaving please), and schedules are very much open. These budget live-aboard trips can be arranged through most dive shops in Puerto Galera and Boracay, and through Whitetip Divers in Manila.

For the more sophisticated diver, there is no shortage of superb, customised live-aboard dive vessels offering the absolute maximum comfort and service. Fine dining, luxurious appointments and professional expertise are very much the order of the day on these boats: some even carry E-6 film processing on board too.

Every year, groups of divers return from around the world to take advantage of the excellent value offered by Philippine live-aboards.

Manila and Cebu are the main centers for live-aboard bookings: embarkation points depend on where the vessel is working.

Live-aboards operating in the Philippines currently include:

MV *Island Explorer*, MV *Big Blue*, MV *Oceanic Explorer* (swidive@imanila.com.ph; http://www.scubaworld.com.ph) are all operated by Scuba World.

MY *Tristar*, one of the most luxurious live-aboards operating in the country, is owned and managed by: Tristar Sea Ventures Corp., U/G 48 Cityland Pasong Tamo Cond., 6264 Estacion St., Makati City, Tel: (02) 844 5074; 844 5159; Fax: (02) 752 2552. Has been cruising the 'Visayan Triangle' full-time for years.

MY *Tabibuga* (georgewegmann@hotmail.com) is a 70-foot (22-meter) all-steel construction motor vessel with one six berth and four two berth cabins. The *"Tabby"* is a mid-priced live-aboard boat that mostly visits the Sibuyan Sea, Apo Reef and Coron.

MV *Eagle 5* (www.eagleoffshore.com.ph), although not a full-time live-aboard, the 107-ft (34-meter) Eagle 5 is very well set up for divers with 2 x 15 cfm compressors and 36 tanks, as well as a complete wardrobe of Shimano rods and reels for sport fishing. Available for charter year round. Tel: (02) 721 1991; telefax 721 1969, eagle@diver.com.ph.

Singapore   Country code: 65

Hardly the dive mecca of Southeast Asia, Singapore is nevertheless an important center for diving concerns. Because of its location in the heart of the region, it is never far from Asia's favorite dive sites.

Singapore's Changi Airport has become the air hub of Southeast Asia. Connections are fast and efficient, and the airport is a fine place to relax between flights. Because of the competition among the republic's many travel agents, travelers have the pick of economic air fares.

All prices in Singapore dollars.

A duty-free republic

Perhaps Singapore's greatest attraction is its duty-free shopping. With the exception of cigarettes, alcohol and a few sundry items which probably would not attract the average shopper, all goods are duty-free. This does not, however, always mean they are cheap. Bargaining is still *de rigeur* in many shops and it is up to the shopper to ensure he gets a bargain.

Over the last decade, dive shops have burgeoned in Singapore as the sport has become more and more popular. Today there are over 20 dive shops selling equipment, dive courses, organizing equipment repair and servicing as well as providing a range of services for both amateur and professional diver. Most are excellent and run by knowledgeable professionals (often dive instructors themselves) who will advise and help shoppers. They are also good places to talk to fellow divers, and many have their fingers on the pulse of diving out of Singapore itself. While many dive shops run Open Water certification courses (PADI is the most popular), some offer Advanced Courses which can be done either in Singapore or in the rather more attractive waters of neighboring territories. Tioman and Aur are popular destinations, while some operators will even fly as far as Bali, Lombok and Manado to run specialized courses.

The republic grew up on its maritime trading facilities—it was first colonized by the British in 1819 when Stamford Raffles established a trading post—and over the years developed into one of the top three busiest

commercial ports worldwide. Strangely, however, it did not develop particularly as a leisure center for sailing. But with a growing middle class, and the development of tourist resorts in neighboring countries, leisure cruising began to develop. In addition, Singapore unveiled a new marine terminal for cruise ships in 1992 which underwrote its belief that it can also become the Southeast Asian hub for cruising.

Diving in Singapore

Despite variable and often low visibility caused by run-off and shipping activities, Singapore offers the observant diver unexpectedly rewarding encounters. Seahorses, turtles, cuttlefish, barracuda, eels, clownfish, copper-banded butterflyfish, angelfish and a variety of corals and sponges, not to mention several wrecks, are accessible within 10 minutes by high-speed day boat. Several small craft ranging from the slower local "bumboats" to custom-made, high-speed vessels run two-tank day trips over weekends and public holidays, from the leisure marinas around the island. Bigger boats take divers further afield into Indonesian or Malaysian waters.

Diving from Singapore

In Indonesia, there is good diving around Pulau Bintan (just 4 hours away), particularly around southern sites such as Mapor Island, accessible by live-aboard boat. Further afield, the Anambas Islands provide fine diving, and it is worth going there for a minimum of

ALITIES

GAPORE

5 days. The nearest Malaysian dive sites are around Pulau Aur (approximately 8 to 10 hours by boat) and slightly further afield to Tioman (11 hours away).

Boats making regular dive trips from Singapore are generally of a local design (boats that were previously designed for fishing), converted to accommodate up to 8 to 12 divers in cabins, and with deck space for tanks and recreational activities. The skipper or his mate will provide good basic Asian meals and handle the diving side of the operation. Few are luxurious, but most are comfortable and will leave Singapore in the evening so that by motoring overnight the diving clientele can jump into the water first thing the following day.

There are also a number of more luxurious boats for hire—either well equipped yachts or motor cruisers—that can be chartered by the day or week or which offer weekend live-aboard trips. Nowadays it is common for a yacht or cruiser to have dive equipment on board (as well as windsurf boards and other marine toys), but they may not all have compressors, which would restrict the number of dives possible.Chartering a yacht or cruiser offers divers the opportunity to travel further afield. Apart from the East Coast of Malaysia and the neighboring Riau Archipelago, the east and western shores of Thailand are also possible destinations.

General information

The island republic of Singapore is located 137 km north of the Equator. It covers a total of 682 sq km and comprises some 59 islets of which the island of Singapore is about 580 sq km. Much of the main island is urban though there are still pockets of primary and secondary tropical forests surrounding the three main water reservoirs. A recent census records some 4 million permanent residents in the republic and annual tourist arrivals of over 5 million. Of the permanent citizens and residents, 76 percent are Chinese, 14 percent are Malay and 7 percent are Indian.

Singapore has 11 public holidays annually, celebrating Hindu, Buddhist, Muslim and Christian holidays as well as its National Day on 9 August. While this means that most people are on holiday, shops and restaurants are almost always open with the exception of the two public holidays when the majority Chinese population celebrate Chinese New Year.

Smaller shops and stores are generally open from 10 am to 7 pm, 6 or 7 days a week while supermarkets and large department stores will stay open to 9 or 10 pm.

Climate

Singapore is a tropical island with relatively uniform temperatures year round. The average daily temperature is 26.7°C. From December to March the northwest monsoon blows, bringing slightly cooler temperatures and the heaviest precipitation. Rain generally falls in short, sharp showers. From June to September, the southwest monsoon brings lighter winds and less rainfall. The humidity is always high—averaging 84.4 percent.

Access

Most visitors arrive directly at Changi Airport, where taxis can take them directly into town (20 minutes). The average cost is around S$17. A public bus also operates to Orchard Road at a cost of S$1.30: it takes just over 1 hour. The MRT train also travels to downtown and takes about 30 minutes.

Money

The Singapore dollar (S$) is the republic's currency. Banks open 9.30 am to 3.30 pm, Monday to Friday and 9.30 to 11.30 am on Saturdays. Money changers will change international currencies, and ATMs can issue currency for those with international credit cards. At the time of this writing, US$1=S$1.65.

Getting around

Singapore has an excellent system of public buses, a relatively new and very fast mass rapid transit system (MRT) and more than 12,000 metered taxis. By international levels, fares on the public buses and the MRT are very economical, as are those by metered taxi. Currently flagfall is S$2.40.

Accommodations

Accommodation in Singapore is geared to meet the needs of most purses, but while there is some budget accommodation, much is targeted at the business traveler. Of the many hundred registered hotels in Singapore, over 50 are in the 4- and 5-star luxury category. Prices for a room vary from as little as S$60 for a basic room in a Chinese-run hotel to over S$1,000 for a fine room in the grand old lady of Singapore, Raffles Hotel. If you select a hotel when you arrive (and that is very easy at Changi Airport), you should expect to pay in the S$150 to S$200 range. However, if you secure a booking prior to leaving home through a travel agent, you will find that the real cost of the room will be much nearer the S$70 to S$120 mark.

Food

Singapore has one of the greatest diversity of restaurants and cafes in Southeast Asia. And more importantly, the quality of cuisine in the republic is unfailingly high. There are over 170 markets serving food from individual stalls, as well as thousands of restaurants and cafes. Meals in these hawker centers can cost as little as S$3.00. Singaporean food is a happy mix of Malay, Chinese and Indian cooking, with an extra accent on spice. Seafood is a particular speciality.

Dive operators

Dive shops all over the republic offer dive gear, courses, publications, and dive tours. Listed below, in alphabetical order, are four we can recommend.

Abyss Scuba International Pte Ltd 373 Joo Chiat Place, Singapore 428029, Tel: 6348-4762, Fax : 6348-4763, Web:www.abyss.com.sg Email: divers@abyss.com.sg

Big Bubble Centre 68 Neil Road, Singapore 088836, Tel: (+65) 6222-6862, Website: www.bigbubble.com Email: bbcdiver@starhub.net.sg Live-aboard trips to Malaysia. PADI 5-Star Dive Centre.

Diventures Scuba Blk 12 Pandan Loop #01-17, Singapore 128230, Tel: (65) 6778-0661, Fax: (65) 6778-0662, email: diven@singnet.com.sg web: www.diventures.com.sg

Marsden Bros Dive Centre 113 Holland Road, Singapore 278556, Tel: 6475-0050, Fax: 6475-0020, email: marsbros@pacific.net.sg web: www.marsbros.com An expatriate owned and operated PADI dive center offering a full range of PADI courses,

including specialties such as nitrox, naturalist and wreck diving, are available. Equipment shop. The high-speed, custom-made catamaran *Typhoon* takes divers on day and night dives around Singapore. Escorted tours to dive sites such as Sipadan are available. Since 1994 the *Reclaim II* has pioneered diving in the area. From April to October, she travels to the Riau archipelago every weekend, and is also available for charter. Encounters with dolphins, Spanish mackerel, tuna, bumphead parrotfish, blue-spotted stingrays, batfish, several species of shark and outstanding soft and hard corals are frequent. Dive sites range from shallow, pristine reefs to dramatic drop-offs.

Built in Terengganu, Malaysia, in 1991, this 56-foot motor yacht has spacious teak decks, 3 air-conditioned cabins sleeping 8 passengers, 2 bathrooms, a galley and dining area. Onboard diving equipment includes 2 compressors, and tanks, weights and equipment available for hire. *Reclaim II* is powered by twin 240hp diesel engines and equipped with GPS, radar, autopilot, sonar, forward-looking sounder, generator, VHF radio, CD player and inflatable dinghy.

The live-aboard trips are distinguished by her professional and fun crew, which includes expatriate zoologists and PADI instructors; excellent cuisine; and adventure diving in secluded waters. All meals are included.

Pro Diving Services Tel: 6291-2261, email: prodiving@pacific.net.sg. Operated by William Ong. In addition to a full range of dive courses, Pro Diving sells a comprehensive selection of gear and can also offer advice on where to dive from Singapore.

Scuba Corner Block 809 French Road #05-150 Kitchener Complex, Singapore 200809, Tel: 6338-6563, Fax: 6298-9671, email:info@scubacorner.com.sg Web: www.scubacorner.com.sg Scuba equipment service & repair centre.

SEA & SEA Underwater Camera Equipment 1 Coleman Street #02-13, The Adelphi, Singapore 179803, Tel: 6337-6334, Fax: 6339-1869, email: seansea@pacific.net.sg

Seadive Adventures Unit #01-03 Republic of SingaporeYacht Club, 52 West Coast Ferry Road, email: seadive@singnet.com.sg Web: http://coldfusion.seadiveadventures.com/index.cfm

Thailand Country Code: 66

You'll find Thailand an easy country to travel in as the tourism industry here is well developed and well organized. The people of Thailand are extremely friendly and polite, and crime problems are relatively rare. English is widely spoken in tourist areas, but keep your requests—and language and grammar—simple. Above all, avoid becoming frustrated and losing your temper as this will lead to doors of communication rapidly closing. The attitude of *jai yen,* or "keep your cool," will go a long way towards making your time here more pleasant and enjoyable. Unless noted, prices in US$.

Cultural considerations

Thais are very proud of their heritage—and rightly so. The country has never been colonized, but was briefly occupied by the Japanese during World War II, and Thais are happy with their freedom and their way of life. Show respect and consideration and you will receive it in return.

Customs and habits in Thailand are often quite different from those of other countries and can be difficult for travelers to understand. Respect these customs and beliefs—even if they may not immediately make sense to you—and you'll find your time in Thailand more enjoyable, fulfilling, and I dare say, educational.

Always remove your shoes before entering a Thai house or a temple, even if your hosts insist it is not necessary. Removing your shoes before boarding a dive boat will also show that you know what's going on.

The head of a Thai is considered the highest point—literally and spiritually—while the feet are considered the lowest. Therefore you should never touch a Thai on the head, even children, and make an effort not to point to or touch objects or people with your feet.

The *wai* (putting your hands together with flat palms in a prayer like position) is a traditional and beautiful form of greeting in Thailand. Rules for who *wai*s who are complicated, even for Thais, but it is generally not appropriate to pay this form of respect to children, to waiters, housekeepers or those younger than yourself or of a lower social station. It is appropriate, however, to *wai* persons older than you in many situations, especially those who have been extra kind to you. For example, if you are invited into a Thai home, it is very polite to *wai* your hosts upon entering and leaving. It is rare that a tourist is ever obligated to perform a *wai,* as you are a guest in this country. However, just like a handshake in Western countries, it is an important part of Thai culture and a little bit of understanding goes a long way.

The Thai Royal Family is highly respected and loved, and it is in extremely poor taste to make denigrating remarks about it, even in jest. Never desecrate an image of the King or Queen of Thailand, which you will often find hanging proudly in many shops and places of business. Even stepping on a rolling coin, which bears the image of the King, is considered rude and should be avoided.

Air travel

Don Muang airport in Bangkok is one of the busiest airports in the world, and hundreds of flights arrive daily from virtually every major country. Thai Airways International is the national airline, and it is consistently named one of the best airlines in the world. Singapore, whose national airline is also a world champion in passenger service, is also a great place to make your entry to Southeast Asia, as Changi Airport offers multiple connecting flights to Bangkok and Phuket everyday.

Air travel within Thailand is convenient and relatively inexpensive. The Phuket airport receives at least five flights a day (the number varies between the high and low seasons) from Bangkok year-round. Phuket's ever-expanding airport receives international flights as well, from Hong Kong, Japan, Taiwan, Singapore, Malaysia, and Europe. Flights are available to and from Koh Samui and Pattaya on Bangkok Airways.

The Thai Airways office telephone number in Bangkok is 66-2/513-0121 and in Phuket, 66-76/211-195.

Land travel

Ground transportation in Thailand is very well organized, and both the trains and buses are relatively comfortable and efficient. Travel by train is probably the most comfortable and least expensive, but since the trains are often full they must be booked in advance. The state government runs the rail system, and booking trains can be less convenient than privately run buses.

Buses are common and go everywhere that's anywhere. Buses run in three different classes: *tamada* (normal), *ae* (air-conditioned), and VIP (the best). The most comfortable are the new double-decker VIP buses and their usage is common on most major routes. Be sure to bring warm clothes, however, as Thai air-conditioned buses are notorious for their extremely low temperatures!

Rot too (mini-vans) are widely available as means of transport between tourist destinations, but the majority of these drivers are extremely unprofessional and drive as if they are in a car race. Caution and a strong stomach are advised when traveling this way.

Motorbike and car rental is available in most tourist areas—where there are roads, of course. If you can, buy insurance. Be careful at all times when driving, due to the dual hazards of tourists not paying attention and reckless Thai drivers. Motorcycles are a fun and cheap way to get around, provided you are experienced on two wheels. Thailand is not a good place to learn. A license is usually not required, but rental agencies will take your passport as a deposit against damage.

Local taxis and buses are widely available, and prices vary from place to place. One thing you'll notice quickly: Thais rarely walk. Thus, transportation is readily available anyplace you find people.

Sea travel

Ferries travel to Koh Phi Phi, Koh Samui, Koh Tao, etc. on a daily basis. Any travel agent can book them. Obviously, some boats are more comfortable and safer than others.

Visas

All travelers must have a passport valid for at least six months. For stays shorter than 30 days, visas are not required for Southeast Asian citizens and for most Europeans and North Americans. Visas are required for stays longer than 30 days, although some nationalities, such as Scandinavians, are exempt and given 90 days upon arrival. Check with the Thai embassy in your own country before departure since entry rules do change often. Altogether, the visa process is simple, convenient and inexpensive.

Health

Thailand is a tropical country and there are certain health issues travelers should be aware of. Check with your health department before leaving. Malaria and other mosquito-borne diseases are only a problem in remote areas like the jungles of northern Thailand, islands near the Cambodian border, and Koh Tao north of Koh Samui. It can be a problem in Myanmar if you spend any time on shore. If traveling to the Mergui Archipelago, see your doctor for the latest recommendations on what medication to take. We do suggest that you bring along a good supply of mosquito repellent, sun cream, and a hat.

Bottled water is widely available, and you are well advised to drink only this type. Tap water is rarely—if ever—clean enough for western stomachs. All water served in hotels, guest houses, restaurants, and dive boats is bottled, usually coming from large 20-liter containers to help control the plastic waste problems. If in doubt, ask.

Health care, including dental work in Thailand is widely available and inexpensive. Most first-aid supplies are easily purchased virtually everywhere. Any prescription medicines you need, of course, should be brought from home.

Dive emergencies

While there are three working recompression chambers in Thailand, there is no air evacuation, at least on any reliable basis. Therefore, transport time can be very lengthy, depending on your location. Even in the Similan Islands, which is relatively close to the chamber in Phuket, evacuation may take 6 hours or more; more distant areas will take even longer. Considering the lengthy transport times, it should go without saying to dive conservatively; do everything you can to avoid a dive accident!

Chamber contact information:

Pattaya

Apakorn Kiatiwong Naval Hospital
Sattahip, Chonburi
Tel: 38-601185; 26 km east of Pattaya; urgent care available 24 hours

Bangkok

Dept. of Underwater & Aviation Medicine, Phra Pinklao Naval Hospital, Taksin Rd, Thonburi, Bangkok
Tel: 02-460-0000 through 19, ext. 341, or 02-460-1105; open 24 hours

Phuket

Hyperbaric Services Thailand, 233 Raj-U-thit 200 Pee Road, Patong Beach, Phuket, 83150 Thailand
Tel: 076-342-518, Fax: 076-342-519
After hours emergency number: 01-693-1306
Email: sssphk@loxinfo.co.th

Samui

Hyperbaric Services Thailand, 34.8 Moo 4, Bo Phut, Ko Samui, Suratthani 843120 Thailand
Tel: 077-427-427, Fax: 077-427-377
After hours emergency number: 01-606-3476
Email: hstsamui@loxinfo.co.th

Note: keep in mind that the Hyperbaric Services Thailand charge over US$800 per hour for treatment, so insurance must be purchased before traveling. Government operated chambers charge much less, but are only in the Bangkok Area. Dive insurance is very inexpensive through DAN (insurance is available worldwide) and well worth it in case of a problem, real or perceived. See more about DAN below.

Weather

Thailand has three seasons; cool, hot, and rainy. The best time to visit the west coast is between October and May; the best time to visit the east coast is February to August. The summer months of July and August are usually very pleasant, although it tends to rain in the evenings. September is not the best time on the islands, as it tends to be rainy and the seas are generally too rough for swimming or diving.

Most of the good dive sites are on islands far enough offshore to be unaffected by runoff, and rain makes no difference to the water clarity. Visibility in the Similans, for example, is actually greatest during the summer months—despite the evening rains.

Clothing

Although shorts and T-shirts are appropriate for dive boats and the beaches, Thais tend to dress more formally, and are actually offended by revealing clothing, especially when worn by women. Do try to be aware of your surroundings, and avoid giving offense. Topless and nude sunbathing are officially against the law, but they are widespread, especially in backpacker's hangouts. Thai people are very forgiving, but this does not mean these practices are accepted. Especially if you are on a beach with a majority of Thais, please wear a bathing suit.

What to bring

Try to pack as lightly as possible, as the climate is very agreeable—except near the northern borders in December and January, and warm clothes are for rent there if you are planning a trek.

The diving industry is very competitive in Thailand, and equipment, usually in very good shape, is available for rent no matter where you dive. Spares are readily available in Phuket, Samui, and Koh Tao these days, but are not always convenient to buy; it is best to bring things like extra mask and fin straps, o-rings, etc. Most centers rent wet suits.

A 3 mm wet suit (even a shorty or surfing style) or a Lycra suit is adequate for diving all year-round. Keep in mind, however, that Lycra offers little or no thermal protection, and these suits are not adequate if you plan to dive three or more times per day. A full-length neoprene suit is probably best for serious diving.

Power in Thailand is 220 VAC. Although some of the more expensive dive boats offer 110 VAC, you should bring a proper adapter if you have 110V equipment. Note: Inexpensive "shaver" type adapters will not work for such devices as laptop computers and rechargers for underwater flashes. Bring the proper type. Most places stock batteries.

As of this update, many, many more dive shops are concentrating on the retail dive gear business. Prices vary, and if you are considering buying equipment while in Thailand, it's a good idea to have an idea of what it would cost at home first. In general, however, prices are competitive, and many items will be far cheaper than they would be at home. Unlike even a few years ago, selection is now excellent.

Photography

Underwater photography services have not expanded as rapidly as other services over the past few years, and it's still difficult to rent a camera in most places, but more and more dive centers are getting "point and shoot" cameras. Film is developed everywhere, but professional labs are only available in Bangkok. Film is widely available, but it is rarely stored cold, and is not usually very cheap. Again, batteries are rarely a problem, although batteries for the Nikonos are for some reason difficult to find. Batteries for diving computers are now easy to find in Phuket, but not in other areas. Most live-aboards have adequate power for charging strobe batteries.

Communications

Due to recent changes in the phone system country-wide, it is now necessary to dial the city or province code before the number wherever you are. For example, if you are in Phuket, you must dial 076 before every number dialed. The same thing goes if you are trying to call Phuket from Bangkok, 076 before the number. Charges are 3 baht per call locally, or from province to province, 8 to 12 baht per call. These are charges per call, not per minute.

Mobile phone prefixes are either 01 or 09. Mobile phone charges are between 3 and 12 baht per minute to call out, but there are no charges for receiving calls on your mobile phone. Thailand uses the GSM system among others, so your European phone will work here. Americans will just have to wait.

If you call from overseas, do not dial the "0" after the country code (66). So, to call Bangkok from overseas you would dial +662+the number. From inside Thailand, 02+the number.

Internet access

Accessing email or the web in Thailand is relatively cheap and very painless. There are hundreds of internet cafes in all tourist areas, and most other areas as well. Prices range from 20 to 60 baht per hour; at hotels, often more. Not all hotel rooms have phone jacks which can be used for laptop computers or Palm devices. If this is a concern, check with the hotel before booking.

Money exchange

Until recently, the Thai baht remained very steady against the US dollar. In 1996 the baht, along with every other Asian currency, started changing daily against most major currencies. Only time will tell if currencies stabilize again. As of this writing, at an exchange rate of US$1=baht 43.5, Thailand represents a bargain for those traveling with US or European currencies.

Changing money is easy, except in extremely remote areas (where you probably don't need much money anyway). Credit cards are widely accepted and dive centers normally do not add a service charge, though many hotels and other shops will.

Accommodations

Thailand has some of the best hotels in the world, and service is often of the highest standard. Thailand is a country with many levels of economy, and the choice of what class you want to fit into is definitely yours. Divers generally select one of the many inexpensive and comfortable guest houses or bungalows, although fancy hotels are certainly available.

On the islands, room rates range from 300 to 1,500 baht per night ($6 to $35 at the time of this writing) for a basic bungalow with cold water and a fan to 1,500 to 3,500 baht ($35 to $80) for a more comfortable hotel with hot water and air-conditioning. If you want to hang out in luxury with the heavy players, figure 12,000 baht ($275) a night or more. If you are interested in the more expensive hotels, booking in advance through an agent can save you 50 percent or more. It pays to book in advance.

Food

Thai cuisine is famous the world over for its remarkable variety and often blistering flavor. Experiment as often as you can. Southern Thailand—where the diving happens—is famous for its fresh seafood. Food is usually very inexpensive, but like everywhere in the world, you can pay more for atmosphere.

Rice is the staple, and is served with almost every dish that is ordered here. Many different varieties of rice are available, depending on what kind of food you're ordering. Curries are absolutely fantastic in Thailand, and vary in degree of spiciness from mild and sweet to fiery.

Quite often the best food available is right off the streetside. Thais are extremely creative in business, and it is common to see Thai families set up a portable restaurant on a street corner. Some will have a more permanent *kwait diaw* (noodle) shop on the sidewalk. This type of food is often fresher that what you will find in the more expensive restaurants because the food stalls have no refrigerators, and must buy their ingredients fresh everyday. Don't be afraid to experiment, even if that means trying the fried silkworms (astonishingly tasty with a cold Singha beer).

For those with more traditional tastes, in all the tourist areas most international cuisines are available, including American steak, Italian pasta, German schnitzel, and Swedish meatballs. McDonalds, if you must, is also available country wide as is KFC, Pizza Hut, and Swensen's to name a few.

Thailand is famous for its fruits, and even if you've traveled widely in the tropics, you will see fruits here that you have never encountered before. Thais have very creative ways to prepare fruit dishes, and the best season for unusual fruit is March to September. A favorite, and delicious, spring-time dish is *kao neaow matmuang,* a concoction of fresh mango slices on a bed of rice marinated in coconut milk overnight. You should also try the durian, an ugly and horrible-smelling fruit that many Asians insist is the best fruit in the universe. See for yourself.

Live-aboard boats in Thailand offer some of the finest food anywhere, and often people come back time and time again not only for the diving, but for the incredible meals that are served onboard.

Dive operators

Professional diving services are the norm in Thailand. The industry has exploded over the past 10 years or so and the standard of service and professionalism is unequaled in Southeast Asia. Most dive centers are affiliated with PADI, but SSI and NAUI instruction are available in many places. Prices vary depending on what you are do, where you are go, and how comfortable you want to be.

It is always best to contact diving centers to arrange your holiday before arriving, since at certain times of the year—especially in Phuket—dive boats are frequently full. If you are planning to join a live-aboard to the Andaman Islands, Burma Banks, or the Similan Islands, booking ahead is essential.

Most diving activities are supervised by a diving guide, either Thai or *falang* (Western foreigner, pronounced "FAH-lahng" in Thai) who speak a variety of languages. If you are a beginner, it is generally suggested that you find out as much about the dive site and the guide as possible before booking. Not all dive sites in Thailand are suitable for beginners, and like anywhere, not all guides are as competent as others; it pays to look around.

On the longer journeys—which attract more experienced divers—more freedom is usually given to the individual diver, although most dive outfits discourage recreational dives past 40 meters. Technical diving centers have sprung up here and there, so deeper diving is sometimes possible. The problem is finding water deeper than 40 meters in Thailand.

All the listed dive centers offer beginning dive courses, and some offer advanced and professional-level instruction. All courses are generally of high quality, and the prices are reasonable. One advantage of learning in Thailand is that the class size is small—typically 4 to 6 students, or even fewer. However, in Ko Tao, diving instruction is such a huge business that class sizes are often bigger than in other places.

Live-aboards

Keep in mind that live-aboard dive boats, no matter how large, do not have a lot of space for luggage storage. Most dive operators recommend soft-sided luggage on the boat, but will allow you to store extra bags at the dive center. Since live-aboard diving is casual, only a few T-shirts, shorts, and possibly a sweatshirt for the evenings are necessary. Generally, the less you bring with you , the more comfortable you will be.

Divers Alert Network (DAN)

DAN is an international membership association of individuals and organizations sharing a common interest in diving and safety. It operates a 24-hour diving emergency hotline in the US: 1-919-684-8111 or 1-919-684-4DAN (4326). The latter accepts collect calls in a dive emergency. Though DAN does not directly provide any medical care, it does provide advice on early treatment, evacuation, and hyperbaric treatment of diving-related injuries. Divers should contact DAN for assistance as soon as a diving emergency is suspected.

DAN membership is reasonably priced and includes DAN TravelAssist, a membership benefit that covers medical air evacuation from anywhere in the world for any illness or injury. For a small additional fee, divers can get secondary insurance coverage for decompression illness. For membership questions, contact DAN at 1-800-446-2671 in the US or 1-919-684-2948 elsewhere.

DAN Southeast Asia is located in Australia and is the office to contact in an emergency in this area. However, if you wish to join DAN or purchase DAN insurance, you'll need to contact your local area office. They also have an excellent web site with international links at www.diversalertnetwork.org.

DAN Southeast Asia-Pacific Contact Information:

Divers Alert Network SE Asia-Pacific, 49A Karnak Road (PO Box 384), Ashburton, Victoria 3147, Australia
Email: danseap@danseap.com.au
Web: www.danseap.com.au
Tel: +61-3-9886 9166, Fax: +61-3-9886 9155
After hours emergencies: +61-3-9828 2958

Environmental considerations

Protecting the environment is a fairly new concept in Thailand (and all of Southeast Asia), but fortunately more and more people are beginning be aware of the value of Thailand's unique natural environment, and more importantly, starting to do something about preserving it. Divers have long been aware of damage to coral reefs through dynamite fishing and anchoring, but only recently have dive centers starting thinking about the damage that can be done by divers themselves. Thailand now has some of the most environmentally progressive dive shops in the world, which has helped keep our reefs healthy and beautiful.

When diving here, please try to respect the wishes of the diving community by not gathering or collecting any corals or shells, even from the beaches. Of course, never buy marine items from shell shops, as this will only encourages the proprietors to order more stock.

Please do not spear fish. Although some argue that spearfishing is not damaging because it is selective, it tends to frighten fish and make them unapproachable. Also, since spearfishing is selective, the pressure is felt only on larger animals, and only on certain species. This can upset the ecological balance of the reef.

On land, you'll find that like in most countries, Thailand has its share of plastic garbage. Although this is a worldwide problem, make an effort to do your part. Take your own bag or backpack to the store, and buy a canteen or reusable plastic container to hold drinking water during trips to the beach (your hotel will be more than happy to fill this up for you, especially if you explain why you are doing it this way). Think about where this plastic will end up. Don't take an out of sight, out of mind attitude, because you just may see that bottle washed up on your favorite beach the next day.

Finally, most islands in Thailand have a year-round fresh water shortage. Please do not waste water. You may see green tropical foliage surrounding you, but there is very little water in the ground. Shorten your showers, turn off the water while shaving, and generally be conscious of water use.

National park fees

As of this writing, the Thai Government has imposed fees to enter any national park in Thailand, and there are often user fees charged as well. The charge is supposed to be 200 baht (US$4.50) per entry for Thais or foreigners and so far, it is being enforced—a strange concept here in Thailand. Expect to pay 200 baht for each national park you visit, no matter how small it is.

Like many government policies in Thailand, this has not really been thought out properly. Some tour operators from Phuket, for example, may enter up to five national parks on a daily tour, and these "national parks" may just be a nice waterfall. This means, for a day of visiting waterfalls, there could be a 1,000 baht (US$23) per person. And, this is per day, making national parks here in Thailand more expensive to visit than Yosemite National Park in the USA!

Divers are also getting jabbed. To dive in the Similan or Surin Islands, each diver must pay a 200 baht entrance fee, plus a 200 baht per day "user" fee. This means that a four-day trip to Similan and Surin will cost an additional 1,200 baht, payable in cash upon boarding the boat. What the government is going to do with 20 million baht (over US$450,000) in collected fees in 2002 is still under debate. All we can do is hope that the money is used wisely, and that a portion of it goes towards protecting the environment.

Bangkok City code: 02

Getting there

Many connecting flights are available out of Don Muang Airport. Check with your travel agent for schedules and destinations. Reservations are recommended almost all year around.

Getting around

Book your taxi at one of the offices inside the airport—ignore touts. Fares downtown run about 500 to 700 baht per car from services inside the terminal, 250 to 350 baht if you use the public taxis (metered plus a surcharge) locaed outside of all terminals. There is also a new airport bus which will drop you off at many locations in Bangkok for 100 baht. For those who want to save this fare, walk across the overpass to the bus stop and take a bus into town for almost nothing (less than 15 baht). Be warned, however, that this takes a long time. A train is also available for around 20 baht, but you will be hard-pressed to get anyone in the airport to explain this option to you. The train station is visible from the overpass on the departure level. Free transport is available from the domestic terminal to the international, and vice versa. Do not be fooled into paying upwards of 150 baht for this short journey. There is a walk way between the terminals which takes about 10 minutes.

Metered taxis are available throughout Bangkok, and are extremely comfortable (air-conditioned) and convenient. Depending on the time of day, it can cost as little as 120 baht to get you back to the airport from downtown. Make sure the meter is on before you start your journey, and if no meter is available, discuss the price before you begin your journey. Bargaining is possible in many instances, but keep smiling!

The Tollway or freeway system can save a lot of time, and the charge is about 70 baht to downtown from the airport. If you are in a hurry, or traffic is bad, ask the driver to use the "tollway" (same word in Thai) and give him the amount he asks for. This is never included in the fare unless you book transportation from an agency or hotel, but it's wise to check.

Phuket City code: 076

Some 890 km south of the capital, Phuket is accessible by land, sea, and air. Frequent daily buses ply the route from Bangkok. Fares cost as little 200 baht for the 14-hour journey in a non-airconditioned bus; 650 baht for a seat in a VIP air-conditioned bus. Buses depart from the Southern Bus Terminal, Sanitwongse Road, in Bangkok and arrive in Phuket Town at the bus station on Phang-Nga Road.

Trains also connect Bangkok with Surat Thani (3.5 hours by car northeast of Phuket) and Hat Yai (7 hours by car southeast of Phuket) in the south of Thailand. From these points travelers can catch an inter-provincial bus to Phuket. Total cost of train and bus is about 700 baht.

At least ten flights daily connect Bangkok's Don Muang Domestic Airport with Phuket. Cost of a single ticket is 2,730 baht. Reservations in Bangkok at Tel: 66-2/280-0070; in Phuket at Tel: 66-76/211-195. In addition, Phuket's modern international airport welcomes flights from more than 12 international destinations including two daily flights from Singapore.

Accommodations and food

Phuket has probably the widest range of accommodation anywhere in Thailand, from exclusive lodging at the Aman Puri Resort for more than $1,000 per day to multiple local guest houses for often less than $4 per day—and everything in between. The most popular (and crowded) beach is Patong, the center for entertainment, shopping and night life. To the south you'll find Kata-Karon, which is quieter and classier, and the home of Club Med. An integrated resort near the airport (Bang Tao Beach) offers first-class international hotels and many amenities for travelers. These include the Sheraton, Laguna Beach Resort, and the Dusit Laguna, all of which will spoil you to your heart's content.

Food is wonderful, diverse, and readily available from noodle shops on street corners, local seafood restaurants right on the ocean, and international-style continental restaurants that will make you feel as if you've never left home. And yes, we finally have a McDonald's and a Starbucks for those of you who insist, right on Patong Beach.

Phuket is most famous for its seafood for obvious reasons. However it is not just the availability of seafood that makes it popular. Phuket's locals have many exciting, special recipes and preparation techniques that motivate even Thais from Bangkok to make that special trip to Phuket. Keep in the mind that the more seafood you eat, the less fish there are to see in the ocean, although many products are farmed. Divers please note.

Dive operators

Most of Phuket's diving centers offer one-day trips to the Racha Islands, Shark Point, *King Cruiser* Wreck, and Koh Phi Phi. In addition, most of the dive centers listed here can provide live-aboard diving to the Similan Islands and beyond, as well as Burma. Some of these centers can arrange charters to the Andaman Islands as well.

All of the dive centers here offer excellent diving instruction and most of them offer courses all the way up to the instructor level. Underwater photography courses are available, especially on the better live-aboard dive boats, some of which have on-board professional photographers.

Phuket is Thailand's center for live-aboard diving, and several of the operators offer boats that cater to a very select group of divers. These boats feature modern navigational systems, international radio communications and safety features, and the stability to travel the open oceans. They also offer first-class service, crew, accommodation, and meals.

Prices in Phuket for a two-dive day trip are pretty much fixed at $70 to $100, which includes hotel pick-up, lunch, tanks and weights, and a qualified divemaster. Two-day trips are just over double this—about $160—and include food and accommodation, a night dive, and a total of at least four day dives. Gear rental runs $20 to $30 per day. Boats certainly vary in quality, so it's best to check with individual dive centers for their particular package.

Live-aboard prices vary dramatically—and the services, destinations, and quality of the boat vary dramatically as well. Expect to pay a minimum of $110 per day for journeys to the Similan Islands on a basic boat, and between $225 and $350 a day for trips to the Mergui Archipelago, Burma Banks or Andaman Islands on a very comfortable boat. There are many boats in Phuket now around US$160 to US$200 range which are well worth the price due the higher level of comfort. The more comfortable you want to be, the safer you want to be, and the further you want to go—the more you pay.

The following operators, listed in alphabetical order, are recommended:

Dive Asia, P.O. Box 70, Karon, 83100 Phuket
info@diveasia.com
www.diveasia.com
Tel: 076 330 598, Fax: 076 284033
Day trips, live-aboards, Burma, Nitrox, IDCs, diving courses, rebreather, and courses on Draeger Ray and Dolphin units.

Calypso Divers, 109/17 Taina Road, Kata Center, 83100 Phuket
info@calypsophuket.com
www.calypsophuket.com
Tel: 076 330 869, Fax: 076 330 869
Live-aboards, day trips, two-day trips to Phi Phi, courses.

Fantasea Divers Co. Ltd., 43/20 Mu 5, Viset Road, Tambon Rawai, 83130 Phuket
info@fantasea.net
www.fantasea.net
Tel: 076 281 388, Fax: 076 281 389
Luxury live-aboard dive cruises in the Andaman Sea and Myanmar between December and May. Luxury live-aboard dive cruises in the Gulf of Thailand between June and November.

Genesis Live-aboards Co. Ltd., P.O. Box 002, Karon Post Office, 83100 Phuket
info@genesis1phuket.com
www.genesis1phuket.com
Tel: 076 280 607, Fax: 076 280 607
Luxury 6 days/7nights and 9 days/10 nights liveaboard cruises in Burma & Thailand.

High Class Adventure Phuket, 66/6 Bangla Square, Patong, 83150 Phuket
info@highclass-adventure.com
www.highclass-adventure.com
Tel: 076 344 337, Fax: 076 344 337
Live-aboards, daytrips, diving-education, shops in Khao Lak and Phuket.

Kon-Tiki Co. Ltd., 42/14-15 Mu 5, Viset Road, Rawai, 83130 Phuket
www.kon-tiki-diving.com
info@kon-tiki-diving.com
Tel: 076 280 366, Fax: 076 280 357
Day trips, live-aboards Courses, IDCs.

Santana diving & canoeing, 222 Tawee-wong Road "Sea Pearl Plaza", Patong Beach, 83150 Phuket
info@santanaphuket.com
www.santanaphuket.com
Tel: 076 294 220, Fax: 076 340 360
Web: santanaphuket.com
Live-aboard trips to Thailand and Burma, instruction, IDCs, day trips.

Scuba Cat Diving, Patong Beach Road (30 meters south of McDonalds), Patong, 83150 Phuket
patonglp@scubacat.com
www.scubacat.com
Tel: 076 293 120, Fax: 076 293 122
PADI courses beginner to Instructor, day trips, short live-aboard trips to the Similans (MV *Scuba Cat*) and longer range to the Similans and beyond (MV *Scuba Adventure*).

Siam Dive n' Sail, 68/14 Patak Road, Mu 2, Soi Sawatdee, behind Club Med, Kata Beach, Karon 83100 Phuket
Tel: 076 330 967, Fax: 076 330 990.
info@siamdivers.com
www.siamdivers.com
Dive center owned by the author of the Thailand section of this book. Most complete web site on live-aboard diving in Thailand and Burma.

South East Asia Scuba Divers, 1/16 Moo 9, Viset Road, Ao Chalong, 83130 Phuket
info@phuketdive.net
www.phuketdive.net
Tel: 076 281 299, Fax: 076 281 298;
Sailing & diving live-aboards, day trips, courses, IDCs, sailing charters.

South East Asia Liveaboards Co. Ltd., 225 Rat-U-Thit Rd, Patong Beach, 83150 Phuket
info@seal-asia.com
www.seal-asia.com
Tel: 076 340 406, Fax: 076 340 586
Live-aboards, daytrips, courses, adventure cruises, kayak safaris, surfing charters.

DIVING BURMA (THE MERGUI ARCHIPELAGO AND THE BURMA BANKS)

Your dive operator will explain the ways and what fors of a trip to the Mergui Archipelago, but as of 2002, this is how it stands:
Some live-aboard trips will depart from and return to Phuket and spend at least two days diving in Thailand on the way up and back. Other trips will depart from Kawthaung (Victoria Point) in Myanmar (Burma).

There are two ways to get to Kawthaung. First, there are daily flights from Bangkok to Ranong in Thailand (7:50 am departure) via Phuket Airways. From there the dive center will make arrangements to take you to a boat which will transfer you in about 20 minutes to Victoria Point. Second, the dive shop may arrange to pick you up in Phuket for the 5-hour drive by minibus or taxi to Ranong, where again, you will cross the channel into Burma.

The Burmese immigration officials require that you bring your passport, a photocopy of the front page of it, as well as your Thai immigration stamp page it, four passport-sized photos and pay a fee—currently US$130 to US$140. Only US cash will be accepted. These fees, not included by the operator because they are subject to change and payable directly to the Burmese officials, cover a Burmese guide, national park and mooring fees, and immigration charges. You are not required to have a Burmese visa to dive in the Archipelago. This is covered in your fees. For more details, please contact your dive operator.

Ko Phi Phi City code: 075

Some dive operators have mobile phones (01 or 09).

Regular ferries and hydrofoil services link Phi Phi with Phuket. Departures from the deep-sea harbor. Most ferries leave around 9 am and take between 90 minutes and 2 hours to reach the island.

Accommodations and food

Places to stay vary widely in Koh Phi Phi as well, though prices are generally higher than in Phuket. On the northern shore of Phi Phi, four resorts offer air-conditioned rooms, first class restaurants, a feel of exclusivity, and fresh-water swimming pools. These run $80 to $250 per night.

As many Western foreigners have settled on the island, the food available varies from traditional Thai and seafood restaurants to hamburger joints with black and white checked floors and excellent bakeries. No sign of McDonald's yet. Authentic Italian pizza and pasta are readily available, as are steaks and seafood. You name it, they have it.

Dive operators

Some diving centres here in Koh Phi Phi now have larger boats to take you to the local sites and to areas further away like Trang and even the Similan Islands. Boat quality is getting better all of the time.

Most of the diving shops are connected with the PADI training organization and at the time of this writing there are two PADI 5-star IDC centers on the island. NAUI and SSI instruction are available on the island as well. Although the majority of the dive centres are professionally run and prices do not differ much between them, as a beginner, a student, or as a serious diver who wants good information about marine life, it pays to check around before committing to a course or diving trip. Bear in mind that you generally get what you pay for, and the quality of instruction and guide service may well be more important to you than the price.

Day trip prices average about $40 per diving day (two dives), and equipment rental is approximately $20 per day. Tanks and weights are normally included.

The following operators, listed in alphabetical order, are recommended. Note: since the island is so small, if you choose to write to any of these diving centers, just write: the name of the shop, the general location (e.g. Tonsai Bay), Krabi 81000, Thailand.

Ao Nang Divers, 143 Moo 2, Ao Nang, 81000 Krabi
info@krabi-seaview.com
www.aonang-divers.com
Tel: 075 637 242, Fax: 075 637 246
Day-trips, courses.

Barakuda Diving Center, PO Box 283 Phi Phi Island, Phuket 83000
dive@barakuda.com
http://www.barakuda.com
Tel: (075) 620 698, Fax: (075) 620 698
Day trips, courses.

Moskito Diving Center & Excalibur Live-Aboards, Phi Phi Island, Ton Sai Bay, 81000, Krabi
info@moskitodiving.com
www.moskitodiving.com
Tel: 075 612 092, Fax: 075 612 092
Liveaboards, day trips, courses.

Visa Diving Center, 77 Moo 7, Phi Phi Island, 81000 Krabi
visatour@hotmail.com

www.phiphidiving.com
Tel: 01 2700 905, Fax: 076 325 209
Day trips, courses.

Phi Phi Scuba Diving Center, Ton Sai Village, Phi Phi Island, 81000 Krabi
info@phiphi-scuba.com
www.phiphi-scuba.com
Tel: 075 612 665
Day trips, courses.

Sea Frog Diving, Ton Sai Bay, Phi Phi Island, 81000 Krabi
seafrogdiving@hotmail.com
www.thaieco-adventure.org/seafrog
Tel. 01 8941921, Fax: 02 259 7553
Day trips, courses, Thai owned shop.

Ko Samui City code: 077

Visitors to Ko Samui have a choice of ways of reaching the island. For years they have arrived at Surat Thani by bus or train, and taken a boat from either Ban Don or nearby Donsak to Samui, and in some cases onward to Ko Pha Ngan. The cost for the 1-hour journey by express boat from Ban Don to Samui is 250 baht ($6). Alternatively travelers may fly from Bangkok to Ko Samui with Bangkok Airways. There are at least two flights a day, and the 1-hour trip costs 3,550 baht ($81). Bangkok Airways flies at least once a day between Phuket and Ko Samui. The cost of this short flight is 1,870 baht ($42). Note that all departing flights from Ko Samui Airport require a 400 baht aiport tax. This is because Samui Airport is a privately owned airport.

Accommodations and food

Samui, like Phuket, has an incredible range of accommodation available. There are still many places with huts right on the beach for sometimes less than $4. And there are incredibly expensive, luxurious accommodations as well. You can probably still spend more money in Phuket if that's your style, but the difference is not much. One very delightful thing about much of the accommodation in Samui is that the hotels have tried to maintain the traditional Thai architectural style, with huge slanting roofs and lots of wood. Even the airport is built in this way, and it makes a charming first impression when you arrive. At the time of this writing, there are no high-rise Miami Beach-style hotels, and let's hope it stays that way.

As in all tourist centers in Thailand, food is available to suit any palate. Samui has great little beachside restaurants that normally show videos in the evenings, and many little funky places run by both foreigners and Thais that serve everything from great pasta to Muslim vegetarian food to pizza. Some of the late-night food carts—restaurants on motorcycles—that hang about outside the discos after midnight offer great barbecued chicken, spring rolls, and deep fried everything. This is just the thing to eat after a few too many Singha beers.

Dive operators

All of Koh Samui's dive centers offer high-quality diving courses and are well organized and reliable. Your diving trips are always supervised by a professional divemaster or instructor.

Travel times to the different destinations such as Sail Rock and the marine park are anywhere between two and three hours. Prices do not tend to vary significantly between the operators unless a speed boat is involved. The average two-dive day trip includes transportation, tanks and weights, and a divemaster, and costs around $70. Gear rental is about $20. Prices are sometimes reduced during the low tourist season between August and January. Most operators now also arrange diving trips to Koh Tao, as well as nearby Koh Phangngan.

The following operators, listed in alphabetical order, are recommended:

Big Blue Diving Co. Ltd., Samui Resotel (Munchies), 17 Moo 3, Bohphut, Chaweng Beach, Koh Samui, Surat Thani 84320
samui@bigbluediving.com
www.bigbluediving.com
Tel: 077 422 617, Fax: 077 422 617
Day trips, courses, IDCs, resort on Ko Tao.

Easy Divers, P.O. Box 61, 84140 Koh Samui, Thailand
samui@thaidive.com
www.thaidive.com
Tel: 077 427 096, Fax: 077 427 418

SIDS Samui International Diving School,
PO BOX 40, 84140 Koh Samui, Thailand
info@planet-scuba.net
www.planet-scuba.net
Tel: (077) 422 386, Fax: (077) 231 242
Day trips, courses , IDCs, overnight dive packages.

The Dive Shop, 167/25 Moo2, Chaweng Beach, Bo Phut, Koh Samui
diveshop@samart.co.th
www.thediveshop.net
Tel: 077 230 232, Fax: 077 230 232
Day trips, 1/2 day trips by speed boat, courses.

Ko Tao City code: 077

Ko Tao is easily accessible from Ko Samui or Ko Phangngan by daily ferry, weather permitting. Cost is between 345 and 550 baht ($8-$134) each way. A speed boat runs every morning from Chumpon and takes 2 hours—400 baht ($9) each way. Buy tickets at the travel agent just outside the train station, and take a local bus as directions to the pier are impossible for a non-Thai speaker.

Accommodations and food

Ko Tao's bungalows tend to be basic, but that, like everywhere else, is changing fast. Most places now have bathrooms inside the rooms, and air-conditioning is more common. The most upmarket hotel in Ko Tao is the Ko Tao Cottages which feature such luxuries as air-conditioning and hot showers. Still, in most places electricity is not available until 6pm and in some places not at all. When on Ko Tao, expect to rough it a little bit.

Although there are not many varieties of restaurants on the island, most of the places serve good, if basic food. Don't expect USDA prime imported beef on any of the tables here. There is a great sandwich shop right in the village of Mae Haad. Ask the locals which is the current favorite, as places open and close all of the time. Every time I visit the island there's a new happening spot.

Dive operators

Koh Tao now has a number of PADI 5-star IDC dive centers, and all shops offer high quality instruction. The boats are becoming better and better on the island as well. Some boats are even equipped with GPS navigation systems, which enable the guides to find hidden underwater pinnacles—normally the best sites—consistently and quickly.

Trip prices hover around $40 per two-tank dive with equipment rental about $20 for the day. Tanks and weights are normally included in the price.

The following operators, listed in alphabetical order, are recommended:

Ban's Diving Resort, Koh Tao, Koh Phang-
nan, 84280 Surat Thani
jonas@bansdiving.com
www.amazingkohtao.com
Tel: 077 456 061, Fax: 077 456 057
Day trips, courses, IDCs, travel services.

Big Blue Diving Co. Ltd., 20/1 Moo1, Koh
Tao Surat Thani 84280
info@bigbluediving.com
www.bigbluediving.com
Tel: 077 456 050, Fax: 077 456 049
Day trips, courses, IDCs, resort on Ko Tao.

Easy Divers, At Lomprayah Jetty, Mae Haad
Town, Ko Tao, 84280 Surat Thani
tao@thaidive.com
|www.thaidive.com
Tel: 077 456 010, Fax 077 456 010
Day trips, courses, IDCs.

**Koh Tao Cottage International Dive Re-
sort**, 19/1 M3 Chalook Baan Kao, Koh Tao
84280 Surat Thani
divektc@samart.co.th
www.kohtaocottage.com
Tel: 077 456 134, Fax: 077 456 133
Day trips, courses, German spoken.

Scuba Junction Dive School, Haad Sairee
Ko Tao, 84280, Suratthani
info@scuba-junction.com
www.scuba-junction.com
Tel: 077 456 164, Fax: 077 456 163
Day trips, courses.

SIDS Planet Scuba Koh Tao, Mae Haad and
Sairee Beach, Ko Tao 84280 Surat Thani
info@planet-scuba.net
www.planet-scuba.net
Tel: 077 456 110, Fax: 077 456 110
Day trips, courses, IDCs, overnight trips.

Pattaya
City code: 038 (Same for Jomtien)

Air-conditioned buses link Pattaya with both
Don Muang International Airport and the
center of Bangkok. Airconditioned and non-
air-conditioned buses from Bangkok depart
from the Ekamai Bus Terminal, Sukhumvit
Road, every half hour and take an average of
just under 2 hours to make the journey. The
trip is getting shorter and shorter all of the
time due to the new tollway system being
built through Chonburi.

Accommodations and food

Pattaya was the first tourist resort built in
Thailand, and its got everything, including the
very posh Royal Cliff Resort. For those on a
budget, there are also many, many small
guest houses, often run by foreigners, which
are available for less than $20 per night. Since
Pattaya is so big, they always have hotel
rooms available and it pays to check with
travel agents to find the best deals.

Although just a few years back Pattaya had
acquired a poor reputation, the government
has done a good job cleaning up the town, and
it's again a very nice place to visit.

Like Phuket, Samui, and Bangkok,
Pattaya has every kind of food available. Like
Bangkok, Pattaya is a 24-hour city, and street
vendors sell everything from fresh tropical
fruit to Chinese noodles, and Indian curries
to fried silkworms. Eating off the carts on the
streets, like everywhere in Thailand, is where
you'll find the most varieties of food prepared
in the most local way. You'll also find great
seafood and steak houses in Pattaya along with
wonderful Japanese restaurants.

And yes, there are McDonald's, Pizza
Hut, Kentucky Fried Chicken, Dunkin' Donuts
and all the rest of the chains. Why people eat
this stuff when they are in the country with
the best food in all the world I'll never know,
but if you've got that homesick feeling, in
Pattaya you may indulge.

Dive operators

This small city was the first place in Thailand
to develop a diving industry, and most of the
operators are well-established. The centers
listed below all offer quality diving instruction.
Most of their business comes from Bangkok,
so the weekends in Pattaya can be quite
crowded, and it pays to book ahead. Some of
the shops offer special weekend dives or live-
aboard trips which get the working diver
back at work early Monday morning.

Because many of the clients of the Pattaya
operators are regular divers coming in from
Bangkok who own their own tanks and
weights, boat prices are generally less than in
other places, but equipment rental is more. If
you need equipment it's about the same,
around $60 to $80 for two-tank dives, but if you
have all of your own equipment, diving in
Pattaya can be quite inexpensive.

Pattaya's dive operators have been
expanding towards Ko Chang. If you want
more information about diving there,

contact anyone of the shops below for current information and prices. Prices range from $60 to $90 per day.

The following operators, listed in alphabetical order, are recommend:

Mermaid's Dive Center, Soi White House, Jomtien Beach, Cholburi, 20260, Thailand
mermaids@loxinfo.co.th
www.mermaiddive.com
Tel: 038 232-219, Fax: 038 232 221

Seafari Dive Center, 359/2 Soi 5, 20260 Pattaya
seafari@inet.co.th
www.01-diving-thailand-seafari.com
Tel: 038 429 060, Fax: 038 361 356
Day trips, courses, wreck diving.

Scuba Pearl Dive Center, 193/165 M10 (Rungland) South Pattaya Road, Pattaya—City, Chonburi, 20260, Thailand
Amtcom@loxinfo.co.th
www.andi.ru
Tel: 038 361 505, Fax: 038 425645
Day trips and instruction. Russian speaking.

Elite Divers Ltd., PO Box 202, Pattaya 20260, Chonburi, Thailand
chandler@loxinfo.co.th
www.divingthailand.com
Tel: 038 367 306, Fax: 038 367 306, Mobile: 09 992 6589
Underwater video-shooting and teaching, day trips, live-aboard, PADI instruction.

Seahorse Dive Center, Moo 4 Kai Bae Beach 10/8, Koh Chang 23120 Trat
www.ede.ch/seahorse
adidive@tr.ksc.co.th
Tel: 01 996 7147
PADI courses, overnight trips to the vertical wreck or to southern. Islands, day trips.

Andaman Islands

There are a few dive centers in the Andaman Islands themselves, but information is sketchy. There is a dive center on Havelock Island, a short ferry ride from Port Blair. They have bungalows and a restaurant which is owned by the dive center, run by two very nice Swiss diving instructors. They offer day trips and courses, but no live-aboards at the time of this writing.

Prices are relatively the same as those in Thailand for both diving and instruction.

Accommodations and food

There are several hotels in the Andamans, but the only real place to stay in Port Blair where the airport is, is the Bay Island Hotel located just above Port Blair in the hills. This is also about the only place to eat as well, except if you're on a live-aboard boat of course. The hotel costs anywhere from $40 up to $80 depending on the package they put together for you, the size and quality of your room, and whether or not you prefer to pay for your meals all in one go. They do have a swimming pool, the staff are very helpful and friendly (although service is only fair), and the rooms are basic, but comfortable. The restaurant and many of the rooms overlook the harbor of Port Blair, providing a truly beautiful view.

The food at the hotel is pretty good; I wouldn't call it gourmet, but the curries are wonderful and they usually set up a buffet in the evenings that features food from all over the world. There is not really any choice—the street carts and curry shops don't look too healthy, and there are no proper restaurants in Port Blair. This, I'm sure, will change, but who knows when?

Dive operators

At the time of this writing, the only way to dive the offshore areas in the Andamans are on a live-aboard boat from Thailand, but due to recent changes in yacht arrivals, it is at this time difficult, if not impossible for charter boats to effectively charter there. The reasons are complicated, but the newest rule that the authorities have imposed is that no diving gear can be brought into the islands. One must use the local shops to rent all gear, including compressors, tanks and even masks! This is of course impossible. Contact one of the dive centers below for the most current information. Details may change monthly.

Andaman Scuba Club Pvt. Ltd., Havelock Island, P.O. Bag # 9, Port Blair, Andaman and Nicobar Islands, India
www.andamanscubaclub.com
info@andamanscubaclub.com
Day trips and courses. This is the one real dive center in the Andamans, run by two Swiss gentlemen, Ueli and Markus. Please note that since there are no telephones on Havelock Island, email takes over one month to answer. Best to write to their postal address.

CHARTERS FROM PHUKET

Siam Dive n' Sail, 68/14 Patak Road, Mu 2, Soi Sawatdee, behind Club Med, Kata Beach, Karon 83100 Phuket
Tel: 076 330 967, Fax: 076 330 990.
info@siamdivers.com
www.siamdivers.com
Sailing, diving, and surfing charters.

South East Asia Scuba Divers, 1/16 Moo 9, Viset Road, Ao Chalong, 83130 Phuket
info@phuketdive.net
www.phuketdive.net
Tel: 076 281 299, Fax: 076 281 298
Sailing, diving, and surfing charters.

South East Asia Liveaboards Co. Ltd., 225 Rat-U-Thit Rd, Patong Beach, 83150 Phuket
info@seal-asia.com
www.seal-asia.com
Tel: 076 340 406, Fax: 076 340 586
Sailing, diving, and surfing charters.

Further Reading

In addition to a good guide, a diver is probably most interested in a fish identification book, to help make some order out of the more than 2,500 species swimming around the reefs of Southeast Asia. There are several excellent resources available.

Reef Fishes

Reef Fishes of the World, by Ewald Lieske and Robert Myers (Periplus Editions, 1994), is a comprehensive guide to over 2,000 species with 2,500 color illustrations. It enables divers and snorkelers to identify the inhabitants of coral reefs wherever they are in the world.

Tropical Reef Fishes of the Western Pacific— Indonesia and Adjacent Waters, by Rudie H. Kuiter is the first extensive guide to the reef fishes of Indonesia.

This compact, handsome book is a manageable 300 pages long, and includes 1,300 excellent color photographs, illustrating 1,027 species including males, females and juveniles, where color or morphological differences exist. *Tropical Reef Fishes* covers more than 50 families of reef fishes, just about every species you are likely to see around Indonesia's reefs down to about 30 meters.

This is an indispensable work. Kuiter is one of the leading authorities on Pacific reef fishes.

Micronesian Reef Fishes

Micronesian Reef Fishes: A Practical Guide to the Identification of the Inshore Marine Fishes of the Tropical Central and Western Pacific, 2d ed., by Robert F. Myers, also belongs in the library of every diver in Indonesia. While Myers has not sought to write a book about Indonesian species, there is a great deal of overlap in the faunas of the two regions, and well over 90 percent of the species discussed can be found in Indonesia.

Myers' book is a model of accuracy and detail, with clear color photos of more than 1,000 species, complete meristics, and a dense 50– 100 word description of the habitat and behavior of each species.

Other Works of Interest

The grandfather of all Indonesian fish guides is of course Bleeker's *Atlas Ichthyologique.* It is still very accurate, although not even close to being portable, or even available. Another very valuable book that became available as we were in production is Gerald R. Allen's *Damselfishes of the World.* This fine book describes and illustrates some 321 damselfish, all that are currently known, including 16 new species. Full meristics, and range and habitat descriptions of all the species are included.

The most available series of books on Indo-Pacific reef life in the United States are those put out by Tropical Fish Hobbyist publications in New Jersey. Unfortunately, these books are problematic due to their editing, misidentified photos and poor organization.

Fishes

Allen, Gerald R. *Butterfly and Angelfishes of the World.* New York: Wiley Interscience, 1979.
——*Damselfishes of the World.* Hong Kong: Mergus, 1991. (Distributed in the United States by Aquarium Systems, 8141 Tyler Blvd., Mentor OH 44060.)
Allen, Gerald R. and Roger C. Steene. *Reef Fishes of the Indian Ocean* (Pacific Marine Fishes, Book 10). Neptune, NJ: T.F.H. Publications, 1988.
Bleeker, Pieter. *Atlas Ichthyologique des Indes Orientales Neerlandaises* (9 volumes). Amsterdam, 1877. (Dr. Bleeker's classic "Atlas." Out of print and very valuable. Look for it at a good library.)
Burgess, Warren E. *Atlas of Marine Aquarium Fishes.* Neptune, NJ: T.F.H. Publications,

1988. (With many inaccuracies and misidentified photos; little scientific value.)

Burgess, Warren E. and Herbert R. Axelrod. *Fishes of the Great Barrier Reef* (Pacific Marine Fishes, Book 7). Neptune, NJ: T.F.H. Publications. 1975.

——*Fishes of Melanesia* (Pacific Marine Fishes Book 7). Neptune, NJ: T.F.H. Publications, 1975.

Carcasson, R. H. *A Guide to Coral Reef Fishes of the Indian and West Pacific Regions.* London: Collins, 1977. (Out of date, hard to recognize fishes from the drawings.)

Myers, Robert F. *Micronesian Reef Fishes: A Practical Guide to the Identification of the Inshore Marine Fishes of the Tropical Central and Western Pacific, 2d ed.* Guam: Coral Graphics, 1991. (Excellent, see text above. Order through Coral Graphics, P.O. Box 21153, Guam Main Facility, Barrigada, Territory of Guam 96921.)

Nelson, J.S. *Fishes of the World.* New York: John Wiley & Sons, 1984.

Piesch, Ted and D.B. Grobecker. *Frogfishes of the World.* Stanford, CA: Stanford University Press, 1987.

Randall, John E., Gerald R. Allen and Roger Steene. *Fishes of the Great Barrier Reef and the Coral Sea.* Bathhurst, Australia: Crawford House Press, University of Hawaii Press, 1990.

Sawada, T. *Fishes in Indonesia.* Japan International Cooperation Agency, 1980.

Schuster W.H. and R.R. Djajadiredja. *Local Common Names for Indonesian Fishes.* Bandung, Java: N.V. Penerbit W. Van Hoeve, 1952.

Weber, M. and de Beaufort, L.F. *The Fishes of the Indo- Australian Archipelago* (11 volumes, 404–607 pages each). Leiden, E.J. Brill. 1913–1962.

Invertebrates

Debelius, Helmut. *Armoured Nights of the Sea.* Kernan Verlag, 1984.

Ditlev, Hans A. *A Field-Guide to the Reef-Building Corals of the Indo-Pacific.* Klampenborg: Scandinavian Science Press, 1980. (Good, compact volume.)

Randall, Richard H. and Robert F. Myers. *Guide to the Coastal Resources of Guam, vol. 2: the Corals.* Guam: University of Guam Press, 1983.

Usher, G.F. "Coral Reef Invertebrates in Indonesia." IUNC/WWF Report, 1984.

Walls, Jerry G., ed. *Encyclopedia of Marine Invertebrates.* Neptune, NJ:T.F.H. Publications, 1982. (The text of this 700-page book is often good. There are several mistakes with photos, however, and many of the names have not been updated. A preponderance of the illustrations are Caribbean.)

Wells, Sue, *et al,* eds. *The IUNC Invertebrate Red Data Book.* Gland, Switzerland: International Union for Conservation of Nature and Natural Resources, 1983.

Wood, Elizabeth M. *Corals of the World.* Neptune, NJ: T.F.H. Publications, 1983.

Ecology

George, G. *Marine Life.* Sydney: Rigby Ltd, 1976 (also: New York: John Wiley & Sons).

Goreau, Thomas F., Nora I. Goreau and Thomas J. Goreau. "Corals and Coral Reefs," *Scientific American* vol. 241, 1979.

Henry, L.E. *Coral Reefs of Malaysia.* Kuala Lumpur: Longman, 1980.

Randall, Richard H. and L.G. Eldredge. *A Marine Survey Of The Shoalwater Habitats of Ambon, Pulau Pombo, Pulau Kasa and Pulau Babi.* Guam: University of Guam Marine Laboratory, 1983.

Salm, R.V. and M. Halim. *Marine Conservation Data Atlas.* IUNV/WWF Project 3108, 1984.

Soegiarto, A. and N. Polunin. "The Marine Environment Of Indonesia." A Report Prepared for the Government of the Republic of Indonesia, under the sponsorship of the IUNC and WWF, 1982.

Umbgrove, J.H.F. "Coral Reefs of the East Indies," *Bulletin Of The Geological Society of America,* vol. 58, 1947.

Wallace, Alfred Russel. *The Malay Archipelago.* Singapore: Oxford University Press, 1986.

Wells, Sue, *et al. Coral Reefs of The World* (3 volumes). Gland, Switzerland: United Nations Environmental Program, 1988.

Whitten, Tony, Muslimin Mustafa and Greg S. Henderson. *The Ecology of the Indonesian Seas (Parts One and Two).* Singapore, Periplus Editions, 1997. A comprehensive review of Indonesian waters and marine life. Part of the *Ecology of Indonesia* series of titles; other volumes include *Java and Bali, Nusa Tenggara and Maluku, Sulawesi* and *Sumatra.*

Wyrtri, K. "Physical Oceanography of the Southeast Asian Waters, Naga Report Vol. 2." La Jolla, CA: University of California, Scripps Institute of Oceanography, 1961.

Index

Map Index